D1500052

THE REALM OF SPIRIT

THE
REALM OF SPIRIT

BOOK FOURTH
OF
REALMS OF BEING

BY

GEORGE SANTAYANA

NEW YORK

CHARLES SCRIBNER'S SONS

1940

Ὁ Ἔρως ὑλικός τίς ἐστι, καὶ δαίμων οὗτός ἐστιν ἐκ ψυχῆς. καθ' ὅσον ἐλλείπει τῷ ἀγαθῷ, ἐφίεται δέ, γεγενημένος.

(Love has something material about it, and this spirit is generated out of the psyche in the measure in which she lacks the good, yet yearns after it.)

PLOTINUS, III, 5, 9.

He who knows Brahma advances towards Brahma everywhere. He comes to the lake of enemies; he crosses it by his mind. When they that know only the present come to that lake, they are drowned.... As one driving swiftly in a chariot looks down on the two wheels revolving, so he too looks down on day and night, on good deeds and evil deeds and on all the pairs of contraries. Free from good deeds, free from evil deeds, knowing Brahma, he advances towards Brahma.

Kaushitaki-Brahmana-Upanishad, I, 4.

Si mens, dum res non existentes ut sibi praesentes imaginatur, simul sciret, res illas revera non existere, hanc sane imaginandi potentiam virtuti suae naturae, non vitio, tribueret; praesertim si haec imaginandi facultas a sola sua natura penderet, hoc est, si haec mentis imaginandi facultas libera esset.

(If the mind, while calling up non-existent things in imagination, were simultaneously aware that those things did not really exist, it would surely attribute this its power of imagining to a virtue, not to a vice, in its nature; especially if this power of imagining were due solely to the nature of mind, that is, if this imaginative power in the mind were free.)

SPINOZA, *Ethics*, Part II, Prop. XVII, Scholium.

Am farbigen Abglanz haben wir das Leben.
(Light, coloured in refraction, makes our life.)

GOETHE, *Faust*, Part II, Act I, Scene I.

PREFACE

THE title of this book may tempt some unwary reader with the hope of tidings from a Spirit-World. Such is not my subject. Although not perhaps without a certain affinity to poets and mystics, I am intellectually a convinced materialist; and the singularity of my book is perhaps this, that it traces in spiritual things only their spiritual quality, whilst planting them, as far as their existence is concerned, unequivocally on natural ground, and showing how they spring out of it.

The realm here to be described is therefore not another world, nor even a hidden metaphysical agency alleged to animate the whole universe, or to create it. What I call spirit is only that inner light of actuality or attention which floods all life as men actually live it on earth. It is roughly the same thing as feeling or thought; it might be called consciousness; it might be identified with the *pensée* or *cogitatio* of Descartes and Spinoza. Yet there is an important circumstance that leads me to prefer the term spirit. In modern philosophy the notion of mind has become confused and treacherous, so that in whatever direction we press it into consistency, mind ceases to be mind. Pushed inwards, it may be reduced to a vanishing ego, the grammatical counterpart, impersonal and empty, of all feelings and objects alike. Driven outwards, mind may be lost in its objects, and identified with the existence and movement of a phenomenal world or the history of events. Again, mind may be conceived dynamically, called will or life, and turned into a magic law or impulsion supposed to compel things to

become what they are. And it may be conceived
analytically and dissolved into a multitude—nowhere
assembled—of separate data, or a series of feelings
each feeling itself, and none feeling any other. Or
instead of data, which after all are thinkable and given,
mind may be dissolved into a diffused unconscious
substance still paradoxically called feeling, out of
which organic bodies and centres of apprehension
might be composed. Yet all these results are abdica-
tions, and living mind is none of those things. It is a
moral stress of varying scope and intensity, full of
will and selectiveness, arising in animal bodies, and
raising their private vicissitudes into a moral experience.
This inner light is indeed requisite for focussing
impressions and rendering them mentally present, but
it is biologically prior to them, vital and central, a
product of combustion, a leaping flame, a fountain and
seat of judgment. I therefore call it spirit; not that I
think it either a substance or a physical power, or
capable of existing by itself, but that it is a personal and
moral focus of life, where the perspectives of nature
are reversed as in a mirror and attached to the fortunes
of the single soul.

My subject is not experience surveyed impartially,
as in a book of descriptive psychology, but experience
viewed at a certain angle, in the measure in which it
torments or educates the spirit. Nor is my subject
the whole of moral philosophy or the life of reason;
for there all forms of health and government would
need to be appreciated, many of which might be, and
might be content to remain, purely spontaneous and
worldly. Without in the least quarrelling with nature,
spirit is in its interests somewhat withdrawn from
nature, as are painting and music and history; the very
study of nature questioning nature and even in loving
and praising nature loving and praising it only for
being friendly to the spirit.

A study of the realm of spirit is therefore an exercise in self-knowledge, and effort on the part of spirit to clarify and to discipline itself. Not so much that a new province is added to moral life (although this happens sometimes in religion, poetry, and music, or even in mathematics) as that the common world takes on a new colour, is focussed in a new centre of interest, as when a man falls in love. This transformation or conversion would not be necessary if the psyche and the world moved in perfect harmony, as they do at certain happy moments in childhood and youth; but revision grows possible and urgent for the spirit as it gets more and more entangled in all the contrarieties of existence. Being always alive, and suffering more or less, spirit then becomes aware of its natural claims and interests, in contrast to the endless miscellany of events. The world turns into a school, life into a pilgrimage, and spirit itself, though it be as native to the world as laughter and tears, feels itself a surprised stranger, a monarch mockingly served, a prisoner tortured, or a lover entranced.

The spirit I speak of is thus nothing hypothetical, nothing mythical or cosmic, "whose dwelling is the light of setting suns", or that "circulates" in "the unenduring clouds", and "knows no insulated spot, no chasm, and no solitude".[1] On the contrary, actual spirit is well acquainted with solitude, with insulation, and with chasms, and this not by any accident; and it dwells, not in setting suns, but in human bodies, bodies breeding a thousand passions and diseases by which the spirit also is tormented, so that it congenitally longs at first for happiness and at last for salvation.

That no fabulous diffusion of spirit over infinite spaces could remove this predicament, in which actual spirit finds itself, is vouched for by Indian speculation. There, heavens and hells are posited *ad libitum*, and

---

[1] Wordsworth.

spirit is in the body.

many gods with many alternative names and virtues. Yet throughout those dazzling confusing spaces, throughout those transmigrations and cataclysms, the spirit takes counsel with itself, observes everything, endures everything, by outlasting everything renounces everything, and by questioning everything liberates itself.   The great thundering governing gods of popular religion are far from being the most advanced of spirits in insight or holiness.   Insight and holiness may appear anywhere, in anchorite or beggar, in prince or poet, even in a child, when once the illusion of the will is pierced, and the bias of time, place, and person is overcome.   All things, in their particular urgency and lure, are then reduced to vain, cruel, and lovely accidents; while the spirit itself withdraws into that infinite potentiality which is the source of its own heat and light.   Seen from there our natural loves are not stultified, they remain a part of what the heart desires, but they no longer stand alone; they have counter-weights in eternity; the truth envelops them; and the joy and sorrow of existence are balanced and lost in the peace of being.

The Indians and the mystics are inspired people, and their language does not always bear critical examination.   There is a paradox, for instance, in spirit seeming to turn against life and to renounce it, when in spirit life has for the first time become quite alive.   But here we fall into a misunderstanding. Spirit can never condemn or undermine natural life; this can be done only by some rival centre of life at the same biological level, tending to steal away matter or energy from its ancestors or neighbours.   Spirit may give warnings, it may be austere or ascetic, but it is never competitive: that would be a sure sign of non-spiritual forces at work.   Spirit requires no new matter or energy besides that of its organ, but only order and harmony in the matter or energy at hand.

It is therefore charitable and sympathetic to whatever forms life may have taken elsewhere. It loves, but its love is not physical and procreative, multiplying commitments ; rather reflective and spiritual, understanding those commitments, absolving them from their mutual guiltiness, and consoling them for their vanity and ultimate dissolution. In so doing it simply fulfils its own commitment to see things as they are. Such healing intelligence destroys nothing; such charity complicates and embitters nothing; it is neither an accomplice nor an accuser of fate. Spiritual insight is possible only at the top of life; but in fulfilling life it reviews life, and in recollection raises existence into a tragic image. Though this be an image of transiency, vanity, and suffering, there is such joy in forming it, that it often seems unutterably beautiful; or the sheer scope and victory of that revelation may drown all vision in light.

Spirit then seems to have passed beyond existence: which is an ambiguous way of speaking. The detail of existence may have lapsed from view in the sheer intensity of concentrated thought; or thought and spirit with it may actually have ceased to exist, death having been ushered in not by ghastly weakness or violent pain but by a last summing up and a grand finale. That is a question of circumstances, more or less noble and pompous. The liberation of spirit that is internal and essential to spirit has nothing to do with death or with another life, but comes at any moment and pervades all times when intuition supplants convention and passion rises into self-knowledge.

The life of spirit thus has a natural movement and natural goals, which I will now endeavour to describe. But let me not be misunderstood, as if I had taken it upon me to censure everything that is not spiritual. However much a naturalist may celebrate or even share the free life of spirit, he cannot consistently assign to it more than a relative importance.   Salvation and enlightenment may be all-important from the spiritual point of view, but this point of view has no absolute pre-eminence in the universe.   It is comparable to our natural interest in human survival, in science, or in some particular art like music: absolutely legitimate interests, physically inevitable at certain junctures, but special and morally optional in the context of things at large.   This relativity is betrayed by a spontaneous variety and a secret contradiction even in the ultimate oracles of spirit.   Pure intellect may say: *I dominate, I am not dominated.*   A pure heart may answer, *I love, I do not ask to be loved.* Buddha may be overheard saying: *Overcome the will, renounce preference, and you have entered Nirvana.* Who shall gainsay these maxims, or improve upon them?   Yet this desire to cease from willing is evidently a form of will.   So are this selfless love, and this pride in understanding.   Thus the inner life of spirit is a part of natural life, inevitable and perhaps tragic.   The contrasts we may draw between it and life in the world can be only partial contrasts.   Spirit pursues a perfection more inward and chastened than worldly arts and ambitions; but it would not exist or have a possible perfection to pursue, if it were not a natural faculty in a natural soul.

CONTENTS

CHAPTER I

THE NATURE OF SPIRIT

EVERYTHING that exists is confined to a specific character at a particular place and time; if it escaped from those bonds it would cease to be itself. Such an escape occurs continually in the realm of matter, where everything gradually lapses into something different; and this continuous flux, with its various tempos, composes the great symphony of nature. In living substance, plasticity and fertility are a virtue: matter might say, with Shelley's cloud, *I change but I never die*. That which dies at every turn is only the negligible cloud-rack of the moment, easily replaced or even improved upon. To lament that individuals or even species should vanish would be natural only to some elegiac poet who clung to lost occasions and to remembered forms, not being ready for the next, and lagging sentimentally behind the glorious march of time, always buoyant with victory and strewn with wreckage.

The case is otherwise when we come to the realm of spirit, as we do in that melancholy poet. Not that spirit is less mobile or elastic than matter. In its ideal vocation, as we shall find, it is infinitely more so. Even in its existence it is as evanescent as any cloud. But the inevitable concentration of existence at each point into something specific rises in the moral world to a higher power. Individuation from being passive and imputed here becomes positive and self-assured. Spirit, in its briefest and feeblest flash, sets up a moral centre for the universe.

Contingence and partiality, in one direction, embitter spiritual life. Why should "I" (that is, spirit in me) be condemned to lodge in this particular body, with these parents and nationality and education and ridiculous fate? Why choose this grotesque centre from which to view the universe? You may say that other people exist in plenty, viewing the universe from their several positions, so that in giving this involuntary pre-eminence to myself I am perhaps not more grotesque than the average man, or even than the most intelligent. But that only makes matters worse, if isolation, partiality, error, and conceit are multiplied indefinitely, and inevitably attached to conscious existence.

In another direction, however, the imprisoned spirit escapes from its cage as no physical fact can escape. Without quitting its accidental station it can look about; it can *imagine* all sorts of things unlike itself; it can take long views over the times and spaces surrounding its temporary home, it can even view itself quizzically from the outside, as in a mirror, and laugh at the odd figure that it cuts. Intelligence is in a humorous position: confinement galls it, it rebels against contingency; yet it sees that without some accidental centre and some specific interests and specific organs, it could neither exist nor have the means of surveying anything. It had better be reconciled to incarnation, if it is at all attached to existence or even to knowledge.

This is the force of intelligence, marvellous if we try to conceive it on the analogy of material being, but perfectly natural and obvious if we look at it congruously and from within.

It is intellectual.

Spirit in each of its instances assumes a transcendental station, and looks out from there on all the world. Wherever it is, is here; whenever it is, is now. Yet *here* and *now*, for intelligence, are not what they are for physical being, or for external indication, a particular, accidental, dead position. For intelligence *here* and *now* are movable essences, to be found wherever spirit may wander; and they name no particular material point, but the centre found, at each point, for all distances and directions. So that the bitterness of confinement is mitigated by a continual change of prisons, and the accident of place by the inevitable vastness of the prospect.

A consequence of this intellectual nature of spirit marks it particularly, or even defines it in popular philosophy. Spirit is invisible, intangible, And unapproachable from the outside. The immaterial. materialist might like to deny its existence; but that is not the inclination of mankind at large. Only, being necessarily familiar with material things, and having shaped language and expectation in conformity with physical happenings, people find it impossible not to materialize the spirit of which they are vividly conscious; so that critical philosophy sometimes, in clearing up the notion of spirit, and removing superstitious and physical analogies, seems to have nothing left. But that comes of being, like the primitive mind, preoccupied with matter, and disinclined to conceive spirit in spiritual terms. This disinclination is not confined to scoffers: religious philosophers also love to materialize spirit, in order to make it seem more solid and important, the pure air of a truly spiritual sphere being far too thin and cold for their lusty constitution.

Let me consider the various ways in which the notion of spirit is apt to be materialized. The sequel will then be less exposed to gross misunderstanding.

Spirits, in folklore, legend, and dreams, are often ghosts; that is, they are visible but intangible spectres of dead, absent, or supernatural persons. Such appari-

tions, for a critical psychologist, might not be physical facts, since the images have their basis in the ob-
Spirit not a ghost. server's brain, and are falsely incorporated into outer space: an error that the waking dreamer himself discovers when he attempts to embrace a ghost and finds nothing but air. Genuine believers in the survival and return of the dead, like doubting Thomas and modern Spiritualists, require their spirits to be tangible as well as visible, to come and go and preserve a continuous physical existence, to eat and especially to talk. Their bodies may be called "spiritual", but are conceived as extracts or magical restitutions of the human body, ethereal, astral, but not immaterial. They move about in another world or in the margins of this world, and are not pure intelligences but complete natural individuals, having a body and a soul.

The native land of ghosts is memory, memory transforming sensations, or drowsily confusing, recasting, or exaggerating old impressions into dreams.
But the landscape open to spirit is ghost-like in being purely ideal. Imagination is fertile; and the old maxim that there is nothing in the mind which was not first in the senses seems to me far from accurate. There is never anything in the mind that *at that time* is not given in a kind of sensation, that is, given directly: but these images are not old images or fragments of old images surviving and recombined, as the fragments of an ancient temple might be built into a modern wall. Images, considered in themselves and objectively, are essences and perfectly immaterial. That which is immaterial has no substance, no persistence, and no effects: it offers no possibility of being stored, divided, redistributed, or recombined. Ideas are not animals that may breed other animals. They may recur, wholly or in part, but only when a living psyche inwardly reverts to much the same movement as on some former occasion. The

given essence will then be the same or nearly the same as formerly. But it must be evoked afresh, and unless evoked it has no existence whatever. It is truly a ghost, belief in it is illusion, and its apparition or specious presence depends entirely on the dreaming psyche that weaves it together.

Dreams, and all the sensuous garments that fancy bestows on nature, are made of stuff much more spiritual than any "spirits" supposed to be persisting and active persons, stealthily re-visiting the earth, or sending messages to it from some neighbouring region. The primitive idea that when the body sleeps the spirit may travel to distant places, and receive monitions concerning secret or future things, though poetical, is true in this sense: that in dreams the contribution that the psyche makes to experience predominates over the contribution ordinarily made by external things. This predominance of the psychic we call *inspiration*; the existence and the rush of it are spirit itself. When this predominance is excessive and persists in waking hours, we go mad; any strong passion, in its recklessness and self-assurance, has madness in it. Yet the same inspiration permeates sensibility and desire, perception and thought, all experience being but a dream controlled, and all reason but fancy domesticated and harnessed to human labours. In dreams, when the spirit seems to travel, it merely smoulders like a fire no longer fanned by the wind: and in that withdrawal and concentra-tion, together with much fragmentary nonsense, it may develop and fancifully express its absolute impulses, building the world nearer to the heart's desire. Hence dreams may be morally prophetic: or a more voluminous inspiration, from the same source, may combine with waking intelligence and art to produce some work of genius. The notion that

Inspiration the voice of the psyche rebuking or idealizing external facts.

spirit can escape from the psyche, or comes into us originally, as Aristotle says, from beyond the gates, merely inverts mythologically a natural truth: namely that the spirit is immaterial and transcendental. It issues from the psyche like the genie from Sinbad's bottle, and becomes, in understanding and in judgment, an authority over its source, and a transcendental centre for making a survey of everything.

That the wildest imaginations are, in their origin, native to matter appears clearly in this, that they are produced by drugs. Nor is this incompatible with their æsthetic or prophetic or intellectual value. The priestess at Delphi inhaled the vapours of her cave before uttering her oracles; other ritual practices have an intentionally hypnotic or narcotic influence; wine and music, martial or religious, notoriously rouse the spirit to boldness and to conviction. Nor is this a scandal, as if pure reason could move either the heart or the world. Pure reason is an ideal brought to light in the spirit by the organization of forces all originally irrational and wild: and this organization in turn is a product of long friction and forced adjustments. So much so, that in human life inspiration and reason come to seem holiday marvels, appearing when some suppressed strain or forbidden harmony is allowed to assert itself, in fancy only, during some lull in action. Prophecy is the swan-song of lost causes. The action that accompanies it has no tendency to fulfil it. If it survives like Hebrew prophecy in later Judaism and in Christianity, it becomes a purely spiritual discipline, mystic where it was martial, and ascetic where it was political. The communism of Plato's Republic could be realized only in the cloister.

Spirit is thus, in a certain sense, the native land of ghosts, of ideas, of phenomena; but it is not at all a visible ghost or phenomenon in its own being. Its own essence is an invisible stress; the vital, intellectual, and moral actuality of each moment.

Another way in which spirit may be materialized is by confusion with the psyche and with those cosmic currents by which the psyche is fed. Wind and breath have given their name to spirit, *Spirit not a fluid.* and most aptly. The air is invisible, yet the winds are a terrible reality, and though they may soon be stilled, the calm supervening is no longer deceptive. I have learned that what seemed vacancy was a reservoir of power, that air, ether, and energy filled that apparent void. I discover that innumerable atoms are floating there, ready to make fresh havoc in the world, or to be breathed in and renew life in my breast. What is this life in me but vital oxygen drawn into my lungs; what is this warm breath exhaled but my very spirit and will? Invisible as it is, does it not quicken my body and inspire all my action? Is it not one with the spirit of the winds howling in the storm or ruffling the sea or carrying seeds far and wide over the fertile earth? Is not the world, then, full of spirits? And is not spirit perhaps the one universal power astir in all things, as it stirs in me?

Such poetic confusions are spontaneous in a candid mind. They may be corrected by science and by logical analysis; but it would be a foolish philosophy that should ignore the continuities and analogies that run through the universe and that at once impress the attentive poet. The principle of life is not exactly wind or air. Life began in the sea and a great seclusion and darkness are requisite for seeds to germinate and for organic patterns to take shape undisturbed. Storms and struggles come afterwards on occasion; a normal order and distribution of elements, or distinct self-defending organisms, must have arisen first. Yet the currents within and without such organisms or such elements remain continuous. A psyche, the organic order and potentiality in a living body, depends upon ambient forces and reacts upon them; and the sense of this dependence and of this reaction is the spirit.

This spirit is something ontologically altogether incongruous with air, ether, energy, motion, or substance. Spirit is the *witness* of the cosmic dance; in respect to that agitation it is transcendental and epiphenomenal; yet it crowns some impulse, raises it to actual unity and totality, and being the fruition of it, could not arise until that organ had matured. An immense concretion of elements to make a habitat and of tropisms to make an animal must have preceded. Being fetched from such depths, spirit feels a profound kinship with its mothering elements. It suffers with the body and it speaks for the heart. Even if it dreams that it travels to distant spheres, it merely reports in a fable the scope of physical sensibility and the depths from which messages are received. In its station, in its interests, in its language, it always remains at home. To say that it travels, or witnesses the distant, is as if we said that the radio conveyed us to the concert which it conveys to us. The travelling, the waves, the transmissions are all physical. How should they be anything else? Instruments are material; even the composer, when he first conceived those accords, was listening to a spontaneous music bred in his psyche out of theoretically traceable impressions, tensions and outbursts of potential energy within him. The chain of these motions is materially uninterrupted, else the composer's imagined music would never have reached our ears; and spiritual union, both in perception and in passion, depends upon physical concordance. The number of spirits that may have lived through the measures of that

It is the moral fruition of physical life.

melody helps me not at all to hear it now; the physical source must be tapped afresh in each case, and the physical receiver must be capable of vibrating afresh to the message.

Spiritualists and mystics are often more perceptive than rationalists; but they are not for that reason perceptive of spiritual things. They are, more probably, supersensitive materially. They feel influences vibrating through the universe to which the din of vulgar affairs has deafened most of us: and they dream of physical survivals and renewals, of physical Elysiums, with endless vistas of warm physical love or physical peace. They hover, they glide, they wallow; and they think themselves spirits. But there is nothing less spiritual than the shallows of indistinction and of torpid oneness. The universe is perforce one, and its parts easily break down and are lost in one another; but such collapse destroys the very possibility of spirit, which is not an ether or a fluid coursing through space, but a moral focus of recollection, discrimination and judgment.

Language in these subjects is particularly ambiguous and charged with emotion; it serves less to discriminate one thing from another than to attribute to one thing, miraculously, the powers and dignities of something else. So the power of nature is often attributed to spirit or identified with it: with a curious result. For if spirit be only the laws or tendencies discoverable in nature, it is only a form to be found in matter, and not an immaterial invisible inward intensity of being. And there is malice in this abuse of language: for we are expected to conceive that laws or tendencies are thoughts (essences being confused with the intuition of essences) and that nature being describable in those intelligible terms is secretly governed by intelligence: so that we may attribute power also to our own

Confusions about the seat of power.

wishes and imaginations, and depute ourselves to be co-rulers of the universe.

Now our *selves*, our organisms or persons, undoubtedly play a more or less efficacious part in physical events. It would be a miracle if our bodies, with so much stored and redistributable energy as they contain, did not redirect by their action all sorts of other motions in the environment. A man habitually identifies himself as much with his body as with his spirit: and since both are called "I", it is no wonder if what happens in each is felt to be also the work of the other. And the connection is radical and intimate in reality; the problem not being how the two happen to be united but in what respects we may justly distinguish them. The difference between myself as a transcendental centre or spirit and myself as a fact in the world is, in one sense, unbridgeable; but not because they are two facts incongruously or miraculously juxtaposed in the same field, but because they are realizations of the same fact in two incomparable realms of being. There is only one fact, more or less complex and extended, an incident in the flux of existence; and this fact lying in the realm of matter by virtue of its origin, place, time, and consequences, contains a transcendental apprehension of all things, in moral terms and in violent perspective, taken from itself as centre. Such sensibility is proper to the natural fact, when this fact is a living animal; but you can no more pass, at the same level, from sensation to matter, than you can pass from extension to duration, from colour to sound, from sound to meaning, or from logic to love. The organization of matter is something logically incomparable with its mere persistence or energy, yet can only exist with the latter; so spirit is logically incomparable with body, yet is a moral integration and dignity accruing to body when body develops a certain degree of organization and of responsiveness to distant things. Nor does spirit, in its new language, discourse about anything save that very world, with all its radiations, in which it has arisen.

Perhaps it is not logically impossible that spirit should exist without a body: but in that case how should spirit come upon any particular images, interests, or categories? If occu- pied with nothing, it would not be a con- scious being; and if occupied with everything possible, that is, with the whole realm of essence at once, it would not be the consciousness of a living soul, having a particular moral destiny, but only a hypostasis of intelligence, abstracted from all particular occasions. But can intelligence be abstracted from particular occasions and from problems set by contingent facts? Logic and mathematics would surely never have taken shape if nature had not compelled attention to dwell on certain forms of objects or of language, and rewarded in practice the elaboration of those forms in thought. Indeed spirit, once abstracted from animal life and independent of all facts, would have forfeited that intensity, trepidation, and movement, that capacity for inquiry and description, which make spirit a focus of knowledge. It would have evaporated into identity with the realm of essence. Even divine spirits, as conceived in human poetry and religion, are thinking, loving, and planning minds, functions which all belong to animal life, and presuppose it.

Treacherous notion of disembodied spirit.

In some speculative myths spirit is represented as a self-existent potentiality pregnant with the seeds of a particular development; so that spirit, as in a dream, gradually creates world upon world, and the experience of them, out of its magic bosom. There is sometimes poetic truth in such myths, but they describe, from some local point

And of "Spirit" in history.

of view, a perspective in the realm of matter, not at
all the history of spirit. Spirit is not a seed, it is
not a potentiality, it is not a power. It is not even—
though this touches more nearly its actual character—
a grammar of thought or divine Logos, predetermining
the structure of creation and its destiny. That, if
found anywhere, would be found in the realm of truth;
but we may doubt that any alleged Logos, or any
psychological system of categories or forms of intuition,
prescribes limits to the truth. It prescribes at best one
type of logic, one set of senses, in which a particular
existent world might be apprehended by its inhabitants.

Yet these myths, as often happens, have a real
foothold in the nature of the facts. They catch
Spirit essentially open and blank. some transcendental privilege or predicament proper to spirit and transfer it,
together with the name of spirit, to the
spheres of matter or truth. Spirit has an
initial vagueness; it awakes, it looks, it waits, it oscil-
lates between universal curiosity and primeval sleep.
Certainly the feelings and images arising are specific;
and spirit has no *a priori* notion of any different
feelings or images to contrast with the given ones.
Yet it is in no way predisposed or limited to these;
it is not essentially, like the psyche, even a slave of
habit, so as to think the given necessary and the not
given impossible. Spirit is infinitely open. And this
is no ontological marvel or mystic affinity of spirit to
the absolute. It is merely the natural indistinction
of primitive wakefulness, of innocent attention. Spirit
is like a child with eyes wide open, heart simple, faith
ready, intellect pure. It does not suspect the trouble
the world is going to give it. It little knows the
contortions, the struggles, the disasters which the
world imposes on itself. There is a horrid confusion
in attributing to spirit the dogged conservatism and
catastrophic evolution of the natural world.

To the primitive blankness of spirit corresponds its eventual hospitality to all sorts of things. But this hospitality is not connivance, not complicity. It is an intellectual hospitality open to all truth, even to all fiction and to all essence, as these things may present themselves. It is not an equal pleasure in them all. Spirit is a product of the psyche; the psyche makes for a specific order and direction of life; spirit congenitally shares in this vitality and this specific impulse. The psyche needs to prepare for all things that may chance in its life: it needs to be universally vigilant, universally retentive. In satisfying this need it forms the spirit, which therefore initially tends to look, to remember, to understand. But the psyche takes this step, so impartial and unprejudiced officially, for a perfectly selfish domestic reason, namely, to prepare the home defences and enlarge the home dominion. The spirit, therefore, is like Goethe's Watchman, who was born to gaze, and possessed all the world in idea, yet was set on that watch-tower for an urgent purpose, with a specific duty to be vigilant. Hence the storms and forest-fires, the invasions or rebellions that he might observe, would not leave him cold, but would distress him in his fidelity, disturb his power of vision, and perhaps bring him and his tower to the ground. Not that spirit trembles for its own being. It is the most volatile of things, and the most evanescent, a flame blown or extinguished by any wind: but no extinction here can prevent it from blazing up there, and its resurrection is as perpetual as its death. What torments it is no selfish fear but a vicarious sympathy with its native psyche and her native world, which it cannot bear to feel dragged hither and thither in tragic confusion, but craves to see everywhere well-ordered and beautiful, *so that it may be better seen and*

It suffers when thwarted in its proper life of free sympathy and understanding.

understood. This is the specific function of spirit,
which it lives by fulfilling, and dies if it cannot somehow fulfil. But as it is unresisting yet indomitable
in its existence, so it is resourceful in its art, and
ultimately victorious; because the worst horrors and
absurdities in the world, when they are past or distant,
so that life here is not physically disturbed by them,
can be raised in the spirit to the level of reflection,
becoming mere pictures of hell and marvellous in
that capacity. Thus a constant suggestion and echo
of sorrow, which cannot but suffuse existence, adds
strange dignity to the tragedy and renders the spirit
freer from the world and surer in its own intrinsic
possessions.

It is not in respect to large cosmic fatalities, such
as war and death, that spirit is most perplexed. Love,
self-sacrifice, and martyrdom are capable of turning
those fatalities into occasions for lyrical joy and tragic
liberation. The worst entanglements, from the spirit's
point of view, arise within the psyche, in what in
religious parlance is called sin. This strangles spirit
at its source, because the psyche is primarily directed
upon all sorts of ambitions irrelevant to spirit, producing stagnation, inflation, self-contradiction, and hatred
of the truth. It is with difficulty that spirit can make
itself heard in such a tumult. Spirit is no random
blast, no irresponsible free demand, but speaks for a
soul reduced to harmony and for the sane mind.
This sanity implies not only integrity within, but also
adjustment to the outer universe. So that whilst
spirit is physically the voice of the soul crying in the
wilderness, it becomes vicariously and morally the
voice of the wilderness admonishing the soul.

Let me tabulate, as briefly as possible, the principal
Glossary   words and ideas that mark the differences, the
of terms.   bonds, and the confusions that exist between
matter and spirit. Such a glossary may help the

reader to criticize his favourite modes of expression and to be patient with those of other people.

BODY. Ancient usage identifies a man with his body, as Homer in the first lines of the Iliad : [1] and in English we still speak of *nobody* and *everybody*. This places man quite correctly in the realm of matter amongst other bodies, but it treats him and them summarily and externally as gross units and dead weights, ignoring their immaterial properties and their subtle physical substance and relations.

ORGANISM. This word still designates the body, since the organization of an organism must exist somewhere and on a particular scale, if it is to exist at all. But a body is an organism only by virtue of its vital power of nutrition and reproduction. By these functions bodily life becomes continuous with the ambient forces on which it feeds and theoretically with the whole dynamic universe. Thus an organism is both a closed system of vital tropes and a nucleus in the general cosmic process.

PSYCHE. The forms of inorganic matter, though distinct from matter logically, are clearly passive: matter may fall into them innumerable times, yet if anywhere disturbed, they show no tendency to reinstate themselves. This tendency defines an organism: its actual form hides a power to maintain or restore that form. This power or potentiality, often concentrated in a seed, dwells in the matter of the organism, but is mysterious; so that for observation the form itself seems to be a power (when locked in that sort of substance or seed) and to work towards its own manifestation. The self-maintaining and reproducing pattern or structure of an organism, conceived as a power, is called a psyche. The psyche, in its moral unity, is a poetic or mythological notion, but needed to mark the hereditary

[1] The wrath of Achilles cast many souls of heroes to Hades and *themselves* to dogs and vultures.

vehement movement in organisms towards specific forms and functions.

ANIMAL. All natural organisms have psyches, and are at the same time in dynamic relations to the whole physical world. When the organism waits for favourable opportunities to unfold itself, the psyche is vegetative; when it goes to seek favourable opportunities, it is animal.

This is an important step in laying the ground for spirit. The unity of the organism subtends the moral unity of the spirit, which raises that unity to an actual and intense existence; the impulse of the psyche, making for a specific perfection of form and action, underlies the spiritual distinction between good and evil; and the power of locomotion gives the spirit occasion for perception and knowledge. Will is no doubt deeper than intelligence in the spirit, as it is in the animal; yet will without intelligence would not be spirit, since it would not distinguish what it willed or what it suffered. So that the passage from vegetation to action seems to produce the passage from a dark physical excitability to the *qui vive* of consciousness.

SOUL. The same thing that looked at from the outside or biologically is called the psyche, looked at morally from within is called the soul. This change of aspect so transforms the object that it might be mistaken for two separate things, one a kind of physical organization and the other a pure spirit. And spirit is in fact involved in feeling and knowing life from the inside: not that spirit is then *self*-conscious, or sees nothing save its own states, but that it is then the medium and focus for apprehension, and imposes on its objects categories and qualities of its own. A psyche, when spirit awakes in it, is turned into a soul. Not only can the career of that psyche now be reviewed in memory, or conceived in prophecy, but many a

private impulse or thought never exhibited to the
world can now be added to one's history; so that
oneself is now not merely the body, its power, and
its experience, but also an invisible guest, the soul,
dwelling in that body and having motions and hopes
of its own. This soul can be conceived to issue out
of the body, to pass into a different body, or to remain
thinking and talking to itself without a body at all.
This, for the psyche, would have been inconceivable;
for, as Aristotle shows, the psyche, or specific form
of organization and movement, in an elephant, can
no more pass into the body of a fly, than the faculty
of cutting can pass from an axe into a lyre, or the
faculty of making music from the lyre into the axe.
The soul, however, having an apparently independent
discoursing and desiring faculty, and a power to
imagine all sorts of non-existent things, may easily
be conceived to pass from one body to another, as by
a change of domicile, and to have had forgotten
incarnations, with an endless future.

SELF OR PERSON. If memory, dreams, and silent
musings seem to detach the soul from bodily life, social
relations and moral qualities may re-attach the soul
to the world, not now biologically but politically.
Politically a man cannot be separated from his body;
but it is not by his bodily faculties that he chiefly
holds his own in society, or conceives his individuality.
He is a person, a self, a character; he has a judicial
and economic status; he lives in his ambitions, affections, and repute. All this again, as in the notion of
the soul, cannot come about without the secret intervention of spirit: yet these ideas, although spirit must
be there to entertain them, are not spiritual ideas;
the interests chiefly concerned are those of animal or
social bodies. Even moral worth or immortal life are
ideals borrowed from animal impulses and animal
conditions. In a different biological setting, or in a

realm of pure spirits, those social duties and services would be impossible: and the will to live forever is nothing but the animal will to go on living expressed reflectively and transferred, somewhat incongruously, to the social self or historical person.

SPIRIT. Psyches, we have said, take on the character of souls when spirit awakes in them. Spirit is an awareness natural to animals, revealing the world and themselves in it. Other names for spirit are consciousness, attention, feeling, thought, or any word that marks the total *inner* difference between being awake or asleep, alive or dead. This difference is morally absolute; but physically the birth of spirit caps a long growth during which excitability and potentiality of various kinds are concentrated in organisms and become transmissible. The *outer* difference between sleeping and waking, life and death, is not absolute; and we may trace certain divergences between the path of transmission for the psyche and the basis of distribution for the spirit. Life follows the seed, through long periods of unconsciousness and moral nonexistence; whereas spirit lives in the quick interplay of each sensitive individual and the world, and often is at its height when, after keen experience, the brain digests the event at leisure, and the body is sexually quiescent or reduced by old age to a mere husk. In the spirit, by definition, there is nothing persistent or potential. It is pure light and perpetual actuality. Yet the intensity and scope of this moral illumination, as well as the choice of characters lighted up, the order of the scenes and how long each shall last, all hang on the preparations nature may have made for this free entertainment.

CHAPTER II

ON COSMIC ANIMISM

LET us admit that something called spirit exists, and exists invisibly, in a manner of its own, by virtue of an intrinsic moral intensity. Its essence lies in willing, suffering, looking, being pleased, absorbed, or offended. It talks to itself inaudibly, evoking and releasing an infinity of fugitive images, yet sometimes proceeding to a conclusion, to the comparatively fixed possession of an idea. Without being a substance separable from the act of feeling or thinking, this spirit lives through time, as in a dream. It remains spirit throughout, not only in its specific character of witness and living light, but in its capacity for recollecting and prefiguring its experience. It forms designs and develops them dramatically in idea, yet in effect it is helpless and evanescent. It awakes and dies down at no command of its own. Its centre seems to travel, passing from one occasion to another and, for all we can see, arising out of nothing, not once only but often, and often lapsing into nothing again.

Whence this fevered existence? When does it arise? In what places does it exist? For how long? With what diversity of dramatic experience and intellectual scope?

These are cosmological questions. Whether there are spirits in the mountain-tops, or in the clouds or in the higher parts of the heavens, or wandering ghosts at night, or souls waiting in limbo for re-incarnation or for the resurrection of their bodies, spirit can never

discover by withdrawing within itself. The more it
is spirit, the less interested it will be in those romantic

The ques-
tion of its
origin and
distribution
is cosmo-
logical.
possibilities. Even the terrible alternative
between heaven and hell for their own souls,
and for those of all mankind, an alternative which many spiritual persons have
faced intellectually, has left them strangely
unperturbed; unless indeed they interpreted that
doctrine spiritually, as representing the torments or
liberation of spirit everywhere and at any time. I
think that, on the other hand, theosophists and spiritualists follow a shrewd instinct when, in support of
their beliefs, they turn to natural science and to physical
phenomena. Matter is the principle of distribution for
spirit as for every other feature of the existing world.
The "other" world, if it exists, is a neighbour or extension of this world, so that inter-communication may
well be possible between the two, travellers may pass
from one to the other, and the change of scene need
not destroy the identity of the characters or the unity
of the play. Supersensitive persons might feel strange
influences descending on them from those remote
regions. Our habitual ignorance cannot abolish what
happens to be unknown to us, or forbid it to exist.
Conjecture is therefore free to imagine as much spirit
in the world as it pleases, or as the analogies of
nature may impose on our dramatic or brotherly sense.

On the other hand, positive belief in imagined
spirits, by pressing poetic apprehension into alleged
truth, transfers the question to empirical and scientific
ground. Such belief has little to do with the subject
of this book, which touches rather the internal economy
of spirit in whatever world and with whatever companions it may chance to dwell. The landscape of
future lives, the private experiences of gods or angels,
would place spiritual dilemmas before the spirit no
less insistently than human experience places them;

and perhaps the same solutions would suggest themselves there also, negative, ascetic, and mystical in heaven as well as on earth. At least, it would probably be so if those spirits were more spiritual than ourselves and less ignorant, rather than merely wilder, happier, and freer. Thus how wide or how thick may be the population of spirits in nature is frankly irrelevant to actual spiritual life, seeking or losing in each instance a path to inward salvation. Yet those cosmological problems cannot help interesting the philosopher who may be investigating from the outside the origin and place of spirit in the universe. I will therefore say a word about them before proceeding to other matters.

In the first place, is spirit *distributed* at all? Might it not be the fundamental locus of all other things? This is what spirit itself is inclined to assert when it becomes thoroughly self-conscious and perceives its transcendental relation to every discovery it may make. The pure insight here is invincible, but hard to maintain pure. The flux of existence prevents. At any moment we may inhale and suck in the whole universe ideally; but exhaling will never restore that universe to its natural reality. Every vista, temporal or spatial, will have been gathered up into the intense present vision in which alone it exists. For discursive thought, however, this concentrated actuality is a blind alley. Emotionally we are enraptured: we have momentarily become God, a truly solitary and unclouded deity; no scheming, commanding, responsible creator or governor of a universe, but a pure fact, a pure possession of all truth, incapable of creating anything; for to create effectually would be to generate something external to oneself, of which this transcendental spirit, by hypothesis, could know nothing. The only possible way for spirit to create is to imagine. Thus conscious-

The transcendental priority of spirit regards only its experience, not its existence or distribution.

ness in making itself the seat and criterion of reality, denies itself the privilege of knowledge.

The truth is that knowledge and consciousness are transcendental in regard to ideas, but not in regard to the objects which furnish the occasion and the external control for those ideas.   It is merely fatuous to identify our ideas with their objects in theory, but it would be tragic if anyone did so in action.   The temptation to do so is real, as we see in dreams; because spirit truly has a vital priority and universality in respect to its eventual knowledge: but this holds only of the single private perspectives, scattered as actual spirit is scattered, along the ups and downs of natural life. Scarcely has imagination in some exalted mystical moments wallowed up all time and change, when that insight lapses, we suffer a jolt, our heaven is clouded over, there is not only thunder and lightning above us, but our very soul begins to cry for help.   It turns out that the spirit that had seemed to compose and deploy the universe is itself an incident in the universe, subject to fortune, and broken into moments and into fragmentary views.   Even if somewhere, in some superhuman instance, it should be able to embrace all things in idea, it surely exists also elsewhere in other instances in which that omniscience is lost and that peace turned to anguish, when the mind's eye, in which all things were supposed to be painted, peers tearful and half-blind into a dreadful past and an unknown future.

A philosophy, then, reposing entirely on the transcendental dignity of spirit would not represent the cosmos as animated, since there would be no cosmos, only dreams generated by ignorance and delusion; and it would not even represent spirit legitimately as animating the conventional history of the world as attested by documents; for the past too would be a creation of the present.   But transcendentalism is

Indian and German idealism represents the cosmos not as animate but as visionary.

seldom taken so strictly.   When the Germans talk of
spirit animating history or even nature, they are not
thinking of the actual spirit in themselves, at that
moment framing that vista.   They are rather giving
the name of spirit, in a metaphorical sense, to some
tendency or principle or law which they vaguely conceive the facts to obey.   Such "spirit" is not a spiritual
reality but what I call an essence or at best a trope:
in itself a conceived rhythm or, if actually executed
by events, a truth about them.   So when the Indians
talk of Brahma as the support and only reality of the
universe, they are evoking something to which, in my
vocabulary, the name of spirit cannot belong.   This
Brahma is a state of deep sleep in which spirit, matter,
and essence seem to lie concentrated and undeveloped.
The dreamer is felt to be deeper than the dream,
physiologically quite truly: but is this non-dreaming
dreamer a spirit?

I know what the Indians might say about Brahma
at once hearing and not hearing, seeing and not seeing, etc.   He *does* hear, in as much as
whenever creatures hear it is only he that
hears in them.   Yet he does *not* hear, since
in his own person he is free from all relativity or privation, seated in no particular station or
organ, and not subject to the false intrusion of sensation or thought: things which are false because founded
on ignorance of all the rest of infinite Being.   Brahma
can lend no ear to these illusions, but annuls them
morally and sleeps on, as the deep sea sleeps on,
unmindful of the vain transitory lights and vain transitory tempests that play upon the surface.   Very well:
I have no quarrel with that intuition, or with any
intuition.   Yet in terms of the logic implicit in common sense, the Brahma so described would become
actual spirit only when somewhat ruffled by circumstances, and actually hearing, etc.   In so far as he

Is Brahma the absolute self truly a spirit?

remained asleep in a dead calm, he would be only the non-existent possibility of spirit, the unused category of thought, the unexemplified essence of any consciousness that might arise eventually.   The profound reality of Brahma in his deep sleep is surely felt to be much more than that.   He pre-eminently exists.   He is precisely what is substantial and solid, warm and vital, in all things: the positive potentiality of all universes and of all thoughts.   Undoubtedly: but then my name for Brahma would not be spirit but matter; because in my system as the name for the *intrinsic ideal possibility of all things* is essence, so the name for the *existing potentiality of specific things* is matter.

This identification may seem extravagant.   The highly subtle notion of Brahma, or transcendental spirit breathing at peace, lies at the opposite pole from stocks and stones, fire and blood.   Yet the Indians themselves often identify Brahma with ether, with breath, or even like Thales, with water.   It is they, not I, that confuse spirit with the primary substance of things.   It has always been under the spell of natural forces that poets have shaped their mythology; and it is still by an intense concentration on mere life, mere duration, or mere dumb existence, that the mystic experiences his identity with the absolute. This identity is hidden, latent, destructive of detail: it is an identity of substance, in a diversity of persons. But the *substance* of spirit is matter as of all other transitory things.   Were the notion of spirit not thus fused with that of substance (as it notoriously was by Parmenides) it could never carry that suggestion of indestructible primacy, power, and intimate secret presence in all things which it evidently carries to the devout mind.

The devout mind is pious and anxious, as well as spiritual; it never therefore quite divorces the idea of salvation from that of safety and profit.   Now safety—a treacherous safety—and profit—a temporary profit—are in the gift of matter, of fortune; and few would worship spirit if they did not understand it to be the very breath and law of material things. But this breath bloweth where it listeth, and this law is ironical, in *Religion not satisfied with the immaterial.* that it destroys everything that it fosters. Thus experience of the world turns a clear spirit away from the world; and substance when recognized in its indefinite and vain fertility invites the spirit to withdraw within itself. There is thus a kind of co-operation and understanding between pure matter and pure spirit. As matter is plastic and blindly prolific, so spirit, in its inviolate transcendental station, is infinitely open and detached from particulars. It offers, as it were, an intangible mirror to matter, like a glass sky traversed by no heavenly bodies but only by reflected images of earth.

Thus the moral safety of spirit, the joy of its inner intellectual liberty, seems to the natural man a sublimated echo of material safety and good fortune. The prophets express salvation in the language of prosperity, as the mystics in that of love. They are not content that heaven and hell should be merely within us, or that insight should be its own reward. Though the chastened spirit may secretly smile, it will be reputed by the pious to work miracles. Philosophical demagogues will promise to turn the most vulgar of generations into gods; and even in the Upanishads the enthusiastic King, quite convinced at the end of each lesson that all things are indifferent, cries to the Brahmin, "I will give thee, O Venerable One, a thousand cows."

I think, then, that in fundamental sympathy with Indian wisdom, we may draw the following distinctions in our own language:

In so far as Brahma is conceived as a universal

readiness for thinking, undetermined to any particular thought, he is the *essence* of pure transcendental spirit,

and non-existent until exemplified in some actual intuition.

In so far as he is conceived to be infinitely pregnant and to contain virtually the characters of all possible beings, but without any distinction of subject from object or any actual intuition, Brahma is pure being or the realm of essence.

In so far as this potentiality is conceived to be something real and extant (since avowedly phenomena are not created by pure spirit but produced naturally by a regular development of works and psychic heredities), Brahma is the inner reality of matter.

In so far as within particular psyches Brahma hears, sees, thinks, and suffers, he is existent spirit. He *exists* only diffused; but it is only by attaining his transcendental dignity and cognitive essence that particular psyches can ever hear, see, think, or suffer actually and in a moral sense; so that it is the one pure quality of spirit, it is Brahma himself, that blows through all living beings, whenever they are stirred to consciousness.

This Indian notion of deity corresponds best to our modern insight into the transcendental nature of spirit; for here subjectivism in logic and sentiment is united with naturalism in the description of the world. But our own religious traditions do better justice to the moral and tragic side of the matter. Spirit does not lose its divine nature by becoming incarnate in man, by being rejected by the world, and by suffering and dying. On the contrary, apart from such incarnation God would remain only a natural power or an infinite essence or a vain ideal. If spirit first renders man divine, humanity first renders God moral. We might even read this meaning into the *filioque* clause of the creed, saying that a Holy Spirit could never have proceeded from the Father, if it had not also proceeded from the Son.

Neither transcendental nor Indian idealism can therefore avail to animate the cosmos. They may profess to reduce it to an illusion or to an unconscious work of the spirit; but spirit itself will thereby forfeit its spiritual nature, until, becoming conscious in the vicissitudes of that too real world, it asserts its spirituality by surmounting them. In its reality, then, spirit will be dispersed, and very thinly, in the world which it is alleged to create. *(Spiritual falsity of pantheism.)*

Might not this dispersion of spirit be admitted and yet the exclusive reality of it be maintained? Might it not exist in an infinite number of instances, with only spiritual relations between them?

I can conceive such a universe, although I know of no philosopher that has described it. Leibniz perhaps came near it, in his ingenious monadology: but his monads were souls, developing through physical time. If he had taken the transcendental unity of spirit seriously, he would have been compelled to break up *(Theory of spiritual monads making up a physical world.)* his personal monads into as many spiritual monads as there were instants of life in each of them; and the relations between these instants, like those between different souls, would have become moral only, subsisting in the realm of truth, without any physical medium of distribution, not even a physical time. Perhaps such was his secret insight, if he ever applied the principle of internal relations to the moments of time; for then the temporal vistas within each moment would correspond with the temporal vistas of all other moments, yet the moments would not occupy distinct dates in any physical time flowing beneath them or through them.

Distribution into separate souls, each with a consecutive life, is by no means essential to spirit. In our world spirit is so distributed, because a certain persistence on the part of an organism must, according to the established order of nature, precede any sensation; and it is from our animal souls and lives that spirit borrows that moral and dramatic character which marks its most vivid moments in ourselves. Indeed, without expectation, memory, and impulsive preference we should hardly give to intuition the name of spirit. On the other hand, in order to exist at one moment spirit does not require to have existed before, or to exist later; and if Leibniz identified spirit with long-lived souls, and souls again with indestructible atoms, this was due to theological and conceptual commitments that need not detain us.

Such a hypothesis is not one to accept or to disprove. It is a fable; yet the remarkable many-sided competence of Leibniz in composing it, distinguished at several crucial points what is congruous with the essence of spirit from what is incongruous. Here is a lesson to learn and, in spite of our modern progressive frivolity, never to unlearn again. It is congruous with spirit to be existentially insulated and soliptistic, yet in its solitude to keep an intellectual outlook over its own career, past and future, and over a world felt to surround and control it; for while spirit is enormously active morally and imaginatively, a great dreamer, and full of obsessing cares, yet it is subject at every turn to external fatalities, to surprises and torments; and even when left relatively free, it often feels within itself a sudden tendency to fall asleep, or a sudden tendency to stretch its normal wakefulness to abnormal lengths, as if it could grow omniscient, divinely balanced, and superior to every accident. All this Leibniz admirably indicates in his myth of the everlasting monads, infinite in number, cut off essentially from one another, but each developing (or perhaps

Respects in which the monadology does justice to spirit.

reverting) through all the stages of slumber, dream and intelligence.

At the same time it is incongruous with spirit to appear or to operate in the physical world; it can never descend from its transcendental station of witness and judge into the region of objects. It lives, indeed, in a natural society; but that fact can never abolish its spiritual solitude, nor the intrinsic centrality of thought in each of its instances. And the counterpart of this spiritual concentration is the infinity of possible instances of thought. Thus the monadology exhibits in a myth the inwardness and transcendental purity of spirit, its spark-like unity and starlike multiplicity; and all later transcendental idealism only elaborates the notion of this solitary thinking monad of Leibniz, thinking its fated world.

Nevertheless this allegiance to the pure notion of spirit involved Leibniz in hopeless difficulties when, turning his radical transcendentalism into a cosmology, he identified his monad first with the psyche and then, even more extravagantly, with the physical atom; so that the light of consciousness, something essentially warm, moral, and volatile, something *spiritual*, became the substance of the cosmos, comminuted, geometrized, galvanized, and persisting *ad infinitum*. In this sphere the notion of a monad without windows repeats the conceptual atomism of Democritus who wished matter to be composed of indestructible geometrical solids. But ideal fixity of any kind is false to the intimately fluid and relational nature of existence. The natural atom is all windows—all windows at least dynamically; and even in the scheme of Democritus it was the motions, shocks, and congeries of the atoms that supplied the needed orchestration for the life of nature. Indeed, the metaphor of being windowless was not altogether happy even for spirit; for although spirit can admit nothing passively from outside, nothing of foreign manufacture, yet its inward inventiveness is fed by external stimuli and made cognitive by anxiety about ulterior things. The unity here is that of outlook; and the counterpart of it is a universal curiosity, an impartial aptness to know and to experience everything whatsoever. If spirit be without windows, or rather without doors, it lives by peering perpetually outwards through that dome of many-coloured but transparent glass which the psyche has built round it. The light, however—and this is the main point—is not that of a sun outside, but of a fire within. It is animal life kindled into flame and dramatizing the world from that focus with the spasmodic chiaroscuro of good and evil.

The monadology of Leibniz appeared at an unfortunate moment, and hardly received the developments it demanded; for scarcely had the universe been analysed in Germany into nothing but souls, when the soul was analysed in England into nothing but perceptions. And it was a just nemesis: because the soul, if anything, is a poetic name for a biological reality, for the psyche, a system of tropes in animal life as observable as the organism and its behaviour. These physical facts are the *natura naturata* of natural history; and the psyche is the same facts synthesized logically into an ideal *natura naturans*. It had therefore been a false step, a step into empty air, to ignore the hereditary formative psyche and to give the name of soul to consciousness, however attenuated or dull this consciousness might be said to be. Degrees of vivacity in feeling are perhaps only relative and imputed; where feeling arises at all, it brings its own standard of intensity. Leibniz had passed in his monadology, founded on the logic of parts and wholes, into a fictitious region; his psychology had become literary,

The psyche, a biological unit, disappears in psychologism.

where perception, introspection, memory, and reasoning exhaust the realities conceived or conceivable. In this literary psychology there is no psyche: there are only images, emotions, dramatic fictions, verbal associations. It was therefore a sort of ironical duty for any shrewd reader of Leibniz to abandon his system, since his critical principle, reducing nature to spiritual monads, reduced his monads at once to passing intuitions; and then we should have only these atomic and homeless intuitions on our hands with which to compose a universe. Our universe would have no souls in it, and no substances or causes; only a cloud of psychological states, existing in no medium and produced by no agency.

Cosmos is not the word to describe such a world; yet the chaos it dissolves into if consistently thought out has one great merit for my present purpose: it is composed exclusively of spirit; an undiluted actuality permeates every part. By examining this system we may see how far spirit alone might go to constitute a world, and by what illusions we might disguise the essential incapacity of spirit to generate itself or to collect its instances into an historical process.

In the first place, there are unavoidable but illegitimate implications in the chief terms that a psychological idealism is compelled to use. The words idealism and idea are themselves illegitimate and constantly ambiguous. An idea is properly an essence, and idealism a system that attributes power to the essences exemplified in things, as if their beauty or clearness had caused matter to assume those forms. But this contradicts the nominalism and the scepticism inherent in any genuine retreat into the passing state of mind. Nor are the names commonly given to these states of mind less misleading. They are not properly "perceptions", for a perception implies an object or an

Yet even literary psychology is saturated with naturalism.

occasion provoking and justifying that perception: whereas in pure psychologism there is never any object save the contents of the mind at the moment, and there is no present occasion, deeper than that state of mind, to determine what that state of mind shall be. "Sensation" and "feeling", in the same way, suggest more than what psychologism can allow: they suggest a plight of the organism, a movement in things, of which the spirit becomes morally aware, without yet discerning any graphic image. Finally, "idea" remains to render confusion worse confounded: for while still often meaning essence it also means intuition, some episode in the life of spirit, or even the whole passing state of the psyche, in which much more may lie fermenting than the discrimination of any recognizable idea.

All this confusion is involuntary and excusable in a philosophy struggling against common sense and the genius of human language. Sometimes an effort is made to clear the air, and adopt fresh and more appropriate categories; and we hear less of states of mind and more of phenomena, data, or even objects. But this path leads away from psychologism and back to essences and things; as by another less honourable path, through "unconscious mind" and psychic powers supposed to be spiritual, we return likewise to mother nature.

Much deeper runs the delusion of having superseded the physical world by a purely spiritual society. Social idealism incoherent. A purely spiritual society is conceivable, but not as modern philosophy may conceive. Such a society would be a community of angels, each singing his note in eternity, notes which might compose a harmony of which each might be somehow aware. But between these intuitive sorrows or joys there would be no temporal sequence, no communication or causation. Every phrase of that

music, though there might be musical perspectives
and infinite undertones within it, would in its existence
be without date or place; and these phrases could
neither physically collect, nor physically separate themselves into parallel series, such as common sense conceives human lives to be. A purely spiritual world
would be a monadology of conscious moments, an
ideal symphony of emotions, conspiring or contrasting,
but never meeting, or merging, or generating one
another. If the romantic society of active colliding
and well-known "spirits" conceived, for instance, by
Berkeley, differs so radically from that celestial swarm
of spiritual atoms, the reason is that naturalism survives illegitimately in the habitual assumptions of all
idealists, as of all men. The stuff of modern idealism
is not ideas, it is not spirits, but novelesque literary
psychology; and this psychology, being biographical,
moves in the frame of physical time and physical
evolution. It describes the supposed inner experience
of human souls, born at one date and buried at another
in particular geographical places; souls travelling with
their bodies like the soul of Locke in his coach between
Oxford and London. The psychological philosopher
may reduce his idea of the physical world to a fiction
of the imagination, symbolizing his spiritual relations
with his own past and future, and with other spirits;
but this reduction he makes dialectically in argument
and on paper. He is absolutely debarred from making it in his real belief or daily conceptions not only
because contrary assumptions are involved and ratified
in action, but because, if he did not make these contrary assumptions, his own social idealism would be
blown to the winds.

Men are animals, and human society is an animal
society. Spirit is undoubtedly incarnate in those men,
and may on occasion withdraw into itself mystically
and disengage itself ascetically from the animal interests

of life; but you cannot have it both ways. If you are wedded to the flesh and to the world, very well, your spirit may enjoy following their fortunes; but then you cannot liberate yourself, save in empty words, from acknowledging their existence and their dominion. It is not by calling them fictions, and still serving them, that you will pass into a spiritual sphere. Your affections, your self-love, your conceit of freedom and immortality would need first to be disinfected and renounced: they are all animal passions, forms of animal lust, pride, and propulsiveness. Then, if what remained or supervened seemed to you bliss, you might say truly that you were a spirit alone with the spirit; and it would not concern you any longer to deny matter, as if you were afraid of it or of the notion of it; for now you would no longer be living competitively within nature against the rest of nature, but speculatively and disinterestedly in sight of the whole; and you would be essentially too much above nature to chafe at being existentially a very small part of it.

The fiction that all is spirit leaves spirit enslaved to matter.

Cosmic animism has therefore no real affinity with spiritual insight or spiritual liberation. Spiritual minds may legitimately give names to all things according to the part these things play in the spiritual drama; but this is poetry to be understood poetically. Any dogmatic assertion of the spiritual texture of things, in turning spirit into power, turns it unwittingly into matter; and the consequences are not confined to a change of vocabulary. The very notion of spirit is thereby lost or infected; and the man in whom spirit seemed to awake becomes again a busybody and a worldling, a partisan and a fanatic, a slave of time, a dupe of place, and a puppet in an evolution which he calls spiritual, but which is really that of the material world.

CHAPTER III

THE NATURAL DISTRIBUTION OF SPIRIT

OLDER and saner than any cosmic idealism is the sense that spirit is universally diffused, not by itself but in union with matter. As consciousness is the inner invisible reality of life in our bodies, might it not be the inner invisible reality of things everywhere? The analogy is tempt- *What is the extent of animation in nature?* ing, and becomes irresistible when, as among kindred living creatures, there is also a close analogy in structure and habit. But the analogy becomes deceptive as we recede from our own species, and ignore the specific conditions of consciousness even in ourselves. We are often unconscious, or almost unconscious : what then quickens consciousness in us, and how far is a similar excitation traceable in nature?

There are sweeping speculative turns of thought by which, without any accurate inspection, we might assure ourselves that something called spirit pervades the universe. If for instance we *Vitality of physical forces.* define life as spontaneous motion, it becomes evident that matter is everywhere alive; and if we define spirit in the primitive materialistic manner, as the principle and cause of motion, it becomes a truism that matter is everywhere instinct with spirit. But such ways of speaking are intolerable in a critical philosophy, and I have already discarded any definition of spirit that identifies it with physical motions or physical forces. The potential and the dynamic, according to my use of terms, are by definition material;

while spirit possesses activity or energy only in the
Aristotelian sense of being a perfect realization or
ultimate fruition of function. The same use of terms,
however, will justify me in saying that a *potentiality* of
spirit lies in all life, perhaps in all matter. This does
not mean that actual spirit, only very faint, pervades
the material world. It means that in the primeval
motions and tensions of matter there are rhythms and
tropes capable of compounding themselves eventually
into living organisms; and we know in our own case
that the fortunes of a living organism have a moral
import; in other words, carry consciousness or spirit
with them.

Throughout nature there are events about which
it is possible to care. The forces producing these
events seem to form a system, as if each part moved
in concert with the other parts, and was affected by
their presence and motion: a permeating physical
responsiveness that may seem to foreshadow perception and will, and certainly prepares the ground for
them. Yet this anticipation is remote. Moral being
arises by virtue of the self-recovery and self-defence
practised by specific creatures; a world, no matter how
organic, if it evolved undisturbed, would have no
occasion for sensation or reaction. Moreover (and
this cuts deeper) we should remember that the dynamic
unity of our world is ignorantly posited by us, as a
condition of rational action within it; [1] so that the
side of physical reality discoverable to us may be
only an excerpt made by our specific sensibility,
leaving out all that is beyond our range; and who
knows how chaotic that residue may be? No wonder,
then, if an image so selected reflects the unity of the
selective eye.

It would be a worse impertinence, however, to
deny positively that the tremor of change running

[1] Cf. *The Realm of Matter*. Chapter II, toward the end.

through the universe may carry with it some conscious thrill and forward assurance, some music of the spheres; and the distinct parts in turn may be variously haunted by some wraith of intelligence or will, on the same ontological plane as spirit in ourselves. If for that reason, we proclaim the universal presence of spirit in matter, at least we should not forget the dictum of Spinoza that the mind of the universe resembles the human mind as the dogstar resembles the barking animal, in name only. Man lives on food, reproducing himself precariously, dying, and struggling not to die. His experience is all born of pressure and care. But a universe lives on itself, without habitat or neighbours; its mind would therefore be entirely free and automatic, subject to no external stimulus and addressed to no external object. As Sirius and a dog are parts of the same realm of matter, so a universal mind and the human mind would fall within the same category of spirit, and deserve that title. But they would be as different, within that sphere, as it is possible to be.

That which the analogy of nature suggests or even imposes is rather that in matter everywhere there must be a *potentiality* of mind. But what is potentiality? A mere possibility (such as the "possibility of sensation" which Mill made the essence of matter) has no existence

Real potentiality of spirit in matter.

or power whatever, except in the language of the philosopher or in his expectations. So with that insidious expression "unconscious mind". This phrase marks something that people are not able or not willing to describe honestly, namely, the *truth* that, under certain additional conditions, a feeling or a thought will arise. The existing facts are either material, and then not to be called states of mind at all; or else (on the hypothesis of psychologism) they are a constellation of previous or contemporary states of mind in the history of spirit: in which case they are not in the least unconscious. But philosophical writing has become so slovenly that perhaps a *forgotten* feeling or thought may be called unconscious, because not given at the present moment: in which case all other people's thoughts are always unconscious, and the greater part of one's own. They are indeed for the most part hidden from one another. But properly "unconscious mind" should be intrinsically latent, a process only potentially conscious. This process is now non-mental, that is to say material; because a real potentiality is the actuality of something else. Potential mind, for a psychological idealist, is therefore an absurdity, since in his view all the real antecedents of any sensation or thought must be actual sensations or thoughts elsewhere. But for a materialist the phrase "potential mind", though clumsy, need not be meaningless. A seed is the seat of a real potentiality; it is not a blank; it is not an ideal possibility or essence, but a moment in a material involution and evolution, materially conditioning, under favourable circumstances, the growth of a particular organism. In this sense we might say truly that the potentiality of mind pervades the universe, since doubtless, if the prerequisite material complexities arose at any point, spirit would arise there. Of this we are instinctively sure whenever an animal is born. If the little creature is alive, the little creature is conscious, or will become conscious when duly shaken. All we need do, therefore, in order to discover the distribution of spirit is to study life, to rehearse its movements as sympathetically as possible, putting ourselves in every creature's place, and seeing if spirit in us is thereby really enlarged, or whether we are merely attributing our trite humanity to nature in moral fables.

This subject is not open to science, but only to discernment and imagination. Moral affinity must be felt morally; and if an animation not moral, and in that sense not human, pervades other parts of the world, we must be content to ignore it. In nature, as in a book, we can discover only such thoughts as we are capable of framing. These will be seldom or never the exact thoughts of the author, or of the other animals; yet an author will have existed, and his thoughts will be recoverable if there is a sufficient likeness between the capacities of the writer and the reader, the speaker and the listener.

True mind reading rests on animal sympathy.

On both sides, at any rate, understanding follows upon inspiration. The most deliberate talker must once have formed his phrases without knowing what they would be; and an intuitive writer, like a sympathetic reader, hears the upwelling thoughts spoken within him, and devoutly listens as he writes. Second thoughts and corrections, contradictions and arguments, merely compare different automatisms that seek to talk one another down. It would be sheer pandemonium, but for two kindly deities that come sooner or later to appease the quarrel. One is Convention, imposing current and communicable ways of talking, apart from actual thought; and the other is Intuition itself, silent and private, surviving the fray and independent of the issue. But neither convention nor actual intuition can penetrate to alien spirit, or disclose its existence. They are tightly subjective and exclusive; and it is only because of their instability that the psyche sometimes passes, in the rough and tumble of life, into the magnetic field of other organisms, and can catch something of their spirit.

The spiritual side of animal life, savage life, ancient or foreign life cannot be approached in the temper of sporting travellers or invading missionaries, or even in that of evolutionary philosophers. We gain nothing by congratulating other creatures on the degree of our special humanity that they may have attained. Insight might

Indefinite elasticity of moral existence.

begin if we could discover or conceive unsuspected
ways of feeling: superhuman courage, fidelity or
patience; superhuman scope of the instincts; infrahuman absoluteness or intermittance of the passions;
even, in so far as such a thing is feasible, some non-
human direction or scale of perception. I can call
these endowments *super-* or *infra*-human, because I
am taking the point of view of spirit as it moves in us;
but nothing gives this criterion authority over those
different impulses and experiments. The life of
spirit is but one ultimate phase of one sort of life.
Could we understand the other directions in which
nature may move, we should possess other criteria by
which our own criterion could be judged, not indeed
with greater authority, but with equal justification.
Even in ourselves order has some plasticity, and
anarchy some allurements. Devils and semi-bestial
gods, nymphs and muses were no empty fancies.
They were inspired dreams of what existence might
be and almost is, either beyond us or in ourselves.

The ancients thought the stars animate and even
divine, because the stars know so perfectly what to do.
Order, where This hardly seems, to us, a sign of intelli-
there is life, gence. We think of mind in romantic
generates modern times as a sort of truant, a dis-
spirit. embodied force, interfered with by real
things and interfering with them from outside. Both
our self-consciousness and our mechanical arts encourage this sentiment. Our intellectuals are rebels, proud
to run out of their orbit. At the same time, we live
amid machines that have uses entirely foreign to their
substance; and our own purposes are artificial, imposed
by a variable society or by some variable idea. If one
artist or leader shows more genius than another, we
think it due to his abstract mind and groundless
originality; as if hands were not concerned in doing
the work, or the labyrinth of fact in imposing the

action. We are nothing if not critics, but without a
criterion for criticism; and we think ideas clever and
persuasive for finding fault with reality rather than
for expressing it. We thus abstract our minds from
ourselves, and imagine that we do as minds what we
can do, or can wish to do, only as animals.

Doubtless the stars are not animals, and here the
rusticity of fancy in the ancients, who had been pastoral
peoples, misled their judgment; but if the stars had
been animals, the fact that they knew perfectly what
to do would have been a mark in them of great intelligence and sovereignty of spirit. Unfortunately, that
relative security and liberty which the stars find in
space cannot be enjoyed by animate bodies on earth;
the spirit native to us is therefore distracted. But it
was a just perception of the ancients that such distraction was a hindrance to spirit, and not, as we moderns
are tempted to think, the cause of spirit or an effect of
it. Mathematical or static order, like any essence, is
in itself lifeless, yet the material process by which such
order is achieved or maintained obeys a trope, and
adumbrates an organism ; so that the apparently static
order of the stars, the mountains, or sublime archi-
tecture properly seems to us a high expression of
spirit, and a great support to it. To conceive such a
harmony, even as static, involves a transitive harmony
of motions and tensions in ourselves. The psyche is
exalted in rehearsing that order; and quite intelligibly,
since organisms exist only by enacting some form of
order and defending it, and the psyche is but a name
for the success of the organism in so doing. When
spirit perceives order in the world, it is therefore
quickened by a sort of concourse and applause electri-
fying all those impulses by which the soul itself and
the spirit first came to exist.

If we were justified, then, in attributing spirit to
movements in nature not on the human scale, it would

be sane and humble in us to think such spirit purer and keener than our own, where those movements were more exact and constant than ours. In the heavens the same idea that described action would fill and satisfy thought; and we might truly say that the stars were guided by a perfect intelligence of their motions and an immortal determination to do their duty. They would have assurance of their destiny forever, and would joyously execute what they foretold. How hazy, how confused, and distressed in comparison, seems a mortal mind! Like all good myths, this notion of the life of the heavens and of Aristotle's God has a moral justification, being the glorification of what tends to occur in us as our minds grow clearer and clearer. Our spirits become freer or, in the cant of to-day, more creative, and we grow happier as our thought and our endeavours express our true potentialities. The psyche has then come to know her resources and her vocation. She is reconciled to herself and to the world in so far as it affects her; she has attained her normal intelligence and virtue. Where these are wanting, we remain tossed by barbaric caprice, benumbed by superstition, rent by internal conflicts. We then cannot help placing our liberty in our ignorance and our pleasures in our vices.

Spirit expresses harmony, but the elements of that harmony must be tensions.

It would be foolish to imagine the spirit dwelling in an absolute void or in the spaces between the worlds or between animals, so that it might slip miraculously into any part of nature at random, breeding grapes out of thistles, or inspiring trees to walk and fishes to speak. How should such absolute spirit, even if it had magic powers, ever decide in its own blank, unattached mind what fiats to issue or in what crises to intervene? If it is to act a part in the drama, it must subserve the passion of the play. It must have, as the poet's mind

It can arise only in an animal psyche.

has, its special memories and affinities, to load the dice, to follow a scent, to crave a particular issue. The place of spirit is in a psyche. There must first be a psyche specifically organized, directed upon a particular type of transmissible and defensible life, rich in definite but unknown potentialities. Spirit is incarnate by nature, not by accident. Otherwise it would not possess the lyrical, moral, impassioned character that makes it spiritual. It is intellectual, it thinks ideas; but it is not a realm of ideas hypostasized. It is alive, nothing if not transitive, always on the wing, watching, comparing, suffering, and laughing. It is the consciousness proper to an animal psyche.

This locus of spirit determines in each case its special vocation, turns it perhaps into a moral or social inspiration, when it might have been, in another body at another time, an irresponsible wild sensibility. Perception, impulse, conscience, and hope anchor spirit inwardly in the earth. It cannot imagine, it cannot *It bears inward witness to this fact by its vital and moral bias.* love, what is not somehow native to its home climate. Even its rebellions and contrary dreams are dictated by its animal predicaments. It is a spiritual symptom of vital strains. Ideas do not ask to be conceived; they threaten nothing to the sleeping mind that may neglect to distinguish them. But on the physical side attention and watchfulness are evidently crucial. They enlarge the capacity of an organism to react upon things, to change with them when necessary, and to change them when possible. And how should a pure spirit gratuitously and even blasphemously have pronounced some parts of the creation good and others evil? And why should it embrace as momentous and agonizing the poor fortunes of a particular earthly creature? Logically, rationally, morally this is a scandal, an insoluble mystery, or even, as some think, a hideous sin, meriting the endless torments that ensue upon it.

Turn to the natural history of the matter, and though the mystery remains, since any fact at bottom must be mysterious, the scandal vanishes; and what a self-torturing conscience thought a sin becomes the innocent, inevitable, beautiful impulse in any rhythmic or living thing to persevere in its existence and to grow into all those complexities and extensions that come naturally in its way. Will is but this impulse raised to consciousness, these inwardly rooted potentialities taking shape, and struggling to be born. The impulse and will, though groundless morally, are not groundless physically, but just what at that point they would naturally be; and the potentialities, though limited and specific, are not gratuitous, but fruitful and genial, if only harsh circumstances or their own conflicts do not crush or distort them. Spirit thus depends for sanity, for sweetness and hope, on that same physical order on which it depends for existence.

Our question concerning the distribution of spirit is now virtually answered. While the criterion for *Provisional* the existence of spirit is internal, namely, *conclusion.* that it finds itself thinking, the criterion for its distribution is public and historical, namely, the observable distribution of those forms of behaviour with which, in our several persons, we find spirit allied. Evidently this criterion, if scientific in its mode of application, is still subjective in its principle, and open to continual revision. Observers have different degrees of dramatic sensibility, and may see spirits everywhere or nowhere. A true interpretation would need to revise all such intuitive mind-reading. Yet mind-reading, in principle, must always remain intuitive; and where such intuition cannot but mislead, because the nature of the observed physical life differs from the physical life of the observer, all that a critic can do is to discount his personal equation and say: I recognize that there must be spirit, or something like spirit, in other regions, and I salute it and transcribe it, as well as I can, into my human terms; but I see that my myths are myths, and bow to the liberty of alien spirit to blow as it listeth.

A close and credible insight into spiritual life can therefore extend only to the limits of a man's race, temperament, and habit. Spontaneity here may then repeat and understand spontaneity there; and what is intrinsically a poetic exercise, not a metaphysical revelation, may become also, by accident, a true sense of ideal union between many minds.

The outer boundaries of our exploration being thus defined, we may consider the distribution of spirit in man at closer quarters.

There is a false traditional problem about what was called the seat of the soul, or in more modern parlance, the exact point in the brain and instant of time at which consciousness should spring out of the body or should impinge upon it from some fourth moral dimension. The ancients were not troubled by this question; and if it had been put to them, perhaps they *Mind though relevant to physical space and time has no position there.* might have replied that they failed to localize actual intuition or moral intensity in the natural world because these things being invisible and pneumatic were not to be found at all in that field. The psyche, indeed, was to be found there; and of the psyche they gave various more or less crude accounts, until Aristotle once for all distinguished form from matter, and identified the psyche (which makes the difference between living and dead bodies) not with any physical substance, but with the form which, in an organism, all suitable substances tended to assume and preserve. Even the psyche, then, was not to be found in nature as a particular thing, as for instance a hot vapour issuing from the lips in crises or at the moment of death; yet it could be discerned there intellectually, as

the form or platonic idea of life in each organism.   In
other words, the psyche was the system of self-renewing
and self-developing tropes reproduced by each species
in each of its individuals.   In these individuals the
psyche was individual, being in each a particular
instance or rehearsal of the hereditary type; in the
species, the psyche was generic, like the group of
faculties which we call human nature.   But as to the
spirit (which Aristotle called intellect or reason) that
was altogether at another level.   Intellect and reason
were the forms of spirit that interested Aristotle, who
had nothing of the poet or sceptic; and he saw that
in that direction at least spirit was altogether transcendental and not to be found in nature even as a form
that matter might acquire.   It was pure act, living
in and for itself, everywhere its own centre, a court
of appeal for perception in which all things sensible
are revised, a dialectical field for imagination in which
all essences thought of appear.

To inquire *where* this court of appeal or field of ideas
may itself lie, is misleading.   Intrinsically, as it
spontaneously asserts itself and fills itself
out, spirit lies nowhere, and has no date.
It is transcendental, that is to say, withdrawn from the sphere of the categories
which it employs, an actual intuition not
having by any possibility a position within
its own field of view.   On the other hand, intuitions
or instances of spirit are events ; something therefore
precedes and introduces them, and they debouch upon
further events.   They are also cognitive and moral;
they proclaim to themselves the existence of a world
which involves them, and which they welcome or
reject.   Therefore, unless they declare themselves to
be illusions and deny their own deliverance (a very
complicated case of spiritual distraction) they really
have, when viewed from the outside, a date and even

It not only
perceives
time but
keeps pace
in its own
way with
physical
changes.

a position in space, at least by courtesy or adoption. For they arise at some particular natural crisis, and are relevant to that crisis in duration, in character, and in scope. They are local and temporal instances of an intellectual light which in its cognitive essence sweeps over all space and time.

Now, since intuitions, viewed from outside and taken as events, have a natural locus, might we not define this locus precisely, specifying the exact movement of the organism that elicits each intuition, and the exact instant at which this intuition begins or ceases? Mustn't anything that begins and ends at all, as every actual thought surely does, begin and end at some indivisible instant?

Yes; and we may wait for science to discover, if it can, the precise cerebral commotions subtending different feelings. The times, and even the places, of those commotions will then be the physical times and places of such feelings. But there are elementary considerations that render this assertion ambiguous. In the first place, mathematical instants are not natural moments. In an infinite empty time all instants would be alike and indiscernible; they could not be individuated, because internally they would be nothing and externally the relations defining them would be identical in every case. To talk of a particular instant is therefore meaningless unless it be the limit between distinguishable events. Secondly, natural moments, to whatever simplicity they be reduced, contain at least this internal complexity, that they occur and have a direction. The act by which they arise is different in quality from that by which they lapse. They come and go: which implies that they have an origin and a sequel, and are moments in a variegated flux. Thirdly, in this flux there may be simultaneous differences in the scale of events, not

But structure in physical and mental series is not such that they can be superposed.

merely notional within one image, but physically
enacted, as the earth in going round the sun also turns
on its axis. These different units could not be contemporary, successive, or coincident, and their scales
could not be compared, if they did not measure the
same substantial flux, and impinge on the same universe
of matter.

Even physical time, then, in which we wish to
deploy the life of spirit, cannot be adequately expressed
in mathematical or graphic terms. The
world is not compacted of essences. The
whole Eleatic problem that stretches it on
the rack of dialectic is sophistical. Sensuous
extension and duration when analysed in
respect to the essence given in them yield
geometrical space and time, themselves pure essences
with no existence of their own. Such imaginary
objects can have no authority over the material forces
that they may serve to indicate or to measure. Matter
flows through these forms and lends them a scale and
tempo that are alien to them, being factual and energetic; whereas mathematical quantities are elastic, and
there is room for the greatest in the least, as there is
not in existing things. The pulses of nature have a
pace of their own that is not to be stayed or hurried,
and events tramp heavily forward, dividing inequi-
vocably by their beat the distance they travel. Each
natural moment lasts as long as it remains itself, and
the next begins with the disappearance of that
essence, as a pain stops when it ceases to be a pain,
and marks its limits without help of latitude or longi-
tude. Yet this weight and momentum of existence
within each natural moment traverse that moment
without the least hindrance from those ideal limits;
on the contrary, the natural moment exists, and is
more than an idea, precisely because it has been
generated and is the momentary form of a substance

*Mathemati-
cal form
does not
exhaust the
being even
of the realm
of matter.*

and a force that immediately pass on, and create the next moment. Such is the proper sense of the word *event*, something that comes out of something else, a phase in which some eternal essence is momentarily manifested in a flux of substance.

Now spirit is a form of life, not a hypostasis of logic, and its roots plunge precisely into that dynamic substrate that unites, creates, and destroys in turn all the gross units of the natural world. If, in its outlook, spirit rests in essences, in its origin it springs from matter; only that those tensions, movements, and natural moments which in the material world exist unawares, in spirit rise into actuality, and the essences hitherto stupidity exemplified now begin to be perceived. This is a glorious transformation, though perhaps tragic; and *actuality* has extraordinary ontological privileges.

An actual moment, or moment of spirit, possesses an internal intensive unity, even when aware only of change and distraction. It is not a fragment more or less superficially distinguishable from its medium and surroundings. On the contrary, it arises and develops from its centre outwards, like fire; it bursts forth like a ray of light and proclaims its existence with a great shout. Its objects may overlap and confuse one another, yet each intuition (even the most confused, when the confusion is conscious) is autonomous and self-formed. Their actuality separates them absolutely, and as each exists because it shines, existentially the chasm between them can never be bridged. It may indeed be bridged ideally in various ways and degrees, in representation: by faith and dramatic imagination; by similarity and common reference to the same facts; by common subsistence and historical relations in the realm of truth. How moments of spirit may spiritually support, contradict,

The intrinsic order of the realm of spirit is described in the Divine Comedy.

or fulfil one another is in fact the proper subject of
this book.   It is fundamentally the same subject as
that of Dante's *Divine Comedy*, treated in critical prose
instead of in a magnificent biographical and cosmic
myth, into which all the fervour and venom of an
unhappy life could be infused together with the
tenderness of a pure poet.   But if we ask what the
vision of Dante conveys in the end, by way of a lesson,
I think we may say it is this: The morphology of spirit,
illustrated by great examples, showing what spirit
suffers and what it gains by existing.   These myriad
lives and these myriad judgments did not produce one
another; they grew severally out of human nature in
various persons and circumstances; yet here all are
marshalled, under the form of eternity, into a hier-
archy, into a ladder of salvation, through which spirit
may mount to divine insight and freedom, but on any
step of which it may halt, down to the depths of rage
and madness.   Dante had the privilege of living in
an age when, over the sea of rage and madness, spirit
moved gloriously and universally acknowledged; also
the privilege of singing in a young language formed by
a Christian people.   These privileges led him, however, to take his great myth as almost a truth of physics;
so that his respect for the sovereignty of spirit becomes
ambiguous and we are not sure how far he is refining
his stubborn will into insight and how far he is bowing
unwillingly to power.   A colder analysis can surmount
that doubt.   The impossibility of other than moral
relations between the moments of spirit follows from
their immaterial nature.   Immateriality lifts them
above the region of interaction, relativity, potentiality,
fusion, or flux.

Therefore moments of spirit cannot be situated by
their external relations.   We must beware of assimilating them to physical events bathed in a medium
that lends them its substance and determines their

position.   An intuition does not borrow its unity or its limits from its neighbours.   In its own realm, it has no neighbours.   It can have only fellow- Every point, witnesses, complementary thoughts, fulfil- as actual, is morally ments real but separate, and enjoyed by central and others.   Each thought feeds on its own fuel, primary. and in the act of seeing or positing other things, which it is powerless to create, it must at each moment create itself.   Its field of view is finite without being circum- scribed, but grows or shrinks with the scope of atten- tion, and changes its structure and contents *ad libitum*, as in a dream.   Not the previous thought, but the contemporary flux in the psyche and in all nature, determines what the next thought shall be.   Other- wise no one could ever sleep, no one could ever die.

All the phases of spiritual existence have time in them, and local colour, though intrinsically no date, because the time and the pictured place are Time, for internal perspectives within each vista.   For them, is not spirit all times are equally present, and its a source but a vision. proper and necessary lodging is, as the *Arabian Nights* have it, "a city among the cities" and above all a heart among the hearts.   Experience becomes many-coloured as spirit passes from moment to moment and from place to place, yet to have had this career and to have been divided into these lives remains an accident of fortune.   Nothing in spirit could choose those circumstances or fix those limits. The potentialities of spiritual life are infinite and no revolutions in nature can exhaust them; while on the other hand the deeper we go down towards the roots of spirit and the more freely it is suffered to speak, so much the surer and more consistent its oracles become; because the original potentialities of spirit being infinite, they are everywhere the same.

Thus the goodly company of spirits is aptly repre- sented as a gathering of rapturous persons in one

E

assembly, sitting in ranks according to the degree of their achieved enlightenment and charity, while in dark caverns beneath writhe all the writhings ever endured. The occasions are not forgotten, as we see in the speeches of the various souls in Dante. They are remembered and judged, but they are neither re-enacted nor continued. The continuation that is relevant is found realized in the brother-spirits, sitting in the rank above. Or in a more heathen image, we may conceive the inherent relations of spiritual moments to one another as a monadology or legion of daemons, Ariels and Calibans, all free and homeless, each solitary, save for the absorbing presence to it of its imagined world; each spinning in its own thoughts, like a madman, half-prophetic, half-impossible things. This inner isolation of spirit in the wildest rush of life, this essential absence of continuity or derivation between thought and thought, throws them all the more absolutely into the arms of physical nature. There they have arisen, and from there they have drawn their variety. Yet in arising they have escaped that net, each of them has seen the light, no matter how lurid; and their prerogative of being immaterial and intellectual forbids us to distribute them in physical time or space otherwise than by their signifi-cation. Each will be, in a moral sense, lost in its theme, riveted to its object, united with what it loves: yet these more or less rhetorical expressions would never suggest themselves, and would lack all point, if they were literally true. It is only because spirit is really not in those places or in those objects, that its occasional absorption in them becomes remarkable; and in the very act of remarking it, spirit recovers its independence, retreats to its transcendental station and wonders at the bewitchment that could seem to disperse it so helplessly amid all those beasts and all those catastrophes.

CHAPTER IV

THE WILL

THE word soul or psyche is a literary symbol standing for the unconscious organic destiny present in living seeds and in living bodies. In this sense the ancients could reasonably speak of a Soul of the World, since the world has a recognizable though imperfect order of movements, full of power and beauty. To this animating form or dominant system of tropes, we may give the more modern name of universal Will, provided we are aware of using this term poetically, after the descriptive manner of Schopenhauer and other German philosophers. I will scrupulously write the word, when used in this sense, with a capital, and understand by it *the observable endeavour in things of any sort to develop a specific form and to preserve it.*

    Descriptive use of the word Will.

Such descriptive use of terms like Will and endeavour is less metaphorical than it might seem. Undoubtedly in literary psychology and in sophisticated modern speech these words are meant to designate movements of the spirit, emotions, expectations, wishes, decisions, commands, or prayers. We are here discussing the realm of spirit, and need not stop to repeat that such a moral and imaginative sphere exists, that there is an immaterial intensity in feeling, and an immaterial light in intuition. But spirit once clearly discerned and admitted, how shall we distinguish its various phases? Suppose I am thirsty: my distress, in so far as it is conscious, is a spiritual trial; but what

53

is it about?   About the state of my body; or if perhaps
there is only a dream-image that haunts me, it will be
an image of water and of myself about to drink,
but prevented.   Similarly with every other object of
passion, even the most impersonally moral or political.
There will be some dream-image of what might happen
in the world, how people might be living, how they
might be shouting for joy, and unanimously asserting
everything that I believe.   I may imagine that what I
long for is a union of pure spirits, but that is a verbal
delusion.   Spirits cannot be united unless persons are
distinguished, and persons can be distinguished only
in a physical world.   What I long for is life in a world
to come, peopled by natural bodies.   In my purest
will, I am experiencing one physical process and desiring another.   My behaviour and the events expected
to follow are the sole discoverable parts of the entire
history.   In these only could my conscious will find
evidence of any ideal unanimities.

In using the word Will for these two connected
movements in nature, one in human behaviour, the
other in its effects and conditions, we are not feigning,
then, anything psychological behind or within inanimate processes; we are rather recognizing the original
seat of those conflicts and endeavours which agitate
the spirit only because, in the first place, they agitate
the animal psyche and the material world.[1]

According to this use of terms, the psyche becomes
a particular instance of universal Will, found
whenever the form to be maintained is
organic and preserved by nutrition and reproduction.   Then spirit, too, may be called
an expression of Will, since it arises at a
specially energetic phase in the life of the psyche, namely,

Occasions on which Will in a psyche becomes conscious will or spirit.

---

[1] Hobbes used the word *endeavour* in this way.   Had his usage been
adopted, English philosophy might have begun with behaviourism instead
of ending with it.

when the range of adjustment and control begins
to extend beyond the body; for so long as life remains
purely vegetative it seems to be unconscious. No
doubt there are internal sensations in animals, which
may precede external perception; but no organ would
be morally sensitive or conscious if cut off from the
other organs and from the brain; so that spirit seems
to be allied to *messages*, even if these be internal to one
organism. We may then say that spirit arises whenever Will in one place finds it profitable to mark, trace,
and even imitatively to share the movement of Will
elsewhere. By so doing a psyche anticipates attack
and defence, putting forth telepathic feelers, as it were,
indefinitely far into space and time. To mark, to
trace, or to share any and every movement going on
in the world is precisely the function of spirit; only
that for spirit this marking, tracing, or sharing is
purely ideal, and being ideal may tend to become
adequate to the life of the object; whereas marking
tracing and sharing for the psyche involve only a
material response and an instinctive readjustment.

The concomitance of these two phases, one automatic and the other emotional, blinds us to their complete ontological diversity. Each actually
involves and instantly suggests the other, so   Harmony
that under the name of either the entire   conditioned
natural event may be safely indicated. But   by difference.
to indicate an event is not to describe it, much less to
analyse it. Any feature, any nickname or gesture,
suffices to represent to the cursory mind the most
complex of facts; and we thread our way automatically
through the world, by the help of a few superficial
signals to which we hardly attend, while our thoughts
go woolgathering or are lost in the haze of bodily
sensation. When rarely, in reflective moments, we
realize our spiritual solitude, we begin to wonder how
nature (all brute accidents) ever came to confront spirit

(all ideal demands); and the contrast between these conjoined enemies becomes mysterious to us, or even scandalous.   Perhaps then we grow speculative, and attempt to reduce nature to a figment of mind, as if the world were an idea to be easily downed or exorcised by another idea; or perhaps we dream of introducing spirit, like a mighty blast, amid the tempests of nature, so as to direct or to pacify them.   But these are the illusions of egotism; abounding in its own sense, and ignorant of its foundations.   The foundations of spirit are in the life of nature; nothing could be more natural or spontaneous than this running hypostasis of vital changes into prophetic and symbolic intuitions.   The world is not only a patient artist in its structure but a rapt poet in its sentiment.   Why should it not be? And how should this ever be the case with us if, in essence and potentially, it were not the case in our ancestral substance?   Such, whether sophisticated people call it natural or miraculous, is at any rate the fact.   Tensions, movements, unities that in the realm of matter are mere forms or tropes, give birth to intensive, moral, and conscious echoes in the realm of spirit.   Thereby the fertility of the physical order ceases to be vain, and proves itself to be greater than our partisan minds like at first to admit.   In reality, substance and form, mechanism and lyric actuality are interwoven and contrasted in nature's own way: with radical freedom, since opportunity was infinite; yet with blind perseverance, since when one experiment is afoot why should another experiment interrupt it? There is time and there is room for everything in infinity, even for ourselves.

We have therefore no occasion to deny or to minimize the difference between mind and matter. Peace between disparate things is not to be secured by assimilating them.   Assimilation would destroy at least one of them, and probably both, and the result would

not be a harmony but a material confluence of
uniform parts.   If reality were all of one kind, elements
could agree only by repeating one another _{Ways in}
or by moving in the same current, like the which
drops of water in a river.   The Will in each ^{specific Wills}
molecule—the force by which it coheres— to universal
would be unaffected by the direction in which ^{Will.}
the molecule as a whole might be carried, so long as
it was not disrupted; and the politics of the world would
remain entirely indifferent to the citizens.   Such indifference brings with it a negative peace; the part is
not troubled by the whole, and the whole need not
trouble about itself, since in the dynamic sphere accom-
modation imposes itself automatically at every moment
and is necessarily perfect.   Universal Will, by definition, cannot but be realized, being a name for the
continually renewed balance and resultant of all forces.
    Wholly different are the conditions of harmony
when molecules have become plastic organisms, and
organisms, always imperfect, have reached great
elaboration in incomparable directions.   In their fortunes they must continue to conform involuntarily to
universal Will, but their different Wills are partly
defeated in the process.   Compromise may soften this
partial defeat by accepting it.   We then surrender a
native potentiality for the sake of something more
opportune, which may graft itself on the original stem
and create a new Will no less genuine than the old one.
Or if the original Will was strongly organized, the compromise may be only provisional, as when a conquered
nationality sullenly vegetates, until an occasion comes
for recovering its independence, or as a married pair
chafes under the yoke, meditating freedom.   But all alien
forces are not hostile to a healthy Will that nature has
adopted and rendered perennial.   Adaptation far from
being a compromise or a mutilation, may be a happy
development, bringing out latent faculties of the psyche,

and enriching life with an increased relevance and
responsiveness to different orders of things.   A system
of moral relations, lying in the realm of truth, will then
be found radiating from each organic being, multiplying
its connections and increasing its distinction; because
these relations will be based on the native affinities of
each psyche, and selected freely, so that the more life
expands in those congenial lines the more it becomes
what it willed to be.

Such is the harmony possible among disparate
things, a correlation of different orders of beings,
rendering each more distinct, and the whole more
diversified.   Out of such a harmony, established at the
biological level, spirit was born; and the farther and
the more perfectly that harmony can spread round the
psyche, the better the Will in spirit is fulfilled.   Nothing could be ontologically more unlike nature than
spirit is; yet nothing could be better able to mould
itself, in its own ideal manner, to every detail and
convolution in nature, so as to survey it and know it;
nothing could diversify and enrich nature more radically, adding a moral dimension to what would otherwise be merely material; and nothing could more freely
or triumphantly express its own Will than spirit does
by at once feeling and transcending the Will of everything else.

If spirit in us could be entirely dominant we should
esteem everything in nature as if it were the inmost part
of ourselves, and everything in ourselves as
if it were the remotest and the least part of
nature.   But the actual life of spirit is all
compromise, being continually stopped in its flights,
and enslaved by some particular passion or illusion.
To that extent spirit is not spiritual and exists only
in a thwarted effort to be born.   Once clear, however,
even if only for a moment and in some particular
direction, it is out of sight of compromise.   It is fed

<small>Pure spirit
would find
no enemies.</small>

by everything while it wakes and disturbed by nothing while it sleeps. Its existence becomes a pure gain both to itself and to the world that contains it and that thereby completes, in self-knowledge, the cycle of its normal life.

But here we come upon a paradox: that spirit, the most inward of things and the most vital, should find its purest affinities in remote and abstract regions, in mathematics, in music, in truth, in the wider aspects of nature and history, and should find its greatest enemies, its worst torments, at home. The stars are more friendly to it than the mountains, the mountains than the town, the town than the workshop or the garret; and its irreconcilable foes are its own body and its own passions. Yet this was inevitable, in view of the animal roots of spirit in the psyche. An animal organism, in developing smell, sight, and hearing, adjusts itself to external things merely in confirming and steadying its own life. This sensibility to the not-self arises entirely in the self's service. Those far-reaching senses are not speculative in their Will, but defensive or aggressive; and the mechanism that generates and supports them necessarily subserves the welfare of the body. If it did not, it would tend to destroy that body and to annul itself. Yet meantime, by that useful trick of exact adaptation and imitative sympathy, the psyche has automatically generated spiritual sympathy and true intelligence, without in the least requiring these gifts or profiting by them. A purely ideal consciousness of things not hers has sprung up within herself. She has given birth to a spirit that potentially, in its intellectual vocation, infinitely transcends her.

How does this come about? Under what auspices does a moral dimension, mechanically non-existent and biologically idle, attach itself to physical life? I think an answer, of a certain kind, is not far to seek. Every-

Radical divergence of Will in spirit from Will in the psyche as a whole.

thing finite, in the bosom of the infinite, reckons without its host. The great residuum that it ignores
nevertheless continues to beat against those bounds, like the sea upon a coral island. And not only from the outside. There is probably an infinity surging within as well as one laughing round the corner. Now a very tight and simple organism might resist this double solicitation almost for ever, or might reappear perpetually almost without change; but the more complex an organism becomes, the more it will lean upon external support, and the more everything in it will come to be an index to the things that it is not. There are commitments and dangers enough in vegetative life; but these are immensely extended by the organ of spirit, by the whole perceptive, aggressive, and teachably reflex machinery of the animal psyche. The human race in particular has entered upon an ambitious and glorious career, acquiring a dominion over the universe perceptively and over the earth industrially that would seem incredible if it were not actual.

Such enterprise on the psyche's part was no blunder, unless we judge life itself to be a blunder. Nature has simply explored the possibilities of organization and run the inevitable risk of confusion and disaster. This is normal, as is also the inner conflict and strain that so complex an equipment, with its parts working intermittently, imposes upon the psyche. A visit to the Zoo may convince anybody that this is no prerogative of man, much less a miraculous inroad of spirit into nature. All those odd animals are seen straining under the burden of their oddity. Many of them are already almost extinct; many others were extinct long ago. Perhaps the oddity of man—that interest of his in things not edible which issues in art and intelligence—may also prove fatal; and if so far, on the whole, the experiment

Non-psychic processes surrounding and permeating the psyche help to evoke spirit.

The price of this sensitiveness is moral distraction.

has proved physically useful, it has been at the price of terrible inner conflicts, reaching war and organized tyranny in the race and madness in the individual. In no other creature, probably, is the natural soul so much distracted. In no other has the margin of life encroached so much upon the text; no clean clear margin, such as we may suppose sleep and the placid stretches of contented idleness to be for other animals, but a margin crowded with comments and contradictions and caricatures and cross-references, demanding that we attend to everything at once and live not bravely forward, as other animals do, but continually looking backward, or far ahead, or suspiciously, greedily, impertinently, and frivolously in every direction.

We talk of "life" as if it were unquestionably something precious or even divine. Perhaps a part of the vocation of spirit may be to overcome this prejudice. Life, where it has arisen, is by definition a nucleus of Will, and a point of reference for imputing good and evil; but who should impute good and evil, or in reference to what Will, in those vast cosmic regions that surround and that breed life, so that life itself, before it existed, should be declared a good? Physical life and an animal psyche are not ultimate categories; they are not the primary movements or tensions in the universe. The potentialities of matter far outrun any such temporary tropes. The scale on which the psyche operates is a local scale, and the perceptive organs that she develops are biased selective organs. Many deeper or subtler currents, as well as much vaster harmonies, presumably run through the world, and flow unimpeded through the psyche, as through a sieve. In her special interest she can afford to ignore them. But she lives immersed and saturated in them nevertheless; and it was precisely when she availed herself of some of these currents, at first dis-

The Will in matter is deeper than the specific Will of the psyche even in the psyche itself.

regarded, that her organs of sense acquired their extra-
bodily range.   Then in becoming physically perceptive
she became, against her primary Will, vitally extra-
verted.   She began to live and to suffer where, materially, she was not; her heart, so to speak, began to travel.
All this was in her simply an organic crisis or fever;
but it set her dreaming, as a fever will in a deep sleep.
For the first time she felt a real pang, the birth-pang
of the spirit, and she saw a clear image, her first notion
of a world.   It was a strange self-displacement, like
falling in love.   In her ambition to grow she had
become so great that she discovered her littleness.
And henceforth it was impossible for her to go back or
to draw in her horns.   If in nostalgia for vegetative
peace she now shut her eyes and risked being mistaken,
her new and formidable friends would escape her, and
she might no longer escape her old enemies, because
her shell would have been broken, and now her greater
sensitiveness and more precarious life would have
multiplied their number and exposed her much more
to their attacks.

Thus a pragmatic mechanism that operates with no
reference to the truth nevertheless must meet and bow
Universal   to the truth, in its adjustments; and the truth,
affinities of   having divine prerogatives, grounded more
Will in the   deeply and widely in the universe than any
spirit.   particular life, rewards the respect shown to
it by a miraculous but appropriate gift, namely, by a
vision of the truth.   Clouded as this vision may be, it
is essentially a vision of all reality.   It flashes like sheet-
lightning broadly but unseizably, and only for a moment
in every intuition of the spirit.   With this a disproportionate dignity and ambition breaks in upon animal
life, strangely incongruous, pregnant with repentance
and with exaltation above mortality.   But the psyche
cannot repent, and cannot stop feeding, breeding, and
acting.   She must persist or die; and it is only the

spirit that can repent for her and suffer for her, until it achieves its own liberty.

In this way, like an ignorant girl, the psyche has become a mother without counting the cost either to herself or to her miraculous child; and the spirit has come undesired into the working world that wanted only another slave and is utterly incapable of understanding or respecting the divine changeling that has been brought to it. Evidently for the preservation and welfare of an organism fit reactions suffice; a *sense* of those reactions or their occasions is superfluous. And in fact the core of the human psyche, which is like that of other animals, might decline all responsibility for such a dispersion of affection, or even deny that it existed. Adaptation creates intelligence, but does not know that it does so. When the Will in an animal began to react upon and to mimic external objects, it was bent only on absorbing or on dominating those objects materially; the habit of retracing the environment and as it were, sinking into it and catching its rhythm, was something secondary, instrumental and oblique; and the response was strictly practical, touching only what touched the organism. But such a selection cannot be made beforehand. In exploring you cannot first decide what you shall discover; you must explore everything that offers, and then perhaps select the part that it concerns you to study.

[margin note: Automatic acquisition of this affinity in self-defence.]

Now it is precisely this preliminary but indomitable interest in fact, in form, and in truth for truth's sake that is the Will proper to spirit: a Will that wills heroically what the psyche as a whole willed only conditionally and, as it were, unwillingly. For by sensitively adjusting herself to her opportunities she inevitably bred in herself a frank affinity to other things and even to contrary Wills. She found herself hypnotically rehearsing alien movements, without any possibility of absorbing the substances that so moved. And willy-nilly such an ideal possession of things materially absent is mind; it is spirit. This spirit is spontaneous, disinterested, intellectual in its essence; but it does not live, as sometimes it imagines, on its own resources or by its own power. It is the psyche that creates spirit in becoming materially sensitive to remote things; and it is this living natural individual that in generating spirit renders his vital unity moral, and acquires a mental cognizance of the world and of himself in the midst of it.

We should be antedating the birth of spirit and turning our symbols into myths if we asked whether the psyche *made a mistake* in developing such speculation. She was led into an experiment rich in possibilities and in dangers. It could not be called a mistake even if some day, or in many cases, it proved fatal; because all experiments in the end prove fatal if we regard them as aimed at some specific good; but they all prove fertile as well, since they enable new forms to arise. We shall trace presently some of the conflicts which the Will underlying spirit has caused in the individual and in society; they are biological conflicts, confusions in the play of organic impulses; but it would always be a private judgment, inspired by one or another of these impulses, to say that the psyche *ought* to have remained vegetative, so as to avoid these conflicts, or that in becoming partly disinterested (that is, in generating spirit) she was *false to her own interests*. In her own life, she simply developed new organs—the senses, organic memory, language, the arts—because she had the potency and the occasion to do so; and as to the life of spirit that thereby supervened, she gained and she lost absolutely nothing by it, since spirit is immaterial, neither a drain nor an influence, and merely concomitant to her life, like a shadow, a truth, or a harmony.

If the life of the psyche could ever become *wholly*

Biological automatism not thereby interrupted.

disinterested and sacrificial (which would involve becoming materially passive and barren) the Will achieved would be exclusively the Will in spirit, and in that supreme moment the spirit would live absolutely and sublimely free. But that would mean physical death, or a transport equivalent to a suspension of physical life: a condition that may be approached or traversed, but that cannot be sustained. The Will in spirit therefore does not enjoy the privilege which the Will in the vegetative psyche always retains, the privilege of suspending the experiment by which spirit was evoked, and retreating into unconsciousness. To retreat, or rather to soar, into pure spirit is a continual tendency or goal in intellectual and moral life; it appears in the idea of God, when God is conceived spiritually; it is frequently touched or skirted by the innocent mind; but it cannot be maintained or made the staple of any existence. Spirit is not a substance with a life of its own; if it were, it could never have got entangled in these animal meshes. It is a consciousness of animal aspirations already afoot. Even the aspiration to see, to understand, and to experience everything is at bottom an animal aspiration, that needs to be radically transmuted before it can become a spiritual one. The whole experience of spirit expresses natural predicaments. Spirit suffers hunger and thirst; it hates, it fears, it loves, it inquires, it feels perplexed and forsaken. It is merely the psyche become conscious. Therefore any dream of being pure spirit, omniscient, safe, and joyful, represents only an ideal limit, an ambition intimately involved in being spirit at all, but not attainable in its purity. Sometimes the flame grows brighter, sometimes it sinks, in proportion as the vital synthesis of the moment contracts to the scope of some single interest or trouble, or extends to remoter influences and greater destinies. At best, under the

The Will in spirit not separable from the animal Will.

spell of nature and truth, intuition may almost draw the whole psyche out of her native moulds, and concentrate her energies in intelligence, in fancy, or in worship.

At such moments the Will at work in the spirit becomes unanimous with the Will of nature working *It is the* beyond the animal soul. In religious par- *same Will* lance, it becomes identical with the Will of *enlightened* God. Although the spirit always suffers *about its* more or less and sometimes suffers cruelly, *conditions.* yet in one sense it is less pathetic, less help- lessly wasted, than the vegetative psyche that never suffers consciously, but simply crops out, struggles, and dies. Spirit dies too, but with the knowledge of its essential capacity to rise again, so that it rather sleeps than dies; and all its sufferings in so many incarnations are properly not its own, but those of the animal organism which for the moment it inhabits, and which but for this descent of spirit, would have been con- demned to grow, to work, and to die without ever loving anything ideally, or knowing its own *raison d'être*. The objects we see the psyche pursuing are results in which she would rest, conditions in which she would prosper, not perfections that, before she evoked spirit, she could ever worship or desire. She lives as long as she can, on any terms, until her mechanism snaps; and her struggles are so vainly persistent and desperate pre- cisely because they are blind. Courage, we call this mechanical impulse, and enlist it morally in our hero- isms; but in the psyche it is a mere potentiality of heroism and also of madness. When instinct prompts, she will boldly lay any wager, and double it against any odds. The advent of spirit cannot abolish these vital impulses and mortal dangers; but in raising them into conscious suffering and love, spirit turns the ignominy of blind existence into nobleness, setting before us some object to suffer for and to pursue. In the very act of becom- ing painful, life has become worth living in its own eyes.

CHAPTER V

FREEDOM

THE world continually suffers change, but not complete change; for if it did not preserve some substantial and dynamic continuity it could not be said to subsist through change or even to be a world. But it *exists* by exemplifying various essences successively in a flux; that is to say by an irrational selection, first of the particular character to be presented at any moment, and secondly of the manner in which this contingent character shall be exchanged for the one exemplified next. There is no logical necessity or external compulsion in this process. There is only in certain respects a continuity in movement, quantity and habit, with frequent partial repetitions of form; so that tropes or laws and familiar physical objects may be distinguished in the flux, and may serve in some measure to prophesy how it will presumably flow in the future and how it presumably flowed in the past.

All existence contingent and in that sense free.

From this it follows that every fact and every movement is *free*, since nothing else compelled it to be as it is; and further, each fact or movement is free in positing itself with a certain vehemence or Will, by which it not only exists but seems to enjoy existing and to defy extinction.

Compulsion begins when free action in one direction collides with free action in another. Generative causes never remove freedom; over what should they exercise compulsion? On the contrary, they enable

F

freedom to exist in a new instance and perhaps in a
new form.   Parents do not trespass on a child's liberty
by bringing him into the world.   Did they
produce him organically perfect they would
have endowed him with perfect freedom, as
far as his Will was concerned; and if circumstances soon compelled him to do as he
would not, or not to do as he would, such an external
diminution of liberty would leave his Will no less free
and perhaps more precise and defiant.   The Will can
be enslaved only by one part of it checking or suppressing another part; and this is the sad slavery we inherit
from Adam, namely, vital self-contradiction.   Each
part and act of the Will remains nevertheless an
original phase of the Will of nature.   The relations
between causes and effects, as between parents and
children, are fundamentally fraternal.   One instance
of a law is neither more nor less spontaneous than the
next instance; parents and children belong to the same
species, and grow on the same bough; the parents have
been children, the children are formed to become parents, similar passions animate them and a common fate
overhangs them.   If, then, nature in producing them
has rendered their Will specific and limited, it has not
coerced that Will but asserted it, endowing it with
special capacities and with affinity to particular goods.
Such determination is a prerequisite to bare existence,
much more to freedom or to moral life.

At the same time existence, in making each thing
and each impulse such as it is, has made it impossible
or difficult for it to become anything else,
or to pursue any good except that to which
it is naturally directed: and this, *to spirit*, is a real and
even an intolerable limitation.   For spirit too exists
by virtue of a specific Will, manifested in special
functions and aimed at a special object; and this
object, in the case of spirit, is universal knowledge

*To be free
you must
first be born
and have
some Will in
particular.*

*Special case
of spirit.*

and universal love. Freedom for spirit would therefore require a supernatural station, from which all
perspectives should be equally visible and equally
neutralized; and it would require infrahuman and
superhuman sympathies, by which an infinite variety
of goods might be appreciated and impartially judged.
In man, in any finite creature, spirit is therefore deeply
enslaved. It tastes freedom, and gets some notion of
it, only in those movements of intuition in which the
animal seat and the animal bias of the Will are forgotten
and intelligence and love, as if disembodied, fly to their
objects without hindrance from the flesh, lifting them
out of the past or the future into immediate presence,
and doing them, ideally, absolute justice, without sinking into the limitations or the confused hatreds inseparable from natural existence.

The ideality of spirit, that drops things in order
to retain only their essences, sometimes gives a new
turn to the notion of freedom. As spirit is Phenomena,
free in liberating an idea, we may conceive though con-
that ideas themselves, or some of them, are tingent, have
metaphysical powers; and that the Will in are not free
all nature is due to the action or attraction or causal.
of logical being. Even a power to call oneself into
existence out of nothing is sometimes attributed to
essences or forms, as if that which is always equally
necessary could act, or act freely, or be the cause
of selected and contingent transitory facts. But
phenomena contain no Will or endeavour to persist.
They dawn and fade unconcerned. The force, the
fuel, the food, the machinery all operate beneath those
visible appearances. Thunder itself is but an impotent
sound, fit to frighten children; but there is an invisible
power in heaven that really hurls the bolt. Therefore
philosophical tradition has instinctively placed all initiative and liberty in the Will, not in the Idea. To
attribute power to ideas is superstitious. There is

indeed as much contingency in the *occurrence* of ideas
as in any other event: but the material movements that
exhibit or call forth those ideas have a previous history
and will have subsequent effects, ultimately irrelevant
to those ideas.   The seed and the soil produce the
flower, and a given essence has no more power
to create itself, or to call up another essence, than
have all the other forms that have never seen the
light.

There is a further ground for this superstition about
the power of ideas, namely, that *in the psyche* an idea

Psychology is often a premonition. Some definite im-
of the *idée-* pulse, perhaps moulded and qualified by
force. much experience, is at work in the organism;
an image of what might be or ought to be the issue,
arises beforehand in the spirit; and as the act matures
the image perhaps grows brighter and brighter, acquires
fresh specifications, and finally is swallowed up in the
actual perception of the word, the work, or the action
in which the impulse has terminated materially.   This
perception, though it overwhelms the previous idea by
its force and steadiness, often disappoints; there were
currents in the psyche, vaguely present to the spirit
and beckoning it on, that the result achieved has not
satisfied.   Often, however, when the prophetic mind
was well instructed and rational, what is done is exactly
what was foreseen and intended: something that normally happens in routine and daily actions.   Yet even
here there is sometimes an illusion of success or even
of triumph, where the Will has been really defeated.
The previous state of the soul may have been confused
and painful; there may be a vast relief in the actual
birth of something unforeseen, something that at least
is definite, in which good points may be found, and
which powerfully bends the mind in new directions,
towards what now seems possible, and buries those
unhappy vague aspirations that now would be

grotesque. The chief need of the psyche was to be delivered of her burden: what does it matter in comparison whether the spirit has the satisfaction of seeing realized in matter the very form that it had already seen in thought? Disappointments of this sort may pave the road to a kind of happiness.

If fortune here seems to treat the spirit a little roughly, the spirit may parry the blow, and take a high revenge. When the Will has somehow had its way, the spirit is apt to sink a little; it is dashed by this earthly fulfilment of its hopes. What was celestial has become terrestrial. What we loved unreservedly has been tarnished and scattered: a thousand vulgar idols have usurped its name. We see how much better it would have been to lay up our treasures where moth and rust do not corrupt and thieves break not in or steal. But is this safe treasury to be found in the clouds or in that most uncertain of regions, the future? We may hope for many good things in the future, most of which can hardly be enjoyed by ourselves; but sure possessions are possible only in the present, which for intuition always gives also a glimpse of the eternal. The spiritual value of our disappointments does not lie merely in producing resignation, or reconciling our chastened wills to the issue. The issue probably has its modest worth, which we do well to prize. But the chief good in having been disappointed is that, if we are firm, we remain inconsolable, having aspired and still aspiring to something better than the event. Then against its Will, fortune will have wedded us to beauties it had no power to create, but only to promise. That promise, externally so foolish, has made us inwardly wise, enabling us to break in spirit through the veil of time, and to recognize a sublime nocturnal firmament above the sky. The spirit cannot be bribed by compensations. It does not wish, it does not need, to be consoled. It is con-

Disillusion in victory.

secrated to a perfection which it loves and from which, in its love, it cannot be separated.

The Will visible in matter and in the laws of nature having been originally free, a doubt arises whether this radically free Will, in once asserting itself, bound itself never to change, or whether, being groundless fundamentally, it may at any moment take a new direction. Looked at under the form of eternity, or as it is in truth, this dilemma becomes indifferent. Existence being intrinsically a flux or process, its essence involves a passage from prior to subsequent terms which are not identical; there is therefore essential novelty at every step; and it makes no difference whether we say that each term arises independently or that the trope that involves and unites the two terms arises as a whole. It will in any case take time to develop, and will in any case be the exact development that it turns out to be. On the human scale we contrast mechanism with tropes, because we ignore the process and progression involved in a mechanical change, treating it as a single stroke, one more instance of an old way that things have of happening, like the apple falling, or the smoke coming from a fire. But the simplest event, being a change, has a trope in it, a beginning and an end, a sort of inner teleology, the beginning being a movement towards that end, and the end the culmination of that transition. Mechanism is therefore just as vital as life; and life, seen at a sufficient distance, when generations become moments and only types and totals are visible, becomes perfectly mechanical. The only question touches the scale of the tropes to be found in nature; and whether the more minute ones continue to run within the larger or whether (as an intuition) the larger transform and obliterate the smaller.

Freedom implies initiative but not variability.

The same optional alternatives appear in theology. Creation may be called a single fiat, since God is conceived to have intended from the beginning all that was to ensue; or we may speak of a gradual creation, since the Will to sustain existence and to continue the same design, must be renewed at each moment, and in each phase of each event.   Creative evolution is nothing but a modern name for progressive creation.

An impression nevertheless prevails that if the energy or direction of existence suddenly changed, freedom would be vindicated; whereas if they never change, nature would appear to be self-hypnotized and mechanized.   It would seem to be as in marriage.   If divorce is possible, the union remains free; but where divorce is out of the question, the vows once made become a fatality.   This is really the case to some extent, because Will in men and women contains many other impulses besides the impulse to live together; and married life involves many commitments that the Will in lovers had ignored.   Therefore, if no divorce is allowed, the marriage contract loads the dice in every subsequent decision and exercises a real constraint over the other impulses of the Will.   But if love wholly unified the soul, as it sometimes thinks it does, so that no comparable passion any longer subsisted, a pledge to love always would be but a claim to immortality, the pure aspiration to be and to remain oneself.   It would postulate spiritual freedom: whereas any eventual inconstancy would signify infection by some alien force. Integrity alone can be morally free, being alone compatible with a radical self-knowledge and the perception of an ultimate good.   Fluctuations in the Will would prove, on the contrary, that the psyche was pregnant with unharmonized passions or had been transformed by some external influence.   It is self-ignorance that leads to actions contrary to one's latent Will, though perhaps willed psychologically; and it is ignorance of the world that leads to actions that, though obedient to

Dispersed freedom hoist with its own petard.

the Will as an impulse, defeat it as a purpose. In both forms ignorance is a cause of helplessness and self-defeat, not (as romantic feeling suggests) a condition of freedom. Without constancy freedom has no momentum or dignity.

On this analogy we may say that, if the same laws of nature always prevailed or if the world had sprung into existence, dynamically complete, the Will in nature would be physically just as free as if force were added in driblets or came in spurts. Moral freedom, however, the universe could not possess unless it were animated by a spirit that saw the whole prophetically and willed it psychologically; in a word, unless God governed it. We are free morally when the spirit in us foresees and intends what we do physically or assents to it while being done: but spiritually we are no less implicated in actions or thoughts which we heartily approve ideally than in those which we perform or utter materially.

A man given to dreaming, planning, imagining, and always talking to himself becomes deeply entangled in such unperformed actions. He may live through many events in fancy that annoy or even torment him, as in nightmares; but even these will have sprung from himself, or from things that have long taken root in him; and when, in the public world, he finds himself actually doing one of those meditated things, or something like it, he will recognize his own work, and feel proud or ashamed of it. Particularly when the thing done was clearly anticipated and planned, with means elaborately conceived to bring it about ; for then the man has consciously lived through the first begetting and long gestation of his action, and knows it for his own child. But this felt responsibility implies not that the action was free but that (according to conventional notions of cause and effect) it was thoroughly explicable, and

Psychic incubation of action.

caused by the man's Will, by the deepest and most ancient currents of his being; so that his action is a perfect mirror and revelation of himself—a revelation of himself perhaps appalling to his own conscience. Had the action been separately free, the whole good-and-evil of it being concentrated in its groundless occurrence, the man would find it unaccountable and say he was bewitched, that his body had been magically led to perform it against his proper and habitual Will. This primal Will in himself, responsible for all he does, thinks, and loves freely, is a part of the universal Will in nature, of the groundless character of fact everywhere; and it would be sophistical to pretend that this part of universal Will was due to the other parts, so that the man was not ultimately responsible for being what he was. Who, then, should be responsible for him? The other facts? Or the other instances of Will, willing things quite different from the Will in him? Or perhaps the trope that records the way in which these various Wills hang together? But a trope is not a power, only a description; it simply puts all the included facts in the places which they have always taken spontaneously.

If we said that origins are responsible for aftergrowths (which is not true either analytically or morally) nothing would be responsible for itself, unless we came at last to a first fact. But that notion is questionable. If ever there was a first fact in time, it was probably the simplest of facts; and in what sense could this whole complicated world, physical and moral, be due to that simplest or vaguest nebula from which it sprang? Logically, morally, and under the form of eternity, all facts are first facts. Some elements and processes in nature are certainly more pervasive than others, and simpler; but the complications ensue of their own accord, because those simpler facts are so related that

Responsibility pervades existence.

a new essence or a new trope comes to be exemplified
in their movement.   A different Will begins to appear
in the world, one that the previous crawling converging
Wills in it had never manifested.   But the cataract
with its force and music utters the Will of nature no
less genuinely, and more loudly, than the brooks and
the raindrops that went to make it up; so that the truly
primal and responsible Will appears in the total reality
and pregnancy of the world, with its groundless
elements and free evolution.   The fiat of God and the
sin of Adam are equally original, and both are omni-
present; for besides the universal Will expressed in all
that happens there is independent conation in the parts,
making for what might have happened if the total
balance of forces had not prevented.

When the unit of action, which is the free fact,
seems to pass from the part to the whole, is the freedom
of the part thereby lost?   Suppose a young
man with a tenor voice, standing on a
mountain-top felt a sudden impulse to sing
high *C*: the vital freedom in that act would
not be questionable.   But suppose he had learned the
aria *Ah*, *quella pira*, and felt a sudden impulse to sing
that: would the high *C*, when it came to crown the
melody, be less freely uttered than in the other case?
Certainly that note would now have been predetermined,
not absolutely, but in case this particular aria remained
throughout the chosen norm of that action.   High *C*
would thus have lost something of its freedom as to
the moment when it should come and even as to its
coming at all; for if you once set out to sing that
particular song this particular challenge cannot be
avoided.   You must strike high *C* at the appointed
moment or fail in having your Will.   On the other
hand your Will now, in spite of being controlled by
that of a dead composer, is much more voluminous
and potent, and far more deeply your Will than would

A free whole
qualifies
freedom in
the parts.

be the emotional impulse to shout high *C* by itself,
without any musical setting. What was an animal cry
has become part of a poetical trope and a dramatic
climax, so that now there is a reason for your high *C*
as well as a cause. Exhilaration may have taken the
form of confidence, and confidence that of defiance
hurled at all the kingdoms of the world and their
wickedness, spread like a map beneath your feet. The
Will expressed now dominates a much larger segment
of your life and of the moral landscape; the spirit out-
poured is more entangled but more richly fed; and this
organization of vital freedom may be a step towards
spiritual liberation.

Freedom is thus present on various scales in all the
forces and tropes in nature: but the psyche being a knot
of forces with a particular vehement organic
rhythm, repels spontaneity elsewhere as com- *Psychic in-*
pulsion, because it obstructs or disregards *justice to*
her own spontaneity. When she becomes *nature at large.*
conscious these harsh contacts and their sources begin
to appear more or less clearly to her spirit, together
with the emotions of surprise, hatred, desire, or pleasure
proper to her movements on such occasions. In
enlightening our vital egoism, spirit must transcend
this egoism, else it could not enlighten it. Things
that to the psyche are obstructive and dark then
recover a new spontaneity in intuition, not their own
physical spontaneity but the proper spontaneity of
spirit in conceiving them; so that the psychic injustice
of treating them as mere lumber or substance to be
devoured is partly redressed by the spirit in its first
sensuous flight, which turns matter into brilliant images
or into comforts and sweets. The world seems alive
to children and poets, but with a weak spectacular
vitality, full of foolish wonders like a dream. In use
and in difficulty this primary fancifulness of spirit is
submerged, and everything appears dead, or obdurately

animated by a stupid mechanical Will.   Other people
and animals, that were the toys of childhood, now seem
brutal and wicked; and the latent capacity of spirit to
be both poetical and scientific, both sympathetic and
firm, comes late to the surface.

In this long enslavement of free fancy to animal Will
arise certain dramatic or moralistic categories—guilt,
merit, effort, purpose, responsibility—that
cause great trouble in philosophy, when they
are reflected backward upon the physical
world.   If things serve a purpose they are
said to *have* it; but could they have had it
before they acquired the properties that make
them useful to that end?   When something costs us
an effort, our *effort* is said to bring it about; but the
effort is imposed on us by our *failure* to perform easily
something that we were already bent upon, and that
would have been better done if it had cost us no effort.
So when action in others or even in ourselves furthers
or defeats our prevalent Will, we call that action right
or wrong, virtuous or guilty.   Free and responsible
for itself, in the first instance, is the gross natural event
from which the injury or the benefit visibly comes: the
man, the action, the accident.   But if motives, antecedents, or laws of nature are surmised to subtend the
visible event, the responsibility spreads, recedes, grows
thinner and more and more radically involved in the
whole texture of nature; until either the total Will in
things, or in the Creator, becomes alone responsible,
or else, to escape that overwhelming momentum,
separate incidental acts of conscious will are invoked,
without inquiring into their causes.

Freedom may then be attributed to spirit as a
physical agent: something that when scrutinized turns
out to be literally inconceivable.   There can be no
physical derivation of a material fact from an immaterial
fact, or vice versa.   The two are not to be found in the

Bewilder-
ment of
spirit that
inherits this
prejudice
contrary to
its own
nature.

same realm of being. In the order of genesis, substance or energy passes, and may be traced, measured, and guided in passing, from one event to another; what follows is a growth from what precedes, partly by inner development, as from a seed, and partly by external accretion or dispersion. A son is not connected with his father merely by similarity and contiguity, though Hume, who was an old bachelor, might let us think so. There is always physical continuity and qualitative inheritance in a natural process, however vast or sudden the transformations. Yet it is logically impossible for matter to move or even to exist without overflowing into other realms of being. Essences must be exemplified, tropes must be adopted, truths must be established; and when the trope is a psyche, spirit too must be evoked, not now by logical necessity but by a free spontaneity in nature, that hypostasizes the moral fortunes of animals into consciousness of those fortunes. Spirit is thus entirely dependent on matter for its existence and distribution, but not by physical derivation; there is only an ontological propriety in this concomitance, to which the self-assertion of spirit contributes an element no less radically distinct and original than the successive phases in the evolution of matter. Matter would never have evolved into animals, had not organization been potential in it from the beginning; and organization would never have awakened consciousness had not essence and truth overarched existence from all eternity, and summed it up, with all its perspectives ready, for spirit to perceive.

Spirit depends on matter for its existence but not for its essence.

There is therefore a spiritual sense in which spirit not only is free and responsible for itself, but extends its connivance and moral dominion over the most distant facts. Not by magic or effort or bluff; only by unanimity. A wish—a consciousness of Will in the spirit—may

True freedom and responsibility of spirit.

easily be fulfilled by a physical event when the wish
has been formed in a psyche accustomed to such events
and ready to prefigure them or, by action, to bring them
about. In a psyche action and readiness for action
have a moral dimension which, by the nature of things,
appears in consciousness. Reflection may then appro-
priately see in a prophetic wish the moral reason or
motive for such events, as warnings may be omens, or
miracles answer to prayer. It was *better* that things
should so happen responsively to a living desire and
as spirit somewhere had invoked them; it was *saner*
and more *reassuring* for that spirit to find itself so
harmonious with fate that its wishes could be granted
and its prophecies fulfilled. But a moral reason or a
prayer answered indicates a harmony, it does not disclose a cause. The Will in the spirit was attuned in
such a case to the dominant or resultant Will in nature:
so that the spirit saw and loved in advance, or in
unison, the very things that nature was primed to
produce.

Where matter and spirit move in harmony spirit
may adopt the Will in nature as the will of God or more
proudly and histrionically as its own will; and the rapt
mystic or the providential leader may feel joyfully
passive or joyfully omnipotent. But when Will here
and Will there are in conflict, each retains such freedom
and responsibility as is proper to its own sphere. Each
felt preference or *idée-force* appearing in consciousness
then figures as a separate instance of local creation,
responsible for its choices, but spiritually only, that is,
responsible for loving that which it loves. The greater
the conflict between Will in the spirit and Will in the
rest of the psyche and of the world, the less responsible
can the spirit feel for subsequent events. Consequences never flow from the mere intent or expectation felt to inspire an action. They flow exclusively
from that action itself in the context of other physical

events; and the contagion or unison often established between spirits is a physical sympathy between persons, who catch each other's attitude and impulse, and feel, no doubt correctly, that they are invisibly sharing the same emotion.

This spiritual union when it exists, is therefore no groundless accident. Lovers are normally of the same race, exercising a sexual influence of attraction, or later perhaps of possession, on one another; and intellectual union, which is no less spiritual than love, likewise has notorious natural causes. Through language, gesture, and gentle suasion of all sorts, the Will beneath spirit spreads and equalizes itself in groups of persons; and unison in habit brings about unison in feeling and thought. Spiritual bonds therefore presuppose and require physical assimilation or correspondence; and since the organs of spirit have a common descent and continual contact in society, we loosely speak as if contact and descent existed within the realm of spirit itself: but that is mere verbal equivocation and confusion of thought. One moment of spirit—one intuition—can no more generate or control another moment than the light actually shed from one candle can generate or extinguish the light actually shed from another. Actuality exhausts itself, as laughter does, or any emotion. The causes that brought it about must renew it, if it is ever to reappear in all its freshness and youth. Those who use the word spirit for physical influences feel a magnetic radiation from the aspect, voice, action, and words of a spirited person; they see him carrying out his threats or his promises, which in their own minds are mere images and words, though in him they were also physical impulses; and they rashly identify those diffusions of energy with spirit itself; for they have so vague a realization of what living spirit would really

It has no magic powers and its supposed effects are the effects of its causes.

be, that they make no bones of turning it from an actual intuition or a moment of consciousness into a mythical person, a trope or a power manifested in matter. But the powers and tropes manifested in matter declare the properties of matter itself: spirit meantime is the invisible but immediate fact that matter with its tropes and powers is being observed, conceived, enjoyed, asserted, or desired: a vitality essentially moral, invisible, and private, absolutely actual and thoroughly unsubstantial, always self-existent and totally vanishing as it lives.

Everybody knows this without saying it, because language and the thought guided by language inevitably fix on objects distinguishable to the senses and moving as wholes on the sensuous scale: and spirit is not one of these objects. Language nevertheless does justice to spirit and serves it by the way, in its grammar and syntax, in its emotion, harmony, and intent: because all these relations, that make words "winged", lift language to the level of truth, and render it a good vehicle for spirit. But the indicative character of words, especially of nouns, tends to create globular units, sensuous or mythical, and leads us superstitiously to regard them as primary facts and separate powers. Now a man, his several actions, and the motives that may be conceived to animate him as he acts, are vague globular units of this conventional kind; and freedom and responsibility are attributed to them as wholes, when each is pointed to or named, without any attempt at analysis. Consciousness, when that is distinguished, takes its place in this catalogue of perfectly mythical familiar themes and individual powers; and it becomes paradoxical, and apparently artificial, to distinguish the spiritual element in a phase of daily life from the material and biological elements in it. Had the man not been conscious, people will say, the man would

Globular literary units not separate powers.

not have acted as he did: and this is evidently true; but not because his consciousness impelled his body materially, but because the impelling vital processes which involved his action also involved ideas and emotions like those that his action, dramatically rehearsed, suggests to our own spirit. Had his vital processes not sufficed to introduce the action, how should they have sufficed to introduce into his mind beforehand an idea of what the action might be, or a desire to perform it? Or how should the sight or the mere name of that action, reaching our eyes or ears by purely material means, suffice to make us conceive that action perfectly and perhaps boil with rage, and before we know it perform another action to match it?

Spirit, like all forms of life, is glad to be born, and does not account it violence to have been brought into existence, although surely that was the most external and absolute of decrees. But spirit could not have existed before it existed, so as freely and intelligently to have chosen to exist. Its freedom is subsequent, internal, and responsible not physically but morally. Universal Will, in evolving spirit, satisfied one of its potential impulses; this impulse is the Will proper to spirit anywhere, the very breath of our moral freedom, when we become free; but much contrariety and compulsion precedes and follows, because the impulse to transcend oneself cannot animate the universe as a whole, but only the most sensitive and delicate of its fibres. The special organ of spirit has an ethereal texture, and its webs are easily rent. Though without primal malice, but fatally, universal Will is everywhere a most stormy and cruel power and constantly contradicts and defeats one of its impulses by another. It therefore proves in a thousand ways a good and an evil to itself. Plants and animals accept this natural chaos, and never swerve from allegiance to their particular Wills; but when

Spirit caught in the war of Will's becomes conscience.

G

spirit comes upon the scene, while it too expresses a
particular movement of Will which it cannot abandon
without ceasing to be spirit, it feels at the same time
more or less clearly the conflicting Wills in other
creatures and most intimately the conflicting Wills in
its own psyche or mother-life. In this region the
question of freedom and responsibility first becomes a
riddle and a torment. Shame, remorse, good resolu-
tions, relapses, excuses, and scruples harass the conscience; and if piety aspires to conform all desires to
the universal Will, the responsibility for these troubles
must be placed, if possible, wholly on the private
movements of each psyche.

This, for a philosophic or theological mind, becomes
difficult. The will of the psyche is evidently animal
and hereditary; and although this fact takes
nothing away from the vital freedom of the
passions, it generalizes the seat of responsibility for them. Each of our sins is not the
first of its kind; human nature is to blame;
and who, if not the Creator, is to blame for
human nature? To say that Adam's fall, or each of our
stumblings, contained an element of absolute freedom
is true analytically, and also expresses the felt spontaneity and self-precipitation of action or thought.
Primal Will asserts itself as decisions or ideas take shape
within us; and it is impossible to imagine anything
freer or more due to itself than this growth and budding
of existence, this self-arrangement of matter, by its
own impulse, into some distinct form, which it is
possible to rest in or to repeat. Such is the Will to
exist and to be something in particular.

Such too is the possible sympathy of a living being
with the forms of surrounding or imaginable things.
Attention, with approval or detestation, attaches in this
way to objects and observed actions by a congenital
right; we half become these things in observing them,

Conflict
between
conscience
and con-
formity to
universal
Will.

and it would be intolerable to us to erase from them the moral colours that they wear in our living world. Yet when we begin to study nature discursively we see those moral colours spread and fade away as it were, from the centres in which they were focussed, and even to mingle and infect one another with the moral character most contrary to their own. The evil and the good, for intuition, lay at first in each act, in each thought, in each creature; but natural history now assures us that those creatures, with their moral temperaments, were products of evolution, and that the merits and demerits we ascribed to them were relative to our own interests or prejudices. Black and white, that were so absolute, now seem to fuse into a cosmic grey. We scarcely know whom to blame or to praise for anything; the basest passions claim their equal rights; and we are no longer sure that we have any reason for caring what becomes of ourselves.

Perplexity is not relieved by putting this moral contradiction into religious terms. Universal Will may be distributed into divine and human actions, each a primary and absolutely free fiat; yet if the divine will is conceived as enlightened by universal knowledge, all human actions also must have been divinely willed, and spiritually accepted as ingredients in the plan of creation. All our sins and troubles would be providential, everything we detest in ourselves would be ultimately desirable, and all guilt and punishment would be a dreadful blessing that spirit in us was bound at once to hate and to love.

Less sophisticated and contorted is the sense of responsibility that prevails in human society. Alien wills cannot easily be conceived as they are *Healthy con-* in actual operation; that would require a *science of* singular triumph of dramatic imagination and *the public.* sympathy. But they are felt as good or evil, kindly or wicked, in relation to the Will dominant in ourselves at that moment; and a repertory of odious or lovely qualities is formed in the public conscience, quite sufficient for political and educational purposes.   Average men, hearty men, men in harmony with their age and nation, assign praise and blame accordingly to gods and to mortals without hesitation.   The freedom and responsibility of these natural agents is assumed, since they move of their own accord; and the same responsibility and freedom are attributed to the passions of one's own psyche, the spontaneity of them being actually experienced.

But for a subtler mind, for one divided against itself or acquainted with alien manners and judgments, the force of this local unilateral conscience soon becomes dubious.   Not the whole of each criminal is criminal, nor of each saint saintly; there is humanity in the foreigner: and both goods and evils have causes and consequences of a moral colour opposite to their own.   A feeble soul may then relax its moral code, blur its sense of what would be best and most beautiful, and having nothing left to fight for, may say that it rises above the fray; but that is impossible for a firm and integrated psyche. Ventilation and enlightenment clarify self-knowledge, as well as understanding of alien things: and self-knowledge is the principle of rational preference.   It binds us with indissoluble bonds to the things we love.

Intelligence may slide into willlessness.

The good being thus sharply defined by its very relativity, the living spirit enjoys the same privilege as all other forms of universal Will, and by its inner freedom fixes the goals of its aspiration. It is constantly, even at its birth, distracted from its own good by the intrusion of other impulses seated in the same psyche; but in so far as it awakes to its proper function, and is loyal to itself, it transmutes all things to its own ends, digesting them and,

Specific ambition of spirit.

like a healthy creature, plucking its appropriate food and rejecting poisons. For even spirit is a form of Will, involved in the functioning of a special organ; so that it too has a native unexpressed vocation, in violation of which it cannot live at ease. Seen from within, this vocation seems so simple and self-justified that it ought to meet with no obstacle, since it antagonizes nothing and interferes with nothing, but innocently wishes to understand and to love everything. Yet in the psyche where it arises this vocation is marginal and impossible to realize steadily. Even the ambition to do so occasionally and ideally within the spirit's house offends the particular passions shouting outside, each with its absolute urgency. Each would monopolize the spirit, which cannot be monopolized, and yet must listen to every call; so that its distress is deeper and more constant than that of psyches without reflection, which as we observe in the brutes, between the spells of their sudden impulses, live serene and apathetic, as if all were well with them.

Nor is the free Will of spirit hampered only by circumstances: it is inwardly divided and confused. It can triumph only by a perpetual sacrifice. Will here must sympathize with all Will and must love with all lovers; yet it must condemn each Will, not for loving that which it loves but for not loving that which it does not love; in other words, for not loving the good in all its possible forms. But all goods cannot be realized or sanely pursued in any particular life. Only the specific goals of that place and hour are proper to that particular concretion of universal Will. To pursue other goods then or there would be treason; and once having been born under that star, and vowed to that allegiance, it would be the height of pusillanimity and obloquy not to destroy, as far as possible, all obstacles to that chosen good. No chosen good could ever be attained otherwise; and what sort of love of all good

would that be, by which the attainment of every
particular good was prevented?

Thus spirit comes upon the most tragic of conflicts,
the conflict between existence and justice. Beneath the
realm of spirit conflicts are whole-hearted
on every side, and universal Will has no
qualms about contradicting and thwarting
itself. That is its business. War is the
father of all things that actually arise, since they arise
by the confluence of forces; and universal Will has no
prior purpose but lives only in the perpetual result.
Spirit, on the contrary, is the prophet of all those things
that should have arisen and that would have arisen if
each vital impulse could have had its way, and reached
its glory; so that while universal Will is always satisfied,
because it had no special aspiration, spirit which is the
breath of all distinct aspirations can never be satisfied,
because only one or another by chance is ever fulfilled,
and that imperfectly.

*It is a
martyr to
every lost
cause.*

Yet spirit speaks for something deeper in nature
than the upshot visible to cursory science or history;
it speaks for *potentialities* in the heart of
matter, that have taken at least a first step
towards expression. Besides, in its own person, it speaks for the *truth* of that total movement in
which these aspirations arise and meet their destiny.
What it cannot speak for, except when hypnotized by
animal impulse and alienated from itself, is any one
aspiration to the exclusion of the others. The aspiration to justice, which is its own essence, would be
stultified by such partiality: yet it would be equally
stultified if we reproached Will at each point for being
specific and exclusive. To be specific and exclusive
is the condition for existing at all, for having a vocation,
and for establishing an interest, even formal and
unconscious, by which to distinguish life from death,
benefit from injury. Spirit itself arises by virtue of

*And share
every joy
achieved.*

such an interest, suffering and triumphing according to that criterion. It has chosen what in its own eyes is the better part, intelligence, sympathy, universality. It has thereby chosen for all others that which their nature, in each case, demands; but for itself spirit has chosen renunciation, not to be preached to others who cannot love it, but to be practised inwardly in its own solitude. The first thing that spirit must renounce, if it would begin to be free, is any claim to domination. Its kingdom is not of this world; and the other world, where its Will is done, is not a second cosmos, another physical environment, but this very emancipation and dominion of spirit over itself, which raises it above care even for its own existence. Suffering is not thereby abolished, either in the world or in the spirit, so long as the spirit lives in any world; but suffering is accepted and spiritually overcome by being understood, and by being preferred to the easy injustice of sharing only one craving, to be satisfied with one sweet.

The freedom and glory of spirit come from its impotence; by its impotence it is guiltless, by its impotence it is universal, by its impotence it is invulnerably supreme. Its essence is to be light, not to be power; and it can never be pure light until it is satisfied with an ideal dominion, not striving to possess or to change the world, but identifying itself only with the truth and beauty that rise unbidden from the world into the realm of spirit.

CHAPTER VI

INTUITION

THE contrast between matter and mind, like a contrast
in sex, is far from defeating a natural union between
them. Nothing could be more intelligible
Physical
basis of
intuition.
to a sympathetic observer than such a
differential harmony, when once he aban-
dons the effort to express either fact in the categories
of the other, or to make them pass into one another
materially, as if they could form a single univocal
sequence. Their conjunction is by a spontaneous
conspiracy of complementary qualities. In the material
order, which is dynamic and continuous, this harmony
cannot be contained, since one of the terms lies in
another realm of being; yet that harmony can be pre-
pared. A manifold of motions and tensions is often
organized in an animal, such that all the elements and
occasions are supplied requisite for a moral experience.
Matter could go no further; but when it has gone so
far, spirit has been generated, and does the rest.
Impressions and reflex actions evoke images, voices
acquire meanings, instincts inspire longings. This
completion is no addition to the material process, but
a moral counterpart of what the process was as a whole,
or as we say, of what it *meant*. Such is the natural
link between matter and mind, that bodily life should
excite feeling, and that perception, emotion, and
thought should report material events.

Significance and sanity are great virtues for spirit
in this world, yet they are not inseparable from it in

its essence. Left to itself spirit would be omniscient, or would think itself so; and (as is perhaps involved in omniscience) it would feel no regret and no desire. A spirit focussed on particular impressions and troubled about particular events is evidently a foster-child of matter. Why should anything be dangerous to spirit? Why should one essence fascinate or another fatigue? Why should spirit be torn away in tears from what it loves, and beset everywhere by what it hates? Yet such are the first experiences of innocent spirit in this world, and the beginning of its inexplicable trials.

Ignored by intuition when free.

At this late day we know well enough what the material causes of these troubles are, so puzzling to the young spirit. The body must be healthy, well fed, well treated, allowed to grow and develop its faculties. Certainly hygiene will prevent many a woe, and a spirit not smothered or maddened by disease ought to manifest more clearly its innate Will or demands. Souls in this respect are like nations: in health they take everything foreign for a challenge, in disease, everything native for an oppression. What then would be the free and native life of spirit, which it enjoys more and more when conditions are favourable and suffers more and more for missing when they are adverse? What is spirit naturally fit to do?

For the sake of clearness let me state at once the conclusion I shall come to: the reader will then see the details more readily in the particular per- spective that concerns us here. This per- spective is not psychological or historical, but religious, or rather what the ancients would have called philosophical. The end in view is liberation, or the attainment, if only in glimpses, of the highest good. The steps are to be regarded as steps towards that end. What profit has the spirit in existing, and who are its true friends and true enemies?

Which demands an inward or moral happi- ness.

To which I reply: The perfect function of spirit is
pure intuition. By the very impulse that generates it,
intuition tends to become pure. It is the movement
of apprehension by which anything is given to consciousness; and there is a natural joy in it, whenever
it can live unimpeded by fatigue or pain, and not
harassed by care, fear, doubt, desire or any other
obsession about the not-given. Distress at its source
and distraction about its objects are the enemies of
spirit; and its salvation comes when it is freed from all
distress or distraction, and becomes pure intuition,
be the theme of that intuition simple or complex, a
breath of morning air or the sum total of possible
knowledge. The datum is never too simple, if it calls
forth a whole-hearted response from the soul, and the
datum is never too complicated, if it does not overtax
and confuse the scope of attention. In both cases
equally, intuition will be alert and happy. We see
this in the play of young children. Combative,
adventurous, or sexual instincts, as yet not ripe and
without fit occasions, overflow in play, and play in its
first impulse is always joyful. Attention is spontaneous, and action is selective, being confined, or
expecting to be confined, to so much as intuition can
victoriously discover, trace, dominate and delight in.

By intuition, the reader will perceive, I do
not mean divination, or a miraculous way of discovering that which sense and intellect
cannot disclose. On the contrary, by intuition I mean direct and obvious possession
of the apparent, without commitments of
any sort about its truth, significance, or material
existence. The deliverance of intuition is some pure
essence. The degree of truth or significance that this
given essence may have, as revealing a world of action,
or as promising other intuitions, is an ulterior question,
morally and cognitively important, but itself, when

*Relevance
to fortune
only an
incidental
advantage.*

consciously considered, distracting the spirit from its native and present happiness. We have undeniably a more compact mind and a stronger will when the themes of our intuitions are relevant to our action, and we see with the clearness of genius the movement of things near us, and of society. If we groped about the world always startled and aggrieved, and if we nursed pure intuition only about imaginary things, we should be sick children, and our thin intuitions would grow thinner and wilder, as our troubles grew thick. Nevertheless in the most masterly mind, in the most victorious soldier or legislator, no profit or peace will come to the spirit except in pure intuition, when that dominated world and that brilliant career appear as if in another man's life: a tale, a vision, in which all passion has become light, and all compulsion deliverance. Worldly victories are full of falseness and anguish; there must be a second victory of intuition over all victories before the spirit can triumph.

Such a triumph over nature and human nature can never be complete, and the moments in which it almost exists are rare. Were intuition possible only at the top, in the wisest moments of life, it might be left to the saints and mystics to tell us about it. But intuition is primitive; it is pervasive; we cannot look or think without evoking it in a thousand directions, for without it we should have no emotions, no images, no beliefs. It would be impossible for us to observe similarities, or conjunctions or movements, or to feel implications. Indeed, it would be impossible for us to feel anything or be conscious at all, since intuition is a name for that spiritual wakefulness by which attention discerns characters and distinguishes one character from another.

Yet it is fortune that controls intuition.

Intuition, then, is always with us, but dispersed over occasions that continually confuse and interrupt it. It is comparatively clear in the poet, in the wit, sometimes in the child ; it is the constant friend of the artist lost in his work. All I need do here is to disentangle it, and consider what it would be if it were pure.

In the first place, for a foundation, we may take the Aristotelian definition of intuition, or of any instance of spirit, as the second entelechy, the perfect actuality, of organic life. Intuition not only exists, but is the most intense form of existence. Existence, by another definition which at least in my view is fundamental, means flux, process, transition. Had we purely static being we should lapse or rise into essences, and should not exist. Now this point might well provoke some controversy, because in the most opposite quarters, in Buddhism and in British philosophy, the existence of spirit is verbally denied, as being a verbal fiction: according to one party there are only illusions and according to the other party only data. Data and illusions, however, involve intuition; otherwise data could not be given and illusions could not deceive. Moral presence, moral actuality is essential to givenness, as moral deceitfulness is essential to illusion. Intuition crowns the bodily movements that underlie it by taking notice, by being a most acute ideal concentration and moral effect of those movements, so that they now cause clear data, quite unlike their own physical texture, to arise and vanish before pure spirit.

First characteristic of intuition: Actuality, or existence concentrated into the sense of existence.

Intuition differs from the graphic or conceptual data so evoked in being itself a process and not an image, an event and not an idea, an existence and not an essence. It lends to those ideal and moral data the only existence of which they are capable: it enables them to appear. It justifies, when once we sharpen our concentration on the actually given, the Berkeleyan reduction of data of intuition to inert ideas or essences; also the moral

Spiritual tension between objects and terms.

discovery that essences, if supposed to exist on their
own account, are illusions. There is an intense reality
involved; but this reality is the life of the psyche,
unconscious save precisely where it culminates in
intuition, and raises ideal essences into obsessions.
These obsessions may be calm, steady, and normal,
as when we look at a material object and study it.
Every eye will not paint an identical picture, but each
picture may be clear and sustained at will, or changing
only as the material object itself changes. At other
times the psyche ferments inwardly under insufficient
control from external facts; and the ghosts then called
up, though plainly visible, prove to have no existence
in nature and no definite reference to anything there.
They signify only some inner agitation of the soul,
and they signify even this only for the psychologist, or
on second thoughts. The datum of intuition, when
fully realized and clarified, reveals nothing but itself
to that intuition. It is an essence, and though it may
be a picture of time it knows no temporal neighbours.
It is an idea, a concept, and not a moment in any
existing or evolving world. Intuition though it always
has a natural ground never can have a natural object,
but only an ideal one. Nature has learned to know
itself at this price, that its knowledge should be indirect
and symbolic. It can describe itself only in words,
and had to invent them in order to think.

If these sensible or intelligible symbols seem unreal
in their ideality, the reality of existence in its turn
seems no less ambiguous, since it continually falls between two stools, is by not-being,
by merely ceasing to be one thing and
becoming something different. In intuition,
however, we have an instance of perfect
actuality, a form of being that preeminently exists and
moves (for it is a discovery, an experience) yet is
precisely the act of arresting and defining some clear

Actuality is a physical movement issuing in a definite datum.

essence. This flash of light issues from sundry processes and tensions coming to a head, and fusing their energies; but the confluence does not remain simply a fact about those processes: it generates a feeling. This feeling continually varies, like its physiological ground; but at each moment it brings some revelation to consciousness, having a precise logical and moral character, absolutely individual and like itself, however nameless and vague it may seem in relation to conventional human categories.

The fruition of an organ, we have noted earlier,[1] cannot arise until that organ has matured. A first sensation is therefore, physiologically, a last event. A full psychic life must have preceded, now perhaps interrupted, or perhaps brought to a head in some sudden movement. The vital background is far more stable, far wider, than the flash of feeling. There was much more to be felt, if we went in for feeling, and it was a mere accident that we felt this in particular. Thus when the Indians tell us that in deep sleep we return to Brahma, we may say that from the point of view of spirit they are describing the birth of spirit itself, representing the absence of consciousness as consciousness in a perfectly placid, equable, infinitely potential equilibrium. Logical vacancy would thus cover vital repletion. So we too, looking at life naturalistically from the outside, may well feel that spirit actually slumbers in all things, in a deep sleep inclined to waking, a sleep, as it were, under tremulous eyelids. This is not a wholly fanciful notion, because something very like such a vacant but positive tension endures in waking life, supplying the background to all ulterior data. The glance of attention would disclose nothing distinct if a constant blank field, the specific datum of expectancy, did not spread round each image, precede it, limit it, contrast with it, and

[1] Chapter I, p. 8.

swallow it up in the end, much as the sea might swallow up an island or the sky a star—data which could never have been given to intuition except within those broader fields.

Intuition is in some sense always a synthesis, even when the datum is an inarticulate feeling, like a scent or a pain. The very simplicity of such data proves this, not indeed, to analysis (because no analysis is possible of the inarticulate) but to common sense, as soon as the very complex natural occasion for such simple feelings has been discovered. Yet the word synthesis is highly ambiguous and misleading, like other Kantian terms that have become convenient or indispensable. The danger is that what occurs in the realm of matter should be interpreted by literary psychology as occurring in the realm of spirit. In the realm of spirit there is no machinery, nothing compounded, dynamic, mysterious, or latent; therefore there is no synthesis at that level; although intuition momentarily manifests in an open datum, all surface, say in joy, intricate processes that have been going on and combining in the animal psyche since the dawn of creation. The joy felt is a unitary effect of a multiple cause, itself felt only as a fountain of joy. A synthesis may therefore be said to have occurred, but not in consciousness. Consciousness gives the result of that synthesis. It does not give the elements nor the process nor the motive for the given formation. Idealists may say that all these unknown things occur in "unconscious mind", "unconscious mind" being an unfortunate name which they give to bodily life, when they are compelled to acknowledge that the body is not merely an image in the mind but a dynamic heritage prior to consciousness and determining the images that shall appear. This dynamic heritage is the psyche, or the process of life considered objectively and as continuous with the

Analysis of synthesis: it is premental.

vital heritage in seeds; it is something obscure but
indubitably real and taking place in the material world.
Being material these processes are not mental; but being
hidden and obscure they are most readily distinguished
by their occasional moral culmination in some feeling
or image.   Feelings and images may then be inter-
polated dramatically, even where certainly they do not
exist, as in thunder and lightning.   Such play of
fancy is spontaneous in myth and in literary psychology;
but to take it literally would be to explain the profound
by the superficial, the dynamic by the pictorial, and
often the real by the fictitious.

Synthesis, conceived as a fusion of existential
elements into a new existential unit, is therefore
incongruous with spirit, and belongs to the
realm of matter.   But before leaving it
there, we may notice something proper and
indeed essential to spirit that might be
confused with an evolutionary synthesis: I
mean the intuition of relations or, as called by another
Kantian name, the transcendental unity of appercep-
tion.   When a datum is complex attention in noticing
the parts sees them in their common field, and initially
qualified by their place there and their mutual relations.
These relations may be static, and then, since spirit is
volatile, it may return again and again to the same
object, emphasizing each time a different feature, and
evoking a different essence.   These successive intuitions can never be synthesized.   They are events, they
are unsubstantial, they blaze for a moment and vanish
into nothing.   But the deliverances of those moments
may supplement one another as descriptions of the
object, or as mere experiences; and a subsequent
intuition, springing from the organic soil so tilled and
fertilized, may repeat those intuitions or variations of
them in a fresh description of the object, or poetic
suggestion of it in its wholeness and in its destiny.

In intuition there is momentary unity of view but no synthesis.

Imagination may thus evolve, and knowledge may increase, not by an impossible synthesis or breeding together of dead intuitions, but by the training of organisms and the complication of instruments, orchestrating a richer but no less fugitive life in the spirit.

When the object is in motion the perpetual variations in intuition have a double source, for besides the continual renewal of apprehension, always with a somewhat different volume, vivacity and point of view, there is the flux of events, replacing one another before the eyes. Suppose I am watching a procession, or *Parts and movements can appear only within the present whole.* listening to music, or floundering through an improvised speech of my own. The vital continuity of consciousness is not suspended, and there is a comparatively stable background, in my sense of the world and myself in it, against which I notice each new feature. And what is most marvellous, when we consider it, many features that have vanished from the world are still present, though fading, in the temporal perspectives of the spirit. I know that this which has come is not that which is gone, and I can specify many a precise detail in which they differ. Even what is coming, or what ought to come, is present vaguely to my sense, and is recognized as normal or as surprising when it actually appears. Thus intuition transcends in scope the sequence of events toppling over one another in the world, so that the picture of that world in imagination is much wider, much clearer, and much fairer than its aspect at any one instant. There is a nexus of events in the realm of matter, as they fuse and generate one another; there is a history of events in the realm of truth, where their essences, their sequence and all their formal relations for ever confront the spirit; and in the realm of spirit there are partial and ever varied recompositions of events, as intuition catches glimpses of them in different perspectives.

H

If intuition, then, pelts a static object with a variety of views, it lifts a fluid object, or a sequence of events, out of the irreparable flux in which it occurs and keeps its essence and its occurrence in mind, as long as the intuition lasts. The selection of features appearing in such an intuition is made for it by the psyche, under the physical influences of the moment; and here there is a real *synthesis* of tensions and processes. In the intuition the given features are not synthesized but discriminated, being first given in solution under that unity of apprehension without which no intuition could exist at all.

The notion that intuition synthesizes its elements, comes of hypostasizing these elements, and imagining

Illusion that them to be separate existents that intuition
data are must pick out and combine in an adventi-
substances. tious way. But neither intuition nor the features distinguishable in its field are physical objects of that sort, meeting and acting upon one another; they are not wooden pawns that a selective hand must take from the box, move about the chess-board, and sweep into the box again for use on another occasion. We are in the realm of spirit. Here the elements found are pure visionary essences and the spirit finding them is pure light of attention. Essences have no hidden temporal persistence; their so-called subsistence is merely their logical identity. Intuition on its side is not an operation performed by some pre-existing intellect. Intellect exists by intellection; and intuition is a moment of created spirit, not a power applied, but a brief life received. A different simile might express these facts better. Intuitions may be likened to soap-bubbles. Soap-bubbles are impossible to synthesize; if they touch they vanish; yet the surface of one may repeat the iridescence visible on the surface of several others. These colours are not taken from the smaller bubbles, and transferred and rearranged

on the larger one: they are reborn in each instance, in
each degree of complexity, according to the circumstances of that more or less similar moment. Of those
lights, of those spheres, nothing endures; but the soap-
suds and the air remain available for bubbles *ad libitum*,
and the colours of the rainbow may be drawn upon
for ever for decoration without being exhausted. The
reshufflings are all material, the pictures are all precarious, and their parts are created and sustained
within them by the same rays and the same tensions
that create the whole.

In waking life and even in sleep intuition is normally uninterrupted, though what is constant there,
amid a stream of changes, is singularly Continuity
vague and nameless. Nothing could be of intuition.
more worthless to spirit than spirit dozing, when all
its specific functions and pleasures are in abeyance.
Yet that dim spark of light, like a *veilleuse* in a sick-
room, keeps alive the sense of a shadowy ambience
from which anything might emerge. Even in alert
consciousness this vague background endures; and
normally any precise observation or distinct thought
is preceded by a momentary pause, as it were for
breath, or to take aim. We thus fall back upon our
physical resources for foothold before we leap. Then,
the observation having been made or the thought
formulated, we relapse into the familiar hum of habitual
living, with that clear moment marked as with a red
letter, to be reverted to if possible upon occasion.
Fundamentally, we must remember, all time and all
existence are open to spirit; and this virtual omnipresence renders something possible which would be
utterly impossible if spirit were not transcendental,
but were lodged successively in each of its data: I
mean, the reference of a memory to its original, and
the possibility of comparing the two and judging the
memory to be inadequate. Do we then have two

intuitions, one of the original and another of the reproduction? And can a third intuition compare the two? Not in the least. Intuitions are not objects, they are moments of spirit, qualitatively similar in their cognitive essence, which is absolutely intellectual and unpresentable to sense. They differ only in their themes. It is these two themes (which may be rival descriptions of the same fact in the posited natural world) that intuition may compare, when it retreats a little from its two former occasions and sees their two deliverances at once, perhaps together with a third view, taken now of the same object. All views thus form one field of imagination and memory, open to repeated inspection and enlargement; and the diversity of such available ideas supplies all the alternatives between which judgment may waver. For as there is only one ultimate ambition of spirit everywhere, to embrace everything as does the truth, so there is but one total object for multiple consideration, namely, the whole course of nature, physical and moral, with the whole history of spirit included in it, and the whole realm of essence spreading beyond, the logical complement of any special universe.

A survey of the successive is a deeply different fact from the successive events surveyed. Before any survey is possible for the spirit, physical experience and organic memory must accumulate, giving the psyche a wider resonance and fresh capacities for reaction: then these, until the psyche begins to decay, may supply a broadened basis for intuition. This is what fails to happen in the fool : no matter how much he may knock about the world or read in the newspapers, he will never put two and two together. His soul has little synthetic power, and his bubbling intuitions will be as bird-like, as shallow, and as absolute at the end as at the beginning. A great increase in science and in

Experience cumulative, intuition comprehensive.

available information therefore does not ensure any
greater wisdom in the public. On the contrary, it
may occasion universal confusion and frivolity.
Materials do not synthesize themselves by being
heaped together; a spark of life, a synthesizing force,
must arise in some organism; and then a spirit awakened
there may rise above the flux, feel events toppling over
one another, perceive their variety, their tendency,
their promise, and live as much in what they have
been and may be as in what, in the passing moment,
they actually are. All minds belong to their time and
place; such is the condition of their existence that
determines their point of view; yet they are minds only
in the measure in which they transcend their physical
station, and can view their place from other places
and their moments from other moments.

Organic rhythms are animated by what we have
agreed to call a Will, which if conscious would appear
to spirit as pleasure or pain, success or
failure. Intuition expresses such a rhythm, Second
characteristic
such a mode of vital appetition. If the trope of intuition:
Vitality.
initiated were never completed, no intuition
or consciousness would arise at all; so that wherever
there is consciousness there is an element of organic
success, a ground for joy. The organ of apprehension
is working successfully. Intuition thus finds itself
sympathetically participating in the process of creation,
and moving with it. This process cannot stop itself,
and its various organs cannot spontaneously rescind
their impetus. Nor can spirit put the brake on them,
as if it were an independent power, or had a prior
bent against the forces that bring it into existence, or
would prefer to sleep on. Sleepiness is an intoxication of the organism. But spirit is light, and light,
while there is fuel, can never be tired of shining. On
the contrary, it clarifies and makes vocal the will that
is at work, and does so faithfully and impartially,

delivering the message it receives, whether of good
or ill omen in the world's affairs.

In primitive will-lessness there could be no Will-
not-to-will, and the eternal indifference of Brahma
It survives   could not prevent the world from arising.
in pure   Rather that deep sleep was secretly prolific;
spirit.   the whole realm of essence enveloped it like
something forgotten yet somehow known which silently
invited dreams of all sorts to unfold themselves. Yet
when will-lessness is not merely the mutual arrest of
innumerable Wills, as perhaps it is in the depths of
matter, but is rather, as in spirit, the fruit of Will
realized, it retains the image and the love of what was
willed, without the propensity to create it. Such clarified will-lessness is the result of experience and discipline, and is will-less only in respect to existence, being
still the Will to understand that which exists. Passions
and dreams are then recovered without illusion, and
experience is gathered together in intuition without
being any longer ignorantly traversed through birth
and death.

There is an oversight possible here that sometimes
vitiates asceticism. The vulgar, we feel, move with
It glories   the blind Will to live; spirit withdraws from
alike in   that vain and horrible struggle and makes
adventure
and in   for peace, or even for non-existence. It
reflection.   *may* do so, but only by a revulsion that is
physical and temporary. A satirist or an elegiac poet
is free to dwell only on what the universal Penelope
does at night, when she destroys her day's work; yet
in Penelope all is not self-contradiction. Her impulse
is not now earnestly to weave and now earnestly to
unweave what she has woven; she is busy without
conviction and destructive without rage. A shrewd
light twinkles in her eye, and her apparent folly serves
to defend her liberty; something heroic and humorous
within triumphs in the very futility of her action. So

intuition profits by the vanity of life and quietly takes note, while the cycles of growth and decay succeed one another. To these vicissitudes it adds something different and positive, that covers both movements alike. It does so by virtue of its own Will, at whatever point it arises, and does not tend either to prolong the ascent or hasten the descent of natural seasons. For intuition springs out of a power, present in animal life, to respond from one centre to influences and inheritances coming from a distance, and to trace relations backwards and forwards, in quality and quantity, over all being. The sensitiveness is physical, the intuition spiritual; the one establishes, the other expresses, a vital harmony in the movement of things. There is therefore no hostility to nature in.spirit; where hostility appears we may justly suspect some earthly demon of desire prompting us to hate all that is not food for our own lusts. In nature lusts and conflicts are inevitable, since everything has a Will of its own; yet to note the variety and contradiction of these Wills is a great feat, a great exaltation for the spirit and a great joy. This joy will indeed be mixed with sorrow so long as the psyche is reluctant to change or to die; and consequently, while the old Adam kicks at the pricks, the organ of spirit, in ascetic discipline, cannot but strive to liberate and vivify itself at the expense of all unreconciled passions. But no passion is warmer than the zeal to see, to discover, to master the truth, to rescue the spirit from confusion and slavery, even at the price of perceiving the vanity of life.

In this book I am deliberately taking the point of view of spirit fully awake, contrasting itself with other things, and aspiring to its own freedom and perfection. That is the supreme question for the inner man; but we must not suppose, or seem to expect, that spirit, or anything else, should have been produced with an

Third characteristic: Moral autonomy in physical dependence.

eye towards its ultimate good.   That good cannot be chosen or pursued until the creature exists whose good it is to be; you must have a native direction before you can have a goal.   Like other natural growths, spirit finds its life taking shape gradually, developing in this direction and in that, retreating, recommencing, piling up great enterprises that collapse in a deluge, or in a confusion of tongues, and only after many readjustments reaching a clear perfection of some particular sort.   Nature will move on, and spirit may be launched into other adventures; but a possible culmination will have been attained under the form of eternity in one art, which will unite for ever in mutual understanding all creatures that at any time or place may have that vocation.   There are many creatures in many circumstances that possess consciousness; but if we find in one instance what such consciousness would become if it were free and favoured by fortune, we have a criterion for judging, or rather for feeling, its virtue wherever it exists.   Intuition, happy in itself and pledged to nothing further, is such a criterion.

This does not mean that pure intuition was established first, for its own sweet sake, and then was rudely disturbed by other processes irrelevant to it. Such is the illusion created in the spirit (an illusion that itself proves a great obstacle to peace) when we presume that, because we are minds, all things ought to minister to us, or even cannot exist save by virtue of our attention to them.   This *ought* is the cry of selfishness, this *cannot* the cry of pride.   Psyches do not become conscious for the sake of consciousness. They become conscious automatically, in acquiring a special organic responsiveness and heed of relations; and this plunges them into a far more agitated and perilous life than they led before, in their vegetative phase.   They are launched into action and passion. Thus spirit is born the twin of trouble.   The pure joy

and knowledge that should come to it can come only
in snatches, or in ultimate concentration and solitude.

Such solitude is not empty; it is solitude in the
presence of anything and everything, the solitude of
the traveller and witness, the essential *Plastic unity*
stranger, whose proper interest is impartial, *and kindly*
but who is caught and jostled in a press of *solitude.*
troubles not really his own. Yet it was impossible,
logically as well as physically, that a living spirit should
exist where there was no Will, no agent, no environment, no contingency and no fatality. These circumstances and prerequisites supply the interest and
theme of the drama. The given predicament might
indeed have been different, and the vital impulse different. Such a diversity does not disturb the intrinsic
ambition of spirit. Wherever it may arise, at every
stage in its manifestation, it will show its true colours
modestly and momentarily here, proudly and systematically there. This moral liberty cannot be forfeited
while intuition subsists, since this liberty is internal.
When on the contrary spirit beats its wings unreconciled against natural bars, it proves how completely it
has been deceived about the direction of its possible
freedom. It might have been singing in that cage.

False starts and failures are not the spirit's fault.
They are its fate, its hereditary slavery, from which it
may be freed if it lives long enough. As a *Spiritual*
first vital harmony brought it forth, a second *freedom*
may redeem it. For we must not suppose *may be*
that any malice animates nature in regard to *docile.*
spirit, or any reluctance to evoke spirit and give it free
rein. On the contrary, the often inopportune existence
of spirit, in some sorry and hopeless plight, proves that
nature is only too well disposed towards such a development; it emanates from incipient harmonies; and every
species of plant and animal, even the most wretched,
shows how persistently nature flows into every possible

shape. Yet the types established are as specific as they are stubborn, since the first stages have to be hereditary and well protected, if the organism is to be widely diffused or highly elaborate; otherwise the endless potentiality of matter would remain chaotic. We must therefore not be surprised at the fixity of Will in us, physical and moral, or at the consequent peril and suffering besetting us on every side. After a season of incubation while our nature takes shape in the dark, we are born into a world that cannot be altogether friendly. There must be not only buffets and denials, but a more subtle assault of circumstances, contaminating the very psyche in which the spirit lives, and creating strange vices and ambitions. Like a child in a den of thieves, spirit is then taught crime as a duty. Intuition is not suffered to be pure. Scarcely has it begun to distinguish an essence, when it is rudely summoned to confuse it with something different, and in this confusion to become impatient instead of joyful, to hate, to fear, and (what is most insidious) to claim *possession* of its objects, as if they were things or pledges, and not innocent essences. So the interrupted life of intuition is entangled with the incongruous rhythms and conflicts of other organs and of alien things. Yet at this level again a second humbler but wiser life of spirit may begin; piety, religion, and science may insinuate themselves beneath free intuition, darkening its face while deepening its meaning, and turning it from vision into faith and knowledge.

There is indeed a sense in which intuition itself is cognitive from the beginning. It is apprehension of something distinct, capable of being recognized and spoken of again. Yet this something might be a pure feeling or idea, enriching the mind, but conveying no knowledge of anything further. In a pregnant and transcendent

Fourth characteristic: Cognition.

sense, therefore, intuition is not knowledge. It is the mere possession of a thought, which need have no object other than the essence revealed in it. So all exercise, play, and fiction, all poetry and music, expand the spirit congenially, give it a tone and cogency perhaps very precious to it, without conveying knowledge of anything else. Yet this purity of intuitive life, though it appears in snatches at any stage, can attain to solidity and permanence only in arts, like language, that have a broad basis and use in the world. The clear profit brought thereby to the spirit may be ultimately only intellectual or æsthetic, a play of ordered imagination; yet imagination has been evoked in the first place by the senses, in physical contact with external things, and it has been corrected and made inveterate by continual experience. Even the purest psychic fictions, such as logic or grammar, would not long hold their own if directly or indirectly they did not reflect the structure of the world. So also a symbolic poet, interested only in the music and emotion of words, must involuntarily feed his art upon nature, if it is to touch his soul.

In some animals perhaps nothing comes to consciousness before the outer senses are stimulated by some sudden change in the environment. Sensation an Intuition then will be an index, in some index even respects, to the assault of an influence and taken for to the character of its source. And prob- a sign. ably not merely a passive index but an active perception; because intuition being essentially cognitive and spiritual, it has an intrinsic light to turn upon anything that may confront it; and the psyche being in this case tensely directed upon the source of stimulation, intuition absorbs that vital intent, and becomes animal faith: a specific assurance and expectancy turned towards the not-given.

That attention should be turned towards the not-

given may seem a contradiction in terms, and would
be such if attention were always pure intuition, since
then the datum would be the whole ob-

The leap of
intent im-
posed on
spirit by
its animal
origin.

ject, and this object a pure essence. But in
fact attention is always attracted, in the first
instance, to the not-yet-given, because the
psyche is struggling with a disturbance
or uneasiness of which she has as yet no idea; and this
idea, when it now begins to take shape, indicates that
disturbance or uneasiness without in the least encom-
passing or exhausting the truth about it. Intuition is
born smothered in intent; and intent is precisely
assurance and expectancy turned towards the not-
given. The act of recoiling precedes any idea of what
that may be from which we recoil; shaken by the blow,
we look to see what has hit us. And the act of grasping,
clinging, or pursuing precedes and guides attention to
the object grasped, clung to, or pursued. *Some*
intuition accompanied the primary movement, else
there would be no consciousness of it; but we hardly
have words for essences so generic and inarticulate as
are given in sheer alarm, lust, impatience, or effort;
these terms, which we say denote "feelings" really
denote, for our adult minds, the occasions and actions
that are visible when we use them. We never name
our own passions, until we catch them in the mirror
of the world. Yet the passions are not unconscious:
across the background of the habitual scene—which
may be a blank—a light, a shadow, a suction, a tension
pass and transform themselves as we live on; and we
act under high pressure of an inward fatality or Will
that is conscious of its fury but not until afterwards of
its acts. Thus attention to the not-given, anxiety,
suspense, precipitation dominate the spirit in the
beginning; and the element of clear intuition, the sense
of what is happening in reality even within the mind,
though always present, remains inarticulate. In this

way it happens that, though the spirit be essentially joyful, it is born, bred, and propagated in distress.

Tension towards the hidden or distant yields intellectual dominion when it becomes clear intuition; but before being dominion it halts usually at interest, inquiry, or pursuit. And this element of suspense constitutes the trans-cendent force of true knowledge, which takes the datum of intuition for a sign of something beyond. Such belief involves a claim, as pure intuition does not; it is subject to danger and error, and therefore never puts the cognitive powers of spirit at ease. Spirit instinctively transposes impressions into images, and beliefs into imaginative heirlooms, as in myth and legend, metaphysics and theology. To meditate on an article of faith is to replace it as far as possible by an intuition. Imagination advances as material refer-ence recedes, until in mystical ecstasy possession renders all faith unnecessary. *Purgatorial trials of knowledge.*

On the other hand *intelligence* essentially requires postulates, and moves in the sphere of belief; and intelligence rather than idle intuition was what the psyche required when she gave birth to spirit. It was in learning to behave intelligently that she stretched those threads of telepathic communication which when duly connected struck the first spark of intuition. And we may say that as intuition is cognitive of essence even when not conveying any knowledge of fact, so it is intelligent and conclusive even when not positing any external object. For intuition is an act and has an organ, so that it executes a movement and traverses duration in merely arising. We cannot see or hear without *tracing* the datum; and tracing it would be profitless to the spirit if retracing it were impossible; since an intuition that lost its themes in the act of evoking them would be at best a spiritual atom adrift in infinity and no part of any spiritual life.

Thus memory, consecutive discourse, allegiance to old loves and to old knowledge belong to the grain of Intuition tends to sublimate knowledge into vision. spiritual reality; yet they contain faith in the not-given, and thereby transcend intuition. For on a small scale or on a large scale intuition is something ultimate, a culmination of many processes that from the spiritual point of view are subsidiary. All that self-transcendence which is involved in action, in belief, in expectation, must itself be transcended and embraced in intuition, before spirit can be happy. When scattered experience is synthesized in memory and scattered aspirations in worship, they become a single panorama and a single love. The whole course of a life is raised to a present datum possessed virtually in all its details by the dramatic imagination, as all the convolutions of a piece of music are retained virtually in the finale. Then a body of positive knowledge of fact acquires the values of fiction: the man has actually lived through the adventures that on his death-bed or in heaven he sees spread before him as a story: but its spiritual reality now swallows up for him the accident of its material enactment, once upon a time, in his accidental person. He accepts and forgives himself, and ceases to repine at his destiny, because a spirit is now awake in him that is not limited or defiled by those obsessions, now no more its own than those of any other creature. Hope and fear have become vision of the truth: and if that vision is itself lurid and burdened with too much thunder, even the vision of the truth can be dismissed, or sublimated into one pattern among a thousand in the realm of fancy.

Since these phases of spirit do not generate one another but each goes with some special phase of organic life, there is no telling by moral analysis in what order spiritual experience may develop. Moral classifications are possible only if the moments of a given history are distinguished by the relative purity of intuition in them. We might arrange them in a circular or spiral order, from intuition empty to intuition filled with all truth; for according to the Indians, who know more about this than we do, deep sleep, being perfect bliss, must be a kind of intuition, yet empty; and I think an intuition filled with the truth (about which we know more than they did) would be perfect bliss too, if our whole psyche were absorbed in conceiving that truth, with no other wish subsisting. And in that case it would be indifferent that this truth happened to be true rather than mere poetry, since it would be only as poetry that the spirit would entertain it. Pure intuition, even when filled in with infinite detail, would thus revert to the perfect peace of pure Being.

The spiral of spiritual experience from innocence to ecstasy.

On this hint we might sketch the earthly round of spirit, descending from heaven empty and open to every illusion, and ascending into heaven full, but thoroughly purified. A deep pre-natal sleep might be first broken by a feeling of pressure, which if intensified would become pain. A sense of inescapable duration, a dread of change or a longing for it, would create temporal perspectives, forward and back, into an oncoming future and a receding past, both ambiguously present, and both unseizable. These would form a ghostly world, to which spirit somehow would feel that it belonged, and from which the real world would be hard to disentangle. Yet those vital emotions and those temporal perspectives would have had no consistence, if they had contained no images, and supplied no recognizable ideal terms in which spirit might describe them. Nature and history would thus gradually take shape before the distracted spirit and would reveal to it the secret of its own destiny. Anxiety and craving would dissolve before this redeeming knowledge, and the universe would be clarified into a complex essence, given pure and untroubled to intuition.   Spirit, so enlightened, would be again at peace.

When the Indians tell us that such peace is bliss we may be inclined to smile or to call them pessimists, as if only the negation of existence could seem to them good.   And when our own religion bids the dead "rest in peace", we may suspect that some early fancy about wandering ghosts survives in our liturgy, contrary to the "hope of glory".   But perhaps we are deceived in our cleverness.   When peace or deep sleep returns to the spirit the multitudinous vibration of nature that supports spirit has not ceased; it continues and will continue for ever; and new occasions for waking and troubling will break out in a thousand places.   Spirit, considered as a natural concomitant of nature, never can rest in peace.   Yet at any point, by its own insight summing up nature, it may achieve tranquillity.   It is only redeemed spirits, *fidelium animæ*, that can rest in peace: it would be senseless to call down peace on the others.   This peace is therefore a quality of life, not of death.   And perhaps the bliss of Brahma might be understood in a similar way, when the sense of identity with what is common to all things causes their differences and oppositions, without being historically destroyed, to be balanced and mutually cancelled in our allegiance; so that Brahma is all things, and yet is none of them.   As warmth is something diffused and inarticulate, born of infinitesimal pervasive vibrations, so deep sleep may be a nameless happiness, brooding over a sea of troubles.   We are justified in distinguishing this state from non-existence not only morally, as escape from all evil, but also physically by virtue of the concourse of Wills in it from all quarters suspended by their mutual incompatibility, yet rich each with its possible good.   This latent infinite

Peace implies harmony not emptiness.

aspiration lifts the deep peace of the universal psyche into a limiting instance of spirit, as if love of all good lived there without experience, and therefore without loss.

Love is hardly in itself an object of intuition, since it becomes conscious only when it is love of something; and yet love is independent in origin from the intuition of its object. It colours this object with a quality which is not beauty, or clearness, such as the joy of pure intuition would endow it with. Love seeks possession.

Fifth characteristic: Piety or attachment to its source.

It experiences a physical affinity between the psyche and the object, and attaches the Will to that object like a child to its mother, prior to any clear idea of it; so that here the spirit is caught in the leash, restrained and called back insistently more to an active influence than to the essence that represents it in intuition. Love suffers and hopes; it is attached in its aspirations to something not spiritual; it clothes this something as best it may in spiritual guise, but constantly with the sense or the fear of a misfit, of a disappointment. We sometimes find that the mother we love is not the mother we should have liked; and spirit at every turn has that painful experience. The estrangement flows from the native predicament of spirit in being incarnate, lodged in a particular place, time, and person, while its intrinsic ambition is universal. Love, like knowledge, is of the contingent by the contingent; both knowledge and love are therefore in one sense distracting, since they bind spirit to something particular and pre-existent, other than the spontaneous play of intuition.

Yet these bonds are the first roots of spontaneity itself, giving existence and specific impulse to the spirit, since the whole power in spirit is natural, as the whole glory of nature is spiritual. Detachment presupposes attachment; but attachment, when it becomes conscious

I

in love or knowledge, has already begun to transcend
the object of attachment, partly by seeing its limitations
and its surroundings in the world, partly by sublimating
it into an idea and turning it from the brute fact that
it was into a part of the furniture of mind.   And how
shall any local personal love become just, sure, and
enlightened?   Not by being disowned (or we should
soon be disowning spirit itself) but by being understood
and seen to be legitimate and beautiful in its place, as
other loves are legitimate and beautiful in their places.

Vital attachment to the life of nature thus has ideal
fidelity for its counterpart in the life of spirit.   Animal
instincts attract attention to specific objects;
action and passion, in passing, leave a settled
propensity in the psyche to repeat those
movements or to recoil from them; and this
quickened attention and these well-learned lessons of
experience sharpen and fix in the mind the terms of its
memory and logic.   In this intellectual field experience
can be cumulative.   Each term retains its meaning;
and when further experience or consideration shows
that essence in a new light, displaying one or another
of its necessary relations to other essences, its identity
is not destroyed but vindicated; since its place and
function are defined more and more perfectly in the
great mosaic of terms composing a coherent language
for that spirit.   It is in the primary nature of intuition
to exhibit something specific, to clarify and define it;
and also to keep that definite term *in mind* (as we say),
not of course in consciousness except occasionally, but
in reserve in the penumbra of essences to which a
reference is possible and which silently buttress the
meaning and quality of every other essence that may
come before us.

Conventionally considered, and from the point of
view of language and material knowledge, human ideas
are vague and shifting, so that no two men can think

Hence mindfulness and coherence in reflection.

alike and no two readings of the same poem can produce
the same impression. But if instead of referring ideas
to conventional standards never actually specified,
we consider each actual intuition in itself, it is necessarily absolutely clear and definite, revealing the precise
essence that it reveals. Some intuitions will be more
prolonged or emphatic than others, so that the essence
given in them may have a better chance of reappearing
in later intuitions, or one almost like it, and of being
designated by some word; and it will be only the
approach to constancy in the meanings of words or
of other signs that will enable the mind to enlarge its
scope and to preserve its acquisitions.

In the life of reason this intrinsic growth within
intuition may be overlooked, because what interests
the moralist is the harmony to be attained between
desire and thought on the one side and nature and
destiny on the other. The ideal for him is psychic
adaptation rather than spiritual freedom, although
spiritual freedom would be achieved, perhaps in some
at first painful or unpalatable form, if social harmony
were once established. Such freedom could be
attained, however, only after a great slaughter and
sacrifice of spirits; and intuition has its intrinsic reality
and value quite as much in the spirits condemned by
circumstances as in the spirits approved and declared
triumphant. Even such wisdom as the discipline of
experience may achieve is bought at a price and is
a terrible drag on the *discursive* freedom of spirit,
clipping its wings for any far migration. Piety, in
domesticating the spirit in one specific region, educates
it to be partial, prejudiced and unjust. It seems to
attach love to illusion, and life to that which by its very
nature is condemned to death. Incompleteness and
distraction thus enter into the heart of spirituality,
contradicting its native vocation to be clear, comprehensive and free.

The great privilege of the immaterial, however, is to be indomitable. As existence can neither abolish any essence by neglecting it, nor smirch it by dragging it down into the flux of change, so animal life cannot annul the discoveries which it has once made. It may extinguish the light of attention and of memory by destroying the organs and records that might have kept that knowledge alive in the world; but the autonomy of spirit, while spirit lives, is inalienable. The things felt will have been felt, the things loved will have been loved, whatever may ensue; and no contrary judgment supervening will ever have the field to itself. Ignorant as it may be of all contradictions, it will be contradicted; unconscious as it may be of alien goods, the alien goods will exist. So that the clouds that traverse the spirit, in being seen, are in one sense abolished: spirit has outflanked them, set them down to be clouds, and thereby vindicated the supremacy of light and of vision.

Sixth characteristic: Intrinsic authority.

Evidently in the absence of intuition there would be no judgment or valuation at all, no spiritual witness to observe the world or to question it. And if the actual observations or questionings made by anybody be referred to some ulterior authority, that authority can be only that of a further intuition. There is, indeed, the dynamic authority or laughter of things, going their way, doing their work, and crushing all judgments: but this is a triumph for them only in our own estimation. They themselves do not boast; they most humbly and uncomplainingly endure their strains and precipitate their cataclysms. So that intuition shines alone in its moral heaven, among other intuitions; and even these do not shine together in any common medium, but only each in each, when they think of one another.

CHAPTER VII

DISTRACTION

In languages derived from the Latin the word distraction bears the pleasant sense of an incidental *divertissement*, or change from compulsory to entertaining ideas. In English the word has preserved a deeper meaning of which I will avail myself here. We are distracted or distraught when torn asunder by contrary and inescapable commitments. From these we may seek refuge in drink, heedlessness, or sport, but still they will poison the sources of our lives, fill our solitude and our dreams, and threaten our sanity. By distraction I understand the alien force that drags the spirit away from the spontaneous exercise of its liberty, and holds it down to the rack of care, doubt, pain, hatred, and vice. And I will distinguish the chief agencies in this distraction, after the picturesque manner of Christian wisdom, as the Flesh, the World, and the Devil.

I have already dropped some hints as to how we may understand this shocking anomaly; for so it would seem to a truly emancipated spirit, to whom everything, including its own movement and destiny, would be an object of sympathetic interest, but never a source of distraction. Such a spirit would laugh at the hypothesis, perhaps suggested to it by the devil, that it would have lived happy had it been left to its own resources, without a body or a world; for in pure spirit there is evidently nothing to determine what experiences may fall to it, what passions or what impulse to go on living or dreaming at all. Universal Will, even, that part at work in spirit, must be irrational, since if it had been a rational agent it would have sought, but never could have found, a reason for being what it was. All appetitions, repulsions, selections, and exclusions must first be automatic: they must precede and occasion the rise of intuition, if intuition is to exist temporally and to have any special themes or career. Emancipated spirit would see clearly that even its emancipation and liberty were gifts of fortune or divine grace; and it would understand at the same time how rare such good fortune is likely to be, and how distracted the life of spirit must be on the whole.

On the whole, but not essentially; for it is only when a certain harmony has been achieved in the psyche that spirit can awake, and this harmony at moments may be almost perfect. There will then be intuition without distraction. You may hear a sound so pure, so musically modulated and sufficient in itself, that no suspicion intervenes of any cause or meaning that this sound might have in the world, much less any thought of yourself hearing, or of your ears or brain. Another day, the sound may be so deafening or piercing that your whole frame winces and trembles, and your hands go up instinctively to the sides of your tortured head. The body has then awakened spirit only to fill it with horrid concern for that body. Yet this was not the body's Will, only an effect of maladjustment in its physical economy and adaptation. When working well, the psyche remains unconscious of instrumentalities. Your ears may perfectly perform their practical function without sound, as sound, coming to consciousness at all. Meaning, objects, ideas, remote reported events will alone fill your imagination. This is normal in interesting conversation: the psyche receives the

Instrumentalities that distract as objects may enrich intuition as influences.

sounds of the language and conveys their messages to the proper quarters, so that intelligent answers or actions follow; but those sounds never reach the spirit, they remain vibrations without ever becoming data; and intuition evokes only the facts or ideas to be reported. If all the machinery of life could be as familiar and as readily handled as one's native language, it would not need to distract or to detain the spirit at all, but would become transparent and unconscious, or else form a separate sphere of objects, such as words are to the grammarian. No doubt the material intervention of that machinery would qualify the movement by which intuition was finally evoked, as the same thing said in English or in French has not the same exact æsthetic or moral essence for the spirit. Yet this atmosphere enveloping ideas forms no separable object in direct apprehension, but only an indescribable aura, due to the total quality of life concerned. These agencies distract only when they interfere with intuition at the desired level: as when in speaking you catch the tone of your own voice, lose the thread, become embarrassed, and detest yourself and all your peculiarities.

The psyche has limited energies and is seldom in perfect health; each of her achievements (of which spirit is one) therefore suffers from a double danger. At the roots, sustenance may fail; only a low or feeble development may be possible, or one in a special eccentric direction which may seem monstrous judged by what would have ensued if the faculty in question had realized all its potentialities equally. There are animals, there are races, there are circumstances in which spirit may take happy but very limited flights; a little wit, a little fancy, a little innocent pleasure; and no repining, no suspicion that bolder flights are missed. If we regarded such limitation as unfortunate or wrong, we should be condemning every phrase of spiritual life possible to man; because all phases are conditioned and limited by the same power of circumstance that keeps the child a child, and the drudge a drudge. The demand that spirit in all creatures should be passing through the phase which we happen to have reached, needs only to be mentioned to be discredited. It is the very opposite of sympathy with human nature; a wretched exhibition of tyrannical conceit and fatuity. Not the limitations of life should trouble the spirit, for those are inseparable from its existence and definiteness; but only the false promises that nature sometimes gives and then betrays, when some budding affection dries up, or some work begun enthusiastically falls to pieces of itself. This amounts to true cruelty on nature's part, offering a gift and then snatching it back; yet the alternation would be no worse than that between sleeping and waking, if development were merely arrested, as when a child dies; something cruel for the parents, but far from distracting and perhaps a blessing to spirit in the child.

Positive distraction rather indicates a second danger that besets the spirit: not so much failing or lapsing, as being deflected, confused, and deceived by contrary vital motions. In such discord, spirit suffers horribly and is indeed, morally, the only sufferer in all the camps. Yet looked at biologically, spirit in its turn is not always guiltless since its organ too may impede or derange other organs. Sometimes consciousness seems to make cowards of us all; life is spoiled by responsibility for life; care, fear, and indecision poison the innocent pleasure of seeing and feeling and playing the game. The day comes when we can no longer play unless we gamble, adding a dark worldly motive to the free sport. All interests are sicklied over by the shadow of contrary interests, all beliefs by contrary suspicions. The sickly

Any impulse, even the highest working out of season, may corrupt the others.

soldier fights without joy and almost without rage; the sickly assassin fires the second shot into his own brain. In all this the paraphernalia of spirit—languages, maxims, theories, information—overwhelm the primary Will. So we find the modern man too dubious, too indifferent, to call a rival out to a duel. He feels constantly challenged within himself; courage has lost all charm and all finality. At the moment of his most confident thrust he perceives that he, too, is wounded, and the sense of moral disaster all round embitters every practical effort.

This is an ulterior complication, and spirit seldom flounders inwardly in that the animal impulses which buoyed it up have forsaken it. Usually these impulses are only too obstreperous and deter- Unemployed emotions. mined; they defy spirit or seduce it. There is a sense in which spirit is always seduced, seduced by the radical current of the Will before it awakes to any clear ideas. It fears, it enjoys, it suffers without knowing about what. Emotion exists first with a cause but without any object; and while this condition is hardly distraction, since there is nothing from which spirit could be distracted, yet it is an uneasy unsatisfied state. Alarm summons attention to something, and attention is baulked if nothing can be found. To feel alarmed, and not know about what, is ignominious, and when the trick becomes habitual in the organism, the spiritual state induced is a form of madness. Yet madness is often only nature unveiled, a wheel in the necessary machinery seen working apart; and here we have but to restore the ideas habitual to the mind for the emotion to seem sane, even if perhaps mis- directed.

Love and hatred are often in this case. We are allured or enraged, yet fundamentally we do not know what it is that allures or enrages us. We may point to some rather ordinary person, or to some rather ordinary event; but why on earth should such devastating feelings overcome us in their presence?   The cause lies in the hidden complexity and casual turns of nature in us, in our unconscious Will: and the cause explains the absence of a reason.   Emotions arise when Will is precipitated suddenly in some fresh direction; and whatever image meets us at the terminus profits by the colour of the emotion with which we view it. The ordinary creature seems divinely beautiful, rare, and significant; the ordinary event seems an intolerable outrage.   The power attributed to those objects is entirely drawn from one's own psyche, ripe for such passions.   Therefore mature moralists, when morality was not itself a mere ignorant emotion, talked about the *madness* of passion, the *guilt* of sin, the *folly* of fashion.   Yet this is a normal madness, an original sin, a sprightly and charming folly.   Life could not have begun or grown interesting without them.   The evil involved is constitutional, and the spirit suffers this distraction because it exists, and is a natural being, an emanation of universal Will.   Universal Will aims initially at anything and everything, and realizes whatever it can realize, imperfectly of course from the point of view of that special aim.   Spirit cannot escape these conditions and this imperfection.   It too has infinite possibilities, and contingent occasions.   Often we cannot but hate the things we love, and hate ourselves for loving them; and we are right in blaming our fallen nature for these contradictions.   It is not in the realm of spirit that they are hatched, but in that of matter, to which our psyches belong.   Our souls are diseased, pursuing things that ultimately repel them.   And the approach to health cannot come by rescinding our nature but by disentangling and harmonizing it as much as possible, as indeed it naturally endeavours to harmonize itself.

In animals universal Will takes the form of a psyche,

which is no separate supernatural principle, but only a moving harmony or equilibrium maintaining itself more or less perfectly in each organism until death breaks it down altogether. The more vigorous this concretion of vital powers, the more violent will be the protest of the whole organism against any attack, from within or without, that tends to disrupt it. A defensive contraction or concentration ensues; and if we suppose a slumbering consciousness to pre-exist in the psyche, it will awake with a sharp cry, a conscious protest, which we call pain. Pain is a first form of distraction; for it is a summons, a disturbance of that placidity in which spirit slept when merely potential; yet this summons brings nothing to spirit that spirit can light up, diversify, make articulate, or turn into knowledge. As an intuition, if such it may be called, pain is empty, yet as a sensation it is intense, arresting, imperative; so that it exemplifies the very essence of evil for the spirit: to exist in vain, to care intensely in the dark, to be prodded into madness about nothing. The birth of spirit is joyful when it is the dawn of light, disclosing a thousand movements and objects that evoke intuition and excite a discerning love, or even a discerning aversion; but to be born blind and kept alive by force with no foothold, falling as it were spasmodically and helplessly through a horrible vacuum, is to suffer pure torment and be subject to a gratuitous tyranny.

Distraction seen pure in pain.

Now this arrest and contraction which for the spirit is a pain for the psyche is a means of safety: by suspending her diffused vegetative task and rushing to withdraw or protect some injured member, she is fighting for her existence. Nothing therefore, from her point of view (but her views are merely habits!) could be less gratuitous and more opportune than this mobilization, which so distracts the spirit; for the spirit was enjoying

Pain comes with some rude summons to defensive action.

life or enjoying sleep, but the psyche was not sleeping or enjoying life, but only living and obeying faithfully an imperious momentum to live on. She has prudently developed a central exchange in the brain, with a whole plan for coordinate action in cases of danger, with particular nerves, pain-nerves, from every quarter to give the alarm and guide defensive operations. That the pain-nerves *hurt*, that they distract the spirit, she neither knows nor cares; the point is that they should instantly call the blood or the muscles or the hand to the affected part, to protect or to heal it; and if this summons *hurts* because it brings so violent a wrench and stoppage of normal functions, that makes no difference, if only the crisis can be passed, and safely restored. The trouble is that even biologically this machinery remains imperfect. The alarm often arrives late, when the damage has been done and a cure is impossible; or it arrives needlessly, when local unconscious processes would suffice to repair that damage. Often, too, the agitation set up becomes a worse evil than its cause, prolonging itself hysterically with perhaps fatal results. We then have an orgy of pain, as in difficult childbirth, in cramp, neuralgia, or madness. I suspect that this is the case always, in some measure, wherever there is pain: far from being a means to remedial action pain is a sign that the available remedies have failed. If biological organization and adjustments were perfect there would evidently be no internal disorders; and in the case of external accidents nature would apply an anæsthetic automatically, leaving the rest of the psyche undisturbed, while the part concerned did its mending in peace. To diffuse trouble is the worst possible means to correcting it. We may say with better reason of pain what Spinoza said of remorse and pity, that it is bad and useless. The *pain* in remorse and pity is futile, but not the spiritual or tragic *perception* of the evil in question:

for this perception indicates no impediment in the psyche now, but on the contrary an enveloping synthesis by which the old calamity and its neutralization in the vast context of truth are present to the spirit, and radically present for ever. Such tragic insight, such pity and remorse, are parts of the highest good. That which is bad and useless is to protract or repeat pain, physical or moral, at its original level, where it still indicates not synthesis but distraction.

If spirit were all, pain would be utterly dark and inexplicable; but even on the lowest plane we may say that to suffer is to learn. We learn at least that we are incarnate; and also that the body is subject to some hostile influence and for the moment helpless before it. Pain expresses disruption, as the sense of relief *Were the defensive reaction perfect it would not be painful.* expresses a gradual recovery of vital harmonies, and joy their sudden expansion. If the organism were well adapted and in perfect health attacks from outside would be stimulating rather than painful. The bugle-call to arms would be positively welcomed, as we welcome a challenge to any game in which we are proficient. Bruises and wounds would then be little felt, or would be borne proudly. Even irreparable losses, like blindness, would not spread their blight over the residue of the soul but would rather provoke a new concentration, with perhaps a finer quality of life. Death itself when it supervened would not be painful or feared. Human horror of death is perhaps something exceptional in the universe, arising only when spirit is called back from its natural flights too often, to nurse the agony and bewail the death of others. Simpler better-knit souls might normally die in battle or in sleep, without making a fuss about it.

In pain, in terror, in all such moral suffering as is akin to pain, the enemy is external. There is no disunion in the alarmed soul. Psyche and spirit

are on the same side, disturbed by the same irruption.
For this reason, when the foreign evil cannot be par-
ried, as in mutilation or approaching death,
it may be met and almost disarmed by a
concentration of life inwards, surrendering
the indefensible outworks, and retreating
in the end to pure spirit which though existentially the flower of the psyche, morally
cannot be caught or finally vanquished, because its
interests are not local.   Illumination at this point may
be reduced, it may be extinguished, but the light is
not thereby corrupted or confused; there is no treason,
no sin.   For the same reason, corporal works of mercy
engage the spirit whole-heartedly and more urgently
than any ideal object of aspiration.   We do not ask
whether the wretch lying robbed and wounded by the
wayside *deserves* to be helped.   He *needs* help, and
that suffices to secure unreservedly our spiritual sympathy.   His calamity is external to him.   In respect to
it, there is integrity in his soul, however distracted and
criminal may have been the business that led him into
this plight.   We disregard these circumstances, which
we feel to have been accidents in that blind life, snares
into which a poor animal soul was drawn insensibly,
filth that clotted and distorted it against its primary
intent.   Now in his extremity the broken ruffian is
again a child.   He asks only to breathe, to sleep, to
be nourished, not to be tormented.   And with that
elementary Will in him the Will in every spirit is
unanimous: all recognize the common enemy, physical
misfortune, physical disaster.   These may reduce the
scope of spirit in each soul, but they remove all anti-
pathy between one soul and another: they inspire
humility in each and charity to all.[1]

Under physical stress souls are simplified and assimilated to one another.

---

[1] This sympathy between psyches at certain levels has nothing miraculous
about it, as if they lost their individuality and became mere channels for a
great reservoir of emotion always actual above them.   It is not as if the
emotions actual in any man could pass on materially to his neighbour.

Trouble thickens when the enemy disturbing the soul is not external, but when one vital impulse is fighting there against another. The spirit then hardly knows its centre, identifies itself now with this interest and now with that, or hangs suspended in an agony of self-contra- *Psychic organization essential but imperfect.* diction. Moralists are accustomed to give names to these rival forces, a few stock names for an infinite variety of passions, and to represent one set or one principle as alone legitimate. This is convenient in pedagogy and roughly represents the dominant morality at a given time in a given society; but even then spirit will be as often on the side of some rebellious impulse as on that of the reigning convention. No form of life can be inherently wrong, since there is no criterion by which to judge except the inherent direction of life. But when life is firmly organized in a special way, as it must be before spirit can appear, some impulses will be indispensable for it, and others disruptive. Hence human morality is quite safely and efficiently estab- lished by human nature, and maintained by swift natural sanctions. It is not, and cannot be, perfectly

Each is moved by his own impulses and instincts; and these in a well- organized animal species will become co-operative without becoming similar, never actually reproducing in the helpful soul the feelings that the suffering soul may endure. Charity in Martha will not repeat, as if by physical contagion, the troubles of her flock, nor will love in Mary repeat the divine virtues of her Master. The surgeon must remain calm, and the worshipper prayerful and dependent. Hence a paradox important in the arts: that the passions most movingly portrayed are passions that nobody has ever felt. Not only does the poet never actually feel the emotion he is expressing —he would not be an artist if he did—but the ideal personage he is enacting, if that personage had existed, would not have felt the pure, the glorified emotions that the author's words or theme suggest to the public. Not that real agonies are less terrible, but they are mixed, broken, *distracted*; and the more intense they are, the nearer they bring the spirit to the edge of disruption, that is to say, of unconsciousness. Each moment is then exhausting and blinding in its intensity; and when the storm is over, calm buries that dreadful past as if at the bottom of the sea. We are neither able nor willing to recall it. But to the sensitive spectator or to the spirit recover- ing its native power in epic memory or tragic imagination, the whole is lifted into the sphere of fable, where ignominious experience becomes a history of chosen issues in a single distinct and memorable life.

uniform, since various modes of life may be equally possible and successful, and human nature may develop in one direction and wither in another. Yet in each society and in each individual there will be obviously radical needs to satisfy and obvious dangers to avoid.

Even fundamental functions, like nutrition and reproduction, since they engage the same organism, may come into conflict, and each will then be distracting to the spirit in so far as it interferes with the other. Nature in some animals prudently makes the two alternate: each peaceful creature spends his life diligently feeding until the rutting season, when he forgets to eat and will fight any rival to the death for the sake of mating.   Evidently to a grazing conscience such love must seem sheer madness, until it discovers that if the mating instinct were suppressed, grazing would soon be extinct also.   Hence in the most acquisitive and well-fed human societies universal and early marriage is doubly approved, not only for peopling the state, but for keeping wild love as much as possible from distracting the thrifty mind.

Initially feeding is much more grossly fleshly than making love and much less sprightly, and the images and emotions that fill the spirit are less varied and interesting. Yet in its extensions the need of nutrition carries the spirit farther afield, in hunting, industry, seafaring, and war; so that the oppression that may ultimately come to the soul from these quarters does not seem due to the demands of the body but rather to the world and its hostility. Love is more intimately inspiring; yet it remains visibly rooted in the body, and fixed upon bodily persons; so that its domination seems unnecessary, foreign, tormenting and perhaps degrading to the spirit.   Strange that the most fanciful and transporting of passions should be called *par excellence* the concupiscence of the flesh!

Conflicts between primary impulses.

In the perfect exercise of any function the instruments are ignored and attention rests directly on the object, the scene, and the volume of vital music concerned in the action.   Such are health and freedom; and then spirit enjoys the life of the flesh without obsession by the flesh.   Frank love is not in the least distracting; it is hearty, joyful, and gay; or if any mood follows in which it is viewed at a certain remove, as an odd performance, it still leaves an after-glow of laughter and affection.   This harmony between flesh and spirit runs very deep; a premonition of it plays no small part in falling in love and in love-making.   We might even say that the final swoon of pleasure celebrated in us this cosmic harmony mystically and for a moment.   But human existence is too complicated for spiritual union to be maintained steadily with infrahuman and trans-personal forces; a too great flood drowns us in uplifting us, and this coveted victory is a real abdication.

The trouble does not come at all from the flesh being concerned; on the contrary, love turns the flesh into loveliness.   It comes entirely from slackness and disorder in the psyche, that cannot time and modulate these impulses so as to keep them pure and friendly to the world in which they flourish.   Hence ill-timed cravings, annoyance, shame, hypocrisy and perpetual dissatisfaction.   I need not mention the turpitudes of mere sensuality, now ignorant and groping, now vicious and weary; for these in themselves are comparatively trivial and disgusting to their own sense; and the invectives and precautions of ascetic moralists often miss the point, since these things are not what the flesh desires but what it is driven to by ill fortune.   Nor need I dwell on the tragic conflicts that distract the spirit when love grows romantic, and passionately resists the irresistible power of time and

Neither matter nor mutation would distract the spirit if the psyche were well ordered.

change.   Pure love is not temporally constant, because time is itself inconstant, and swallows up incessantly every chosen object of love.   Innocent sexual desire, like appetite for food, pursues anything suitable that offers.   It explores, tastes, accepts this, rejects that, and remains always alert.   This playfulness and keenness signify no disdain for what has already been chosen. The spirit cannot forswear any good that it has found, or may find; and no good is truly found until love ceases to be a craving for the unknown and, in face of the known, becomes silent and spiritual.   The object then proves to have been an essence and not an existing person or thing; and among essences there is no jealousy or contradiction, and no decay.

Fidelity to things and persons is a domestic virtue proper to a society centred in the family and its belong-
ings.   Affections are then duties, and posses-
sions responsibilities.   Such ties, like all moral relations, enrich the soul in confining it and offer a suitable though accidental theme for the spirit; but they are not spiritual ties. In marriage love is socialized and moralized into a lifelong partnership which it would be dishonourable to betray; and community of interests and habits buttresses that love into mutual trust and assistance. A household rather smothers the love that established it.   Nature seems to be repressed there more than obeyed; and the family becomes a political institution and a part of the world, where the fortunes of spirit are entangled in all sorts of interests not those of the heart.

Loop-line through domestic morality.

How might the heart be satisfied?   Certainly not by turning from a first union to others at the same incidental level.   To re-excite a passion physically is not to satisfy it morally; rather to discredit it as morally vain.   Licentiousness becomes horribly tedious; yet spirit can never turn its back on love, any more than on life, since it is their supreme manifestation.   It

must accept, honour, transmute and sanctify them.
It will therefore retain in compulsory affections that
element which is original and spontaneous, because
home and country appeal to the heart powerfully, apart
from any duty.   And it will cull from romantic passion
and from loose loves the magic spell in them, without
the deception; that is to say, it will distinguish the
loveliness in things or the charm in persons from the
existing persons and things.   These were the vehicle,
that was the revelation.   And the ideal signification,
for the spiritual man, is not a new illusion, as if he
hoped to pursue the charm and the aroma that have
fled from earth into heaven, and there catch them and
store them safely in his moral museum.   This heavenward evaporation of the good is a metaphor.   Charm
and aroma cannot be removed from themselves; and in
themselves they are incorruptible.   Fortune shows
them for a moment, then hides them; at any time, in
one place or another, they may reappear.   The material
continuity of life and of objects means nothing to
spirit; the point is only that the revelation, wherever it
comes, should be as clear and full as possible.   That
there should be interruptions, that youth should congeal
into old age, and that death should end all for each
person, follows from the nature of existence.   The
flux of things is terrible indeed to the distracted spirit,
compelled to cling and tremble and whine at the
mutations of matter; but those mutations themselves
become musical and comic, if once the spirit can free
itself and perceive its affinity to the eternal.

A grand passion would open the way best to this
transformation: for here the flesh has already conquered
the world, and almost conquered itself, since
the rapt lover becomes a worshipper, as is
proper to spirit.   Yet there is madness in
this devotion, and great suffering, because
the victim is attaching his whole soul to one person

Illusion and revelation in the grand passion.

and to the caprices of that person, and giving to man, or rather to woman, the things that are God's. Yet this very exaggeration tends to break up the illusion, and to disentangle the secret of love. Here is a fever in the spirit, fed secretly by the flesh, but disproportionate altogether to what the flesh can claim or can give, tormented out of all measure by accidents of little moment, and crucified even in victory. And yet what soul that has ever known a great love would wish not to have known it? The illusion was only a false identification, not a false allegiance. It revealed the potential glory of the beautiful.

Gallantry, marriage, and Platonic love are ways in which the flesh endeavours to make its excuses to free spirit, by showing how amiable, how steady, and how pure it can become. Yet the free spirit is not convinced. Not only do the depths probably remain turbid beneath these surfaces, but love itself, which springs from the heart of nature, has lost its youth and ardour and withered into frivolity or habit or dialectic. Better honest lust in its crudity; for though it be an expense of spirit, yet there is spirit in it, genuine enthusiasm that, when cheated and disgraced, can prompt to repentance. So too the drunkard, in whose vice there are moments of spiritual freedom, repents easily and feels himself a miserable fool. The sordid condition into which he lapses gives the lie too sharply to all the jollity and comfort and irresponsibility that he felt in his cups. If comic insight were to enrich the mind, it would need to be developed into sober intelligence, which has the agility and mastership of wit, without mockery or topsy-turvydom. But when insight ends in laughter, laughter itself fatigues, and dies down suddenly, as if it too had caught us in a false trap. We have lost our bearings and we have cheapened the world; which was not what the spirit longed to do with its freedom. If spirit

Futile escapes and disguises.

suffers and dies in the world, this is only because it loves the world, in the sense of loving the light and joy that are possible in it, or would be possible but for the frustration of one blind impulse by another. Evidently retrenchment is necessary, and surrender of impossible claims; and to surrender them laughing is a short cut to victory and takes place at least in one's own soul for the moment. But this happens only at the level of play and of intellect. The chained dogs below keep on barking in their kennels.

Laughter about fleshly things has various phases, and escapes from distraction in more than one direction. There is first the laughter of victory. As the rude boy jeers at his victims, or the soldier boasts and threatens, so the young lusty rogue laughs at his feats. *Comic expressions of love.* He has eluded his vigilant elders, has found a propitious nook, has overcome his own awkwardness and the trembling resistance of his partner. How frank and bold he can be now; how clear the world is going to be for him henceforth, how positive, how manageable, how prosaic! But his laughter soon turns into a dead seriousness. This jollity has opened a long chapter of human responsibility, human conflicts and human sorrows.

There is also, both before and after, the laughter of detachment, of satire, of mockery. We laugh at the ridiculous routine of love-making, its misadventures, its delusions. We laugh at the cuckold's horns and at the prude's hypocrisy. *Satiric descriptions of it.* We laugh at the one old way out, found at last or missed, from every sentimental labyrinth. There is still a kind of victory, though an intellectual and bitter victory, in this shrewd laughter. Wit in us triumphs, yet human nature, deeper down, remains wounded and ill at ease. The tables have been turned, and now the cynic is laughing at the passion that in the bold lover was laughing at the world. Yet not in this case whole-heartedly, because the cynic is divided against himself. Sensuality would not amuse him if he were a free observer, such as the Roman satirists pretended to be. He would then instinctively stop laughing and begin to preach. The flesh would appear to him as a mechanical if not disgusting instrument for keeping the world going; a most wasteful and over-wrought instrument, that often defeated and always confused its rational use. But sourness about the flesh is only a forced and hypocritical sentiment. The flesh forms the raw material of human nature and is impossible to discard. He himself has been haunted and troubled from the tenderest age by ill-satisfied fleshly impulses which still engage his fancy no less than his body: and that is why bawdy talk makes him laugh. He knows that somewhere, somehow the flesh will always take its revenge. His satiric scorn is not really merry; it mocks his secret sympathies, and betrays the spiritual confusion at the root of his being. For here is an indispensable impulse that carries on the world well enough from the point of view of universal Will, yet in the individual, probably in himself, works terrible havoc. He laughs ambiguously, half scorning the pleasures he has enjoyed, and still half craving those he has missed.

Things go better when people live simply, like peasants near the earth, and spirit in them is dumb, or entertained only by a few superstitions and a few festive arts or sporting adventures. The flesh is then too little indulged to seem an enemy. Heaven would be to feast, to drink, to dance, and to make love lustily forever. These passions are thus left to grow wild and hungry amid the weeds; labour and an early marriage keeps them within bounds. Fixed and monotonous circumstances seem to render people's characters also fixed and monotonous. They scold and distrust one another, but they have no time to quarrel each with himself.

Hypertrophe of lust in artificial societies.

They lay all their troubles to illness, poverty, bad weather, and ill luck. But in a crowded artificial society, the flesh, with its sentimental overtones, creates an inner focus of life sharply contrasted with worldly circumstances and duties: and the question becomes debatable whether the flesh distracts a spirit properly attached to family, study, work, and public affairs, or whether these worldly interests distract it from the all-important revelation of love. In any case there is distraction. The race is compelled, under pain of extinction, to keep the sexual impulse alive, and powerful enough to overcome all selfish prudence or moral disgust. Love must be flattered and tempted underhand by a thousand social lures and opportunities, while at the same time it must be outwardly restrained, and limited to conventional forms and thrifty habits.

Nor is the straitjacket imposed by society the worst obstruction: deeper trouble comes from the illusions, revulsions, suspicions, and disasters suffered by love itself when given a free rein. At the lower level, it fixes attention on ignoble sub-human cravings, infects impulse with vice, wastes time and substance and degrades the conscience with ties and memories impossible to acknowledge; while at a higher social level, it attaches duty where the heart is not attached, and attaches the heart where nothing deserves or rewards attachment. Often the ingenuity of love disguises these tragedies by affectionate hypocrisies or accommodations. That is a mild form of repentance, covering the dead sin with flowers; but even avowed repentance is far from solving the problem. A heroic religious asceticism would need to employ the very impulse that it outwardly suppressed, at least if the reform were to be permanent and the new way of life cheerful and sane. Mere repression, without sublimation into a new devotion and enthusiasm, would run great danger of a relapse; or there might ensue a

Inner contrarieties in love.

complete philosophical reversal of that repentance, with a return to the vulgar naturalism that decries all discipline as cruel and barren.

These vital contradictions might be solved by a good moral regimen, austere in principle, like the Catholic Church, but charitable in temper and disillusioned about the motives that must rule the world. In regard to the flesh, the enemy to be taken captive is no accidental vice, like gambling or drunkenness, that might be thoroughly extirpated. It is a force intrinsic to human nature; you must make peace with it some-how, or be perpetually distracted. You must tame it, transmute it, employ it to warm your affections and light up your painted world. It will then continue to live in your sense of potentiality, of charity, of wonder, of mystic joy. And this will be no pious deception. The force that seemed an alien demon tormenting you from within was always the very life of nature breaking out in you, and making you akin to the whole world. It may work havoc in your little person; nature is not sparing of havoc; but it may also enlarge your heart into an inner understanding of all things natural and divine.

The sins of the flesh, though the saddest, are there-fore the friendliest to the spirit. It may renounce, it will never insult them. They were never themselves hostile to the spirit in intention, only childish gropings of an animal soul caught in the world's trap. It is rather the ill consequences of carnal passion that condemn it, than the quality, dumb longing, of the passion itself; so that for the most part it is the world rather than the flesh that renders the flesh a snare. Evidently in respect to hunger and cold the torments of the body are not due to its own defect, but to a treacherous environment, favourable enough to permit life, but too niggardly to foster it. And from this maladaptation

Transition to distrac-tion by the world.

flows the whole slavery of spirit to the world. In sympathy with the flesh, it trembles at the multiform scourges that come from without—from the elements, from wild animals, from the very family with which a seemingly happy instinct has surrounded the individual. It is then this family, become a tribe, that imposes all those duties, initiations, labours, and wars by which spirit is perpetually pulled hither and thither, intoxicated, maddened, and fatigued. Even love in the world cannot be what it was in Eden: it is shadowed now by responsibility and jealousy. It is beset by a thousand rival or contrary interests that gain upon it with time; except perhaps in old age or sickness, when the old simple affection emerges from the ruins, and proves its closer kinship with the soul. So all the other spontaneous powers, in finding their uses, forfeit their freedom. They drag one another like horses harnessed to run abreast; and the new half-hostile impulse of rivalry becomes an artificial spur, turning free play into bitter passion.

Thus the soul acquires her second, her social, body with its transpersonal machinery of language, custom, and industry. I need not stop to describe this political engine; its phases belong in their principle to the realm of matter. As they grow organic and harmonious, they become instruments of reason; and even when most chaotic, since they form a second political organism out of animal bodies already well organized, they engage the spirit of individuals in new adventures, in which not all is distraction. Labour retains an element of art, from which it sprang originally in play; government contains an element of paternal foresight and moral philosophy; and war contains elements of the chase in action and of chivalry in reflection: things all charged with spirit and showing how it can overlay and disinfect the blind complexities of nature. But here we are concerned with the contrary aspect of

politics, when institutions subject the spirit to forced
and useless labour, and pledge it to hideous passions;
so that, while certainly fed with a more complex
experience and stimulated to higher flights of fancy in
religion and philosophy, it is thereby entangled all the
more helplessly in a vain labyrinth, till perhaps it
loses the very notion of freedom or mastery in any
direction.

A fundamental point in which the political and the
physical worlds are alike hostile to spirit is their
instability. Even this hostility, however, is
not absolute, and for two reasons. In the
first place instability lies at the root of life,
and therefore of spirit also.. Were there no
change and no insecurity there could be no expectation
or concern, no interest in what would happen; and
even where the object of interest is static, the interest
in discovering, surveying, describing and redescribing
it, is necessarily a movement. Permanence itself involves a lapse, a duration or continuous passage; yet
the flow may be so equable and silent, it may so
smoothly carry the spirit down a steady current, that
the voyage may seem the very perfection of rest. Were
there less change there would be no spiritual realization
of repose; for eternity lies above or beneath life, and
even to *pass* into eternity (which is the most that spirit,
remaining spirit, can ever do) is still an act and a
transition. If time were ever arrested, the experience
and the thought of eternity would be abolished.

In the second place, the flux of existence, for spirit
in its ultimate insights, is not an evil. Spirit is not
then concerned with its own survival, nor with running
forever its familiar round, like a tame animal. When
free and self-forgetful the spirit ceases to have specific
allegiances, and though each intuition must dart with
fresh zest towards a fresh essence, yet a different
stimulus and a different discovery, when their turn

*Timely
change not
hostile to
spirit.*

comes, will not be less welcome. Spirit in its own
plane feels no inertia, no bonds of habit; those belong
only to its basis in animal life. Mutability in things
and logical or moral instability in the spirit merely
enlarge apprehension, if only the variations do not
intellectually confuse or intercept one another. Intuitions must come one by one, but their themes are all
eternal.

Therefore elegiac sentiment about the yellow leaf
and the nipped flower has little spiritual force, but
merely confesses the lag of the psyche in respect to
the seasons. Spirit may die, but it can never grow
old; nothing obliges it to ruminate upon things past
or persistently to renew impulses now belated. And
vice versa, nothing requires it to be impatient, or to
pine for everything that the present denies. There is
a natural desire and foretaste of such things as the
psyche is ripe for, and spirit will conceive and prophesy
them; but even then insistence on the future, or reliance
on it, is unspiritual. The future will come, probably
not as we now conceive or demand, and then will be
the time for the spirit to enjoy or endure it without
delusion. That the briefest life, when pure, is sufficient, appears in the gladness of health and laughter:
the child, the happy lover, the conquering intellect
rejoice in existing *now*. They are not troubled by any
memento mori, and need no justification in things to
come. The things to come then seem almost as sad
and impertinent as things long past, and actual happiness is too inalienably perfect to tremble at mutation,
even if mutation were remembered. Spirit, thus freed,
surmounts the sophistry of perspectives, by which the
noon would be made to shiver at the thought of twilight.
Real twilight when it comes has its own beauty, vital
and peaceful; but the false twilight of Hades and the
Elysian Fields reflects a sense of privation, and adds
an imputed sadness or unreality to objects that either

exist nowhere or are merely distant and different from our world.

At the same time there is a profound moral gulf between the flux of existence and the life of spirit. In the mind we have foresight and memory, in nature only effects and potentialities. Change when perceived has been synthesized. Contrast, conflict, drama excite thought and fill it with the most interesting themes; but they ruin and torment thought when they work surreptitiously at its foundations, break up its rhythms, swamp it in contradiction and oblivion, and defeat its life without extinguishing it. Representing as it does the victories of the psyche over an inanimate flux and an inorganic environment, spirit lives by transcendence from its centre and responsiveness to outlying things, even to infinity. It would not willingly be cut off from anything or later than the present or earlier than the present, but in the present is contemporaneous with all things and at their very heart. It lives precisely by feeling the co-presence of the successive and the inter-relation of the distant. It would keep all events always present, as it tends to keep them in vivid memory or clear prophecy. The whole and every part are then seen in motion, like episodes in a play; but it would mark a failure in the poet or moralist if he forgot the first act when the second was going on, and had throughout no premonition of the issue. That is the fate of the distracted characters in the play, creatures full of limitations, sentimentality, and impatience, who are trying to preserve the past or command the future, but always in vain, because that which was cannot be again, and that which is coming will have a thousand sources alien to the commanding Will. Spirit envelopes all these sources and all these losses in its virtual omniscience, and while initially living by the life of the parts, corrects

Yet to transcend the flux is the essence of spirit.

the blindness of each by an equal participation in all
the others; so that although its heart is their heart, its
life is not any of their several lives, nor their deaths
its death.   So long as it remains attached to any one
of them blindly, it is defeated in its own Will, and
distracted by the inevitable defeats of the vain Wills
it has adopted.

The world, then, however familiar superficially, is
in its blindness and in its treachery utterly contrary
to the spirit.   The world is not as it looks, it contradicts
what it teaches, it leaves memories which it stultifies,
and excites hopes which it betrays.

There has been great insistence in recent philosophy
on the terms static and dynamic, but so emotionally
that "static" comes to mean not the per-   The dynamic
manent in time but the definite in character, and the
and "dynamic" not that which exercises   static.
force but simply that which changes.   Now instability
in existence is at least as characteristic of mind as of
matter: and if " dynamic" imply only the continual
variation by which one thought yields to another, mind
will also be thoroughly dynamic.   And it will be
dynamic even in an evolutionary or historical sense,
if what is meant be that sometimes, on reflection, we
find in later phases of thought a logical or moral
development of something present in thought earlier.
Such moral progression, with dialectic expansion and
correction, is inevitable where memory exists, and
inherited powers, exercised once, are exercised anew
on a changed object, seen in changing lights.   The
course of experience will be irrelevant to this dialectic,
yet the thread of it will be traceable through the
labyrinth, until it is broken by accident or lost in its
own tangle.   And reflection catching rhymes and
reasons in the chaos of memory, will fix and impose
these tropes on the remembered incidents, or imagine
and interweave other incidents to fill out the chosen

measure. Thus memory is primarily re-apperceptive, and the first histories are epics and fables. These forms of imagined dynamism, these plots and dramas, are themselves static, and composed precisely because, in such forms, events are memorable. Were these patterns not definite and in that sense static, they could not be conceived or recognized. They are essences. If the love of novelty impels us sometimes to reshuffle them or throw them over altogether, we can be aware of superseding them only if we still see them receding in the distance, while we pick up a new buoy by which to measure our voyage. Mere drift without landmarks would hardly be a change, but only a perpetual sensation of drifting. That the landmarks of spirit are ideal and blown up like bubbles from the unfathomed depths of substance and force, is very true; yet that such bubbles rise to the surface so regularly and mark our course with such varied and responsive lights seems to be proof of relatively static laws in the sea and air. The spirit can count on sufficient stability there, at least in the methods of change; and the fixity of its own terms and achievements, once discerned, laughs at temporal mutation. Spirit has no wish and no power to establish permanent things or persons or types in the world; that is the world's business, if it cares to be conservative, as it must be up to a certain point if it is to rise at all out of chaos, yet as it can never be altogether, since it has chaos in its heart. After running through a cycle or two of evolution, the world might perhaps grow weary, if it had any memory; and the spirit is sometimes tempted to despair in its brief but cruel adventures. What need was there that we should distinguish, that we should care, that we should suffer? No need, surely; yet here is an opportunity, if the spirit is free and unclouded, to see wonderful things, and not rashly for idle amusement but with a participation in divine reality, because our ideas are true. Some are true symbolically of the outer world; others, in a free mind, are true to the organic powers of the psyche, expressed in imagination.

There would be nothing distracting in change if it did not involve deception, or contrary views offered at once to reflection about the same reality. That mere experiences should be various or changeful offends nobody, and simply adds to the gaiety of nations. But for a living being concerned about its destiny, superficial and flighty ideas cannot be satisfying; it cannot help aspiring to knowledge of the obscure and momentous powers that control that destiny and produce those ideas. The variety of these would fortify our spiritual peace if only we could survey their sequence and understand their causes. The problem therefore arises how to fix and deepen our conceptions until they truly describe the ways of the world. This would not involve any arrest or monotony in thought, which is itself a movement. Every moment would still yield a fresh sensation and a new perspective, and all would be well if only changes in ideas co-operated to describe consistently the changes in nature and in themselves. The spirit would then gain continually in scope and wisdom, noting and celebrating the truth in new fictions; because knowledge, unlike truth, is essentially mobile and, both in its terms and in its vistas, poetical. Such suitable harmony between the world and the spirit carries us sanely through daily life; it becomes almost perfect when we are intently watching some exciting event, such as a race. Our perceptions then have the appropriate truth, and so have our emotions; since it is neither possible nor desirable that human ideas should be exhaustive, and the mere sense of losing or winning a bet declares correctly the turn that the race has actually taken in respect to our wager.

Rational variations in ideas.

The natural attachment of spirit to the world follows upon its attachment to the flesh, and is no less necessary in its beginnings. The call for food and shelter establishes the first arts and the call for reproduction establishes the family. How draw the line where the interests of the body begin to yield to the interests of society? But as we pass from one to the other, there is a change in the spiritual climate. Bodily passions, including the impulse to strike and to kill, are violent in their assault like thunderstorms in summer, and often leave behind them amazement and remorse, as if an alien demon had possessed us; yet this demon was himself a spirit, and the profound natural roots of such passions lend them a corresponding depth and even sublimity for the soul. We may have been mad, we may have been criminal, yet something marvellous and divine led us on and dazzled us by its glory. Out of these animal impulses the spirit can weave its refined sentiments of love, honour, and worship.

As the dominant influence, however, becomes external, the spirit is drawn further afield, entertained with more knowledge and controlled by stable customs and sanctions; but perhaps the inner fountain of impulse becomes clogged, or dries up altogether. The spirit then resembles a child at school being educated against his will. Perhaps the education succeeds, the lessons grow interesting, compulsory sports absorb every impulse to play, till the mere thought of any pursuit not one of the regular pursuits or any mischief not one of the accepted mischiefs seems strange and repulsive. This might pass for the complete triumph of the world and of a forced morality: but spirit is like Greek fire, it floats on the elements expected to quench it. A tight *Kultur* cannot extinguish it, but merely produces a particularly definite

The world a more external power than the flesh but no less acceptable.

organ for giving it utterance. What is sacrificed at that time and place is only some rival organ that would have had a different spiritual voice. Let the political world do its worst, and while life lasts it will still excite perceptions as clear and feelings as genuine as any that wild nature might have aroused.

The distaste of each temperament or tradition for its rivals is an animal distaste, not to be confused with the interests of spirit in its essence. Spirit is essentially free and potentially infinite; *Suave mari magno.* the nerve of distraction is not the character of the given objects taken in themselves, but the forced attachment of the spirit to their fortunes, which do not really concern it. As a fact, as a pageant, as an object of knowledge no form of the human world would be in the least distracting. The darkest wood does not trouble us, unless we are lost in it, nor the roughest sea, unless we are tossed in it beyond endurance. So the world troubles us by the anxiety and impatience that we feel at its movements, when we are enslaved to interests that are not ours. That the world exists, that it changes, that it struggles with itself for ever and struggles in vain, would only feed and educate the spirit, if the spirit were free. But it is not free: and the causes and degrees of this slavery are the sole ground of division between the Will in nature and the Will in spirit.

Since the Renaissance it has been out of fashion to preach contempt of the world. Writers and academic philosophers are in the world's service, and work for money or reputation; they are no longer impersonal vehicles of an orthodox *Contentment possible in routine.* tradition. There is perhaps an inarticulate feeling in the background that if worldly aims were taxed with vanity, there would be nothing left to live for, and that delusions must be kept up at all costs, or everything would collapse. This feeling, if it exists, is an un-

L

avowed pessimism of the deepest dye. Vanity is not escaped but made inescapable; the contempt that religion preached for the pomps and vanities of this world is merely extended to the pomps and vanities of religion. But if absolutely everything is vain, even the desire to escape from vanity, vanity loses its sting and even its meaning, for the notion that things are vain merely because transitory we have seen to be morally confused and superficial. The nerve of true vanity lies elsewhere: in doing something for a further object which cannot be attained in that way. If the worldling aims at nothing beyond his participation in the world, that participation is not vain. It may be called frivolous or stupid, if something different be demanded; but why demand anything different? The existence of the animals is not vain, nor their world contemptible. If we level our morality down to theirs, we deftly escape the reproaches of the preacher.

Such reversion from society to nature has been itself preached by many a false prophet, from the ancient Cynics to Rousseau and his many emulators. I call this gospel false, not because I think animality or rural simplicity or savage independence inferior or wrong: such forms of life exist and the human race may be destined to revert to them or to re-establish something like them in a paradise of anarchy. But I am considering the possible victory of spirit over distraction. To remove certain distracting circumstances may be a relief, but does not essentially fortify the spirit or enlarge its dominion. On the contrary, reversion to animal or mystical solitude, while not excluding union with nature, grounds this union on rudimentary strength or health in the psyche; and this is not only a precarious harmony, but an unspiritual one, like the placidity or the fussiness of animals. Social life lifts the spirit to a more comprehensive intelligence; there

Belated longings to be primitive.

is more constant transcendence of the self in imagination and a richer, more varied, more dramatic world to imagine and to overcome. Intellect is more spiritual than sentiment. A reality traversed by moral and intellectual conflicts excites the spirit to clear, absorbing, varied dramatizations, teaching it to recognize its presence in many another self. If this be a heightened picture of distraction, it is also a deepened exercise in self-transcendence and renunciation. The better we know the world the more inescapable will be our perception of its tragic and comic character, that is to say, of its vanity as an experience and of its richness as a truth. We see that the only profit in experience is its profit for the spirit.

The poor and the very young may imagine that they would be perfectly free and happy if they had plenty of money. Money would procure all Illusion that necessaries and comforts without labour, and wealth is would open the doors of all beautiful places freedom. and all important persons. The world would be at one's feet; and this, be it noted, is what the spirit dreams of in its innocence, never of lying at the world's feet of its own accord. The world is to be that of the *Arabian Nights*, all magic entertainments and easy conquests. But in reality the rich, unless they are more than rich, are slaves to the world, and captives of their successes and their possessions. They must keep earning their money, or defending it, spending it as the world demands, trembling at losing it or finding it insufficient, and countering the endless claims, obligations, and jealousies that it brings. Civilization is a physical growth, like the mechanism of animal bodies; the achievement is wonderful, but the advantage to the spirit thereby elicited is problematic: there will be much new experience and much new suffering. It was poverty that first bred riches in the process of relieving natural wants and hardships; and riches soon

covered town and country with variety and softness
as verdure covers the earth. They became a great
convenience and a great ornament. Civilization is
something not impossible to enjoy freely and spiritually,
whether we be rich or poor; but in either case freedom
and spirituality will be found only by the way, in
feeling, in thought, in affection, in love of nature and
home and one's art or craft for its own sake. The
empty stage of nature has been set for a human drama,
with all the paraphernalia of industry, government, and
religion; the scene is more elaborate and the story
more interesting. But evolution has exacted a terrible
price for its benefits by creating a new set of artificial
wants and compulsions: the human slavery to labour,
war, politics, morality, and imposed religion.

Free labour or art is a transformation of matter to
suit the mind, and far from involving distraction

But there
may be
spiritual
freedom in
work.

involves the opposite, namely, *application*, or
such a happy bending of the eye and hand
over some material as may turn it to the
service or illustration of some idea. Nor
does labour merely copy ideas already clear in the
mind, something that for the mind would be a vain
repetition. The most precious fruit of application
ripens in the mind itself, where in idleness there
were only vague or uncertain tendencies to settle
into this or that form; an indecision which labour
enlightens as it proceeds, making clear what is possible
and beautiful in each direction, and revealing its own
hidden direction to the mind. For if the marble block
contains all possible figures, the intellect said to direct
the hand has innate predilections, of which it is
initially ignorant, and it is the hand playing with clay,
or the eye catching some casual harmony in nature,
that reveals to the heart what the heart might love.
Free labour or art is simply nature unravelling its
potentialities, both in the world and in the mind, and

unravelling them together, in so far as they are harmonious in the two spheres. Such labour is therefore
a great corrective to distraction, since it concentrates
attention on the possible, and trains the Will to
discriminate and organize its true intentions.

Why then is mankind universally tormented with
having to work or with being out of work? Because
the work is imposed or denied socially, not *It is society*
done or omitted freely and individually; be- *that imposes*
cause the product is lost to sight, and paid *slave labour.*
for in money, an abstract and treacherous medium, too
easily spent, by which all things necessary or unnecessary must be bought ready-made; and above all because, if the product were traced, it would probably be
found to be in the end worthless or worse than worthless. In other words, the working world is distracted
in the highest degree, because people are compelled to
do what they do not wish to do, and compelled to
put up with what does not content them. They
are organized, they know not why, into a system of
universal slave-labour for the production of rubbish.

This anonymous engine, grinding rich and poor
alike, has a great momentum. In places it runs
smoothly and creates what is called progress *Social allegi-*
and prosperity. In other places, its parts *ance secon-*
collide with one another, and we have crises, *dary and*
panics and wars. That such accidents occur *unstable.*
is not itself an accident. Organisms can never be perfect or undeviating in their development. There is
always conflict or tension within the system, since the
elements are, in substance and method of life, older
than the whole, and their private tropes continue to
assert themselves within the larger trope that envelops
them. If this unifying process is anywhere relaxed,
local growths, which we call morbid, or decay and
dissolution, appear in the parts. The animal as a whole
is in turn a dynamic element in the tribe, and always

in potential conflict with his habitat and his neighbours. Every member of a society wears his loyalties
like a garment, which decency and safety do not allow
him to discard; yet he remains naked beneath, a wild
man and a traitor in his natural person. Therefore
any economic or social harmony can be nothing but a
compromise or a truce. Society is not an organism at
the same level as living individuals that nature repro-
duces from seeds and endows with potential consciousness. When presently the social tension (which is itself
biological) has been relaxed, the bodily functions or
private affections or poetic dreams of the individual
will absorb the spirit in their turn; and as spirit is, as
far as possible, all-embracing, very likely the contrary
movements will invade it together, filling it with alternative hatred, now of the world, and now of the
passions opposing the world in the private soul.

This state of moral distraction is evidently worse
than physical suffering in as much as it overflows more
completely into the spiritual sphere. Pain,
however intense, remains an alien storm to
be roundly cursed, defied, or endured, and
leaving a clear sky when it blows over. The spirit
may faint or may stifle, but is not divided against
itself. Carnal pleasures too, which are but welcome
pains, draw the spirit inwards into primal darkness and
indistinction. The world, on the contrary, in its thousand aspects, calls forth interest and intelligence. It
fills the imagination with knowledge, and paints endless
possibilities enticing the Will. Spirit, being the very
flame of life, loves to be excited, and whatever excites
it appears in the first instance *sub specie boni*, as something interesting and wonderful. The world is alive,
beautiful, gay, and tempting. What youth has not
burned with indignation at the folly of the past, which
has spoiled a world that might easily be made so
glorious? When later he finds that the world has again

Consequent moral con- fusion.

taken a wrong turn, or that his own hopes were mis-
guided, or that at its best the world crushes in him
something dearer than any world, the war has passed
into the conscience.   The court that was to pronounce
sentence has become a Babel of quarrelling voices.

This fate overtakes the spirit for having admitted
the world into its councils.   The world is well enough
in its own sphere, being a part of the great
cosmos and a natural complication there; yet
it is very old, and exasperatingly stubborn in
its old ways.   The freshness of each spring,
when spirit stirs anew over the earth, covers
its surface with loveliness without changing
its substance or breaking its cyclical habits.   Such was
not the world that each young soul prefigured, being
enraptured less by what it saw than by what it felt the
capacity to see.   Nor was this feeling spiritually deceptive; only that the object offering itself in each case
was inadequate: worth observing but not worth serving.
Its incorrigible inertia and endless battles put this
world where it belongs; seen in its place and banished
from the heart, it ceases to be an enemy.   It is an
accident, like our brief lives in it, like any game or
any aspect of nature.   We may safely love it when
we know it to be unimportant.   Honour makes us
amateurs on this stage, and not professionals.   With
that proviso, the zest of life is as becoming as it is
innocent.   Even war, since there must be wars, is an
inspiriting thing.   In animal strife the whole psyche
inevitably conspires to defend the body or to pursue
the prey; and by the same natural necessity the young
patriot or soldier glows with the concentrated ardour
of action and hope, shared with his comrades, until
every obstacle is cleared away.   Nature levies this tax
and gives this reward.   It was not spirit that established the earth or divided it or caused the tribes to
multiply and feuds to arise between them; but the task

The world may be served nobly when it has been over-come spiritu-ally.

once set, heroism and martyrdom are easy for the spirit carried forward by the social Will; and the larger the field the nobler seems the ambition.   The work once accomplished, the instrument has done its duty; and death has no terrors for pure spirit, that in enacting each life at once re-kindles and forgets its own light.

Thus in the midst of labour and war—in the worst conflicts of life with matter and of life with life—the spirit is able to rise clear and to attain perfect freedom in art or in heroism.   This possibility shows us once more that spirit does not come from or demand another world, or reject any form of life as unworthy.   It is ready to participate in any undertaking and to rejoice in every achievement.   What it requires is form, distinctness, in that action, so that there may be intuition of its character and of its field: and this intuition in turn cannot attain distinctness and form, cannot become what it aspires to be, unless there is an approach to *wholeness* in the movement that produces it.

This wholeness is approachable in two directions: first, in the occasion, which must be particular and distinguishable from the indefinite flux of events in nature and the infinity of possible growths; and secondly in the depth to which the psyche is engaged on that occasion.   For perfect intuition, for utter wholeness and simplicity of spirit, the psyche must be engaged in its entirety, as when the martyr sacrifices his life, or the poet puts his whole soul into his work.   And it is in this second direction that the world fails to satisfy the spirit even when tolerable harmony exists in the theme proposed. The lover, the soldier, the artist are not redeemed, they are not turned into spiritual men, by the momentary flash of intuition and rapture that may visit them once or twice in their lives.   Nor is it the criminality of the passions concerned that prevents the spirit from accepting them.   It does accept them, and raises them

Easy lapse from borrowed inspirations.

to a lyric actuality, which is as truly spiritual as anything can be. But they betray this inspiration; they
become instantly entangled in all sorts of cares, crimes,
trivialities, and dullness. The hero, if his life is saved,
becomes a commonplace man, the lover takes to drink,
the reformer begins to worry about his income, the
poet about publishers and reviewers; and the spirit,
that seemed for a moment to have found a human
home, is turned out again into the wilderness.

Lack of psychic depth also renders unspiritual
those social interests which might seem most superior,
such as politics, philanthropy, religion, and *The world*
science. As they dawn in the mind these *degrades*
interests are spiritual: enthusiasm for an idea *even science*
or a theory, pious wonder at a story, as in *and religion.*
the religion of a child. But soon, in contact with the
world, such sentiments lose their innocence. Our
charming theory is contradicted by the facts, or by
other theories; we fall out of humour with thought, or
plunge into controversy, where vision daily grows less
and less, and prejudice more and more. And as for
the history of spirit in religion, if it were ever written,
it would make a sad book. In the spellbound child, in
Leopardi's shepherd addressing the moon, in other
shepherds and sailors inventing nymphs and sirens and
gods of the winds, imagination was liberal; it was
poetry touched with wonder and divination. There
was recognition of inscrutable power in things, there
was spontaneous vivid intuition, and there were deep
stirrings of sympathy between the wonders of nature
and the fate of the soul. But this is only one strain in
religion, never entirely lost —because even in the most
artificial constructions of doctrine and precept there is
always some spontaneity, some poetry, some self-surrender; yet the chief source of religion is not spiritual,
liberal, or poetic, but desperately utilitarian. It is
industry appealing to magic, or troubled and made

devious by dreams.   The guiding motives are fear and
hope, with tyrant custom, both in thought and action,
kept alive by the very obscurity of its sources; for when
no man knows whence a compulsion has come, how
can he know what dreadful thing might not happen, if
he rebelled against it?   And here his poetic imagination will be aroused again, not freely now, in the face
of nature, but under the spell of superstition; and he
will invent punishments for his transgressions of custom, over and above those which society imposes, and
fantastic rewards for obedience.   So that religion, in
its radical function, will be an imaginary servant of
personal and social interests: it will have been turned
from poetry into false science and a false sanction for
morals.   We know only too well the prolonged inex-
tricable confusion that will ensue in philosophy; but
how frequent or how pure the rebirth of spirit may be
in that chaos, we cannot tell without such intimate
sympathy with alien lives as is seldom possible at a
distance.   For spirit, though plastic, has a natural simplicity and sameness everywhere; but the prejudices of
the world are local, and unintelligible to one another.

Worldly minds are remarkably teachable in matters
of science.   The truth here does not offend their instinctive faith, as it does in moral philosophy.
In fact the ways of nature are their own
ways.   Nature too is a chaos just mitigated
enough to keep breaking out, on the surface,
into some image of achievement.   The mathematical
and mechanical order that runs through the material
world renders it amenable to industry, but leaves us in
a moral wilderness, piling the earth with ruins of
civilizations whose souls had perished long before
their works.   Yet the worldly Will is not daunted.
It is not speculative, and the pleasure of rummaging
among those ruins and interpreting them controversi-
ally against some other archæologist, quite overcomes

The world can turn science to its own pur- poses.

any sense of futility in those lost arts or in our own. Men of affairs are too familiar with the secrets of the workshop to take any Platonic or religious myth quite seriously. It will serve to give a pleasant answer to the impossible questions of children, or of their own dreams. But in reality each Olympian Jove reputed in turn to rule over us is but a recent god, an invention of the *Zeitgeist*, condemned to fortify his throne with a terrible anxiety. Older and more nebulous deities mock him from their exile, and younger ones, differently grotesque, are taking shape before his eyes and preparing to oust him. There is no resting-place for the feet of time. Nor is there any resting-place for the imagination. Faith too is a temporary investment, and thought a comment by the way. Even the extreme abstraction that physical science acquires in the end, when it becomes a mere rule of thumb for industry or medicine, rather pleases the business man. What is knowledge after all but a good servant to his ambition or to his comfort? It pledges him to nothing. He can give his orders and smoke his excellent cigar with a calm sense that there is nothing in the world better than what he does or truer than what he thinks.

Yet this positivism itself is not safe, and human nature has other impulses that cannot be suppressed. There are ways in which the world may conciliate the spirit. One, the schoolmaster's way, is to give it a half-holiday and let it run off to the mountains and become romantic. Romanticism is not a true religion. It will never liberate the spirit from the world. It will rather paint the world in romantic colours, and let the exciting image make amends for the dreary fact. Chaos itself is something tremendous, tempestuous, a vortex in which it might seem glorious to revolve and to perish. What could be more heroic than to be provisionally free, when you

And can tolerate a little poetry.

are ultimately mad?   And this experience of freedom, where there is moral chaos within as well as without, will seem to vitalize the world for the romantic soul, without seriously deranging human society; because romanticism and the people who cultivate it are only a fly-wheel, and may rather help to balance and adorn the engine which they profess to despise.   Far from rebelling against the world, the romantic idealist simply accepts one of the sops that the world offers to its spirited children, when they threaten to become troublesome.   Pleasure is one such sop, praise is another, the challenge of rivalry and victory is a third: and the comforts of idealism, like those of wealth, bind the soul to the world with a chain all the stronger for being self-forged.   What is the world but a system of self-created interests, each sustaining the other, lest it itself collapse in the void?

Sometimes, however, the safety valve of romanticism defeats its purpose, and the spirit's holiday becomes a perpetual truancy.   The lessons of nature may be too well learned, and may undermine those of the world.   This is to become a philosopher.   Human society, in principle, is but another ant-hill: it clings and grows on the earth's surface like moss on the rocks; its passions, its maxims, its interests are variations on the ferocious or diligent habits of other animals.   Language and science take the place among us of the instincts, to us incomprehensible, that govern insects and birds in their vital economy.   Religion itself, when established in society, is for the spirit only a part of the world.   It perplexes, it constrains, it deceives like all those other pompous institutions by which the world carries on its merciless business. Merciless, casual, blind this whole engine of existence certainly is: yet where anything is allowed for a time to run smoothly or bask peacefully or move grandly,

Philosophy undermines the authority of the world without escaping from it.

beauty and joy radiate from it to the delight of the spirit, which itself radiates, when it can, from the core of life, to observe and to celebrate all that surrounds it.

Philosophy thus strips the human world of all authority and liberates the spirit intellectually; but it cannot strip the world of its power, or even of its ascendancy over the philosopher's soul. He remains an unhappy creature, divided against himself and tempted to play the Pharisee; for in his theoretical pose he professes to dominate the world and benevolently to criticize it, while in his life and person he is hardly less subject than other men to every worldly requirement, vice, and affectation. And in him, this domination of the flesh and the world over the spirit seems less excusable than in simple honest people, in whom it may be positively amiable and a part of the comedy of existence. So it might be in the philosopher too, if he were frank enough to laugh at himself. For he should never forget that intuition is a surface phenomenon in the psyche, extremely mobile, and usually incomplete: a play of images and feelings lost in passing, and leaving only a general sense of being alive in the world, with fixed habits of language and action to vindicate one's personal identity. Distraction itself is hardly felt as an evil in daily life; interruptions rather enliven us, and we are never happier than when we brush away all reflection and turn to something new. There is a blessed poverty even of the heart; it can be robbed of nothing if it possesses nothing. But the animal soul is eminently tenacious; and it communicates this tenacity to the spirit when mental life has become predominant. A certain degree of definition and method are then established in our ideas and aspirations. Irrelevant matters, contradictions, fatigue can then oppress the spirit with a sense of defeat, and distraction becomes a conscious evil.

Perhaps the most insidious way in which the world can distract us is to proclaim loudly how much it needs us. What selfishness for the poet and the philosopher to entrench themselves in their spiritual abstraction, when everywhere else the spirit is suffering and calling for relief! They should be tireless in the service of their fellowmen. Away with your mummified saint! It is a mark of true goodness to live distracted. Such cries are not groundless. Spirit, though it be the function of transcending the self, has a psychic organ, spontaneous like all other organs, and capable of overtaxing the organism as a whole. It is like the Foreign Office in a Government. It may be accused of treason to the country. Many a poor wight thinks too much or feels too much for his own comfort or for doing his work in the world smartly. He may be a dreamer or may go mad. Would that be selfishness in the spirit? Would not an average life in the world have entertained it more and distracted it less? Does it not suffer more keenly and hopelessly than the world does by the hypertrophy of its organ? For the world, this accident means one lunatic more; for the spirit it means *Une Saison en Enfer*. When the world and the spirit part, the world is perhaps no less selfish than the spirit.

Mammon scolds the spirit about its duty.

Unselfishness cannot mean the absence of an organ for the exercise of unselfishness. It may mean the prevalence of social over private interests, shared enthusiasms being called unselfish, and those not shared selfish; and then an intense life in the spirit will be necessarily selfish, because it is rare. Or else, looking at the matter from another angle, we may speak of material, utilitarian, calculated interests on the one hand, and on the other of ideal, impersonal or disinterested interests. The latter might then be called selfless, not because no self possessed them, but because they so possessed the self that all thought of

Analysis of selfishness.

self was banished in pursuing them. Now spirit, by definition, is domination by the not-self, picturing it, fearing or loving it, living absorbed in its life and form. So that to talk of selfishness in the spirit, in this ideal sense, would be a contradiction in terms. To be concerned with the self at all, for spirit, is a horrible distraction, the great disease, the eternal torment. And this slavery to the self would continue unabated, if the world entirely absorbed our love and attention, so that like a distracted mother we rushed to save it, forgetting our own safety. That would be a social impulse overcoming a private one; but it would be merely an exchange of selves and an enlarged selfishness. The same passion that impelled us to help our children or our party, would at the next moment drive us to rend our enemies, to decry all their thoughts, and to detest everything not like ourselves in the universe. The world is a monster of selfishness that in tormenting and devouring its children asks them to be tormented and devoured willingly.

The potential sympathy that spirit has with all life is not purely perceptive but dramatic, because spirit too is a forward movement of attention, developing a theme, and knowing what it is to care and to fail. Yet this sympathy, being spiritual, by no means repeats or imitates the life which it understands, and which probably never understood itself. In the act of surveying and understanding action, spirit raises that action into an image; and the imagination, though likewise a living process, moves at another level. No furtherance or sanction comes from spirit to universal Will. This Will is blind, while spirit virtually perceives the causes and consequences of everything. In feeling the lure, it divines the snare, and in understanding the Will, it understands also the contrary fatality that must ultimately dissolve it. These are

Spirit endures all the passions but tends to understand and to renounce them.

physical monitions; to which is added the inner embarrassment of knowing that all Will is contingent, arbitrary, and doomed to be spiritually unhappy even in its triumphs.

There is therefore a moral as well as a physical reason why spirit must transcend the world's Will in the very act of endowing that Will with a spiritual value. The physical reason is that spirit, being immaterial, cannot have intrinsically any locus in nature or do any work there. It must remain undiscoverable in the object and absent for scientific inspection: while in the subject its presence is transparent and transcendental, being the hither light that discloses nature and the hither sentiment that it inspires. Whence the moral reason for this physical difference of level: that spirit, being the recorder of time, has its heart as well as its intrinsic locus in eternity; so that in rehearsing life, whether in glimpses or in long vistas, it sees each episode as a whole, yet merely as an episode.

When events reach the spirit they have already happened. The contrary might seem to be the case in prophecy; yet the spirit in the prophet—which we must not identify with his psyche or his person—actually sees as a *fait accompli* that which he announces, though the world, and he in his worldly capacity, have not yet got round to that event. Similarly in deliberate decisions and actions, the spirit may feel the rising tide in the psyche surging in this or that direction, till it bursts into some clear idea or word or deed; but that whole process went on in the dark, in the bowels of the world, of which the psyche is a portion; and the spirit, in great excitement and perturbation felt those alternatives and decisions of the Will, sometimes with joy, sometimes with horror: for Will is often like the wave in Racine, and recoils aghast at the monster that it has vomited.

It is by no means a duty in animals to be spiritual. Consciousness may easily remain in them a scattered luminosity, actualizing passing sensations and phenomena without creating any well-ordered *realm* of spirit, any transmissible and developing structures of thought, art, or sentiment.

Conditional need of being intelligent.

If their perceptions did not mislead them, if their expectations were never disappointed, they might be content with an empirical philosophy and a routine of appearances in lieu of truth.   If such a round of images cannot satisfy mankind the reason is not that life without a vision of truth would be essentially ignominious.   It would be ignominious only to a free spirit, to an active intelligence; but if there were no suffering, the disjointed and frivolous perceptions of a passive dream might be perfectly sufficient.   Human empiricists are condemned to find experience often unpleasant, surprising or intolerable; and then their instinct, being wiser than their literary philosophy, looks for a reason, finds it, or imagines what it might be.   Thereby intellect in them awakes from its passive slumber, and posits, behind the miscellany of experience, a realm of matter and a realm of truth.   *Pathos mathos:* the rebuffs that spirit suffers convince it that it was created and that power and truth confront it from outside.

Even more clearly optional is a sense for the beautiful.   If we have it we complicate the simplicity of life, and of satisfaction with whatever may surround us if only it does not physically hurt. Taste would impose sacrifices and labour

Or of noticing the beautiful.

on mankind for the sake of harmonies that would seem foolish to the positivist.   No doubt the essences arrested in intuition probably have some symbolic value in material directions.   They signify health and liveliness in the organ of sense, which in turn produce fitness for action.   The ground of intuition is always a

M

tension, an openness outward, if not physically in space, at least organically towards some ulterior movement, as in words formulating a thought; yet the quickest and most skilful action, like the happiest phrase, comes automatically, and the spirit accepts it with wonder, as if it were a first-born child. In itself this intuition, when it supervenes, rather arrests action in a touch of trance. We pause and must hold our breath for a moment. Then, having found its distance and taken fresh aim, action begins again. There is therefore plenty of intellectual breath in daily life, in working, fighting, travelling, or migrating. Yet this development is not inevitable. Other animals prefer to reinforce their defences at home, without venturing on a perilous life abroad, and they acquire thick skins and shells, happy in their slow surly movements and dull digestions. To feel joy, to let spirit fly up into the air, they would esteem a gratuitous waste of energy.

In this direction the world constantly pulls. It regards spirit with suspicion, keeps it in leash, and would gladly establish behaviourism in philosophy and in fact abolish spirit altogether. It fails in this, because the organism of the individual is natural and has a psyche, while the organization of the world is mechanical, and is not transmitted by seeds over death and birth, but by an external heritage of dead instruments such as books and tools, with compulsory lessons in using them. Such civilization has no psyche and no spirit of its own; so that its spontaneous equilibriums and variations naturally run counter to the perfection of its living members, and to their living spirit. Is it not a great outrage that this stupid world that has no consciousness should be the parent and master of each individual soul, that alone feels, wills, and morally exists?

Incurable conflict between the world and individual Will.

It seems so to the baffled child; yet spirit has no materials or instruments of its own with which to build a better world, except in fancy; and even fancy will dry up and lose its charm if not constantly fed by external contacts. Nor is moral penury the only result of secession from the world; a worse consequence is extravagance and anarchy within the spirit. So long as the passions hide or excuse themselves in terms of some conventional morality, spirit seems to have only the flesh and the world for its enemies; but when each passion begins to assert its primary right to life and to liberty, spirit has come upon an enemy in the spiritual sphere. The devil has entered the stage; for by this personage I understand any enemy of spirit that is internal to spirit.

Rebellion of the latter; and enter, The Devil.

How can such a thing be possible? How should spirit oppose or contradict its own nature? It evidently can never do so; and if it were absolute and self-created (as the devil sometimes suggests) it would necessarily be expressed perfectly in all its forms, since these could spring only from its unimpeded energies. But in fact the spirit is earth-born and essentially incarnate, a phase of some psyche; and the psyche in turn is an organic trope in animals that meets with all sorts of over-excitations and hindrances in carrying out its rhythms. Hence spirit may easily be found speaking here for one incipient passion and there for another within the same soul. Different impulses, contrary thoughts may then cross the spirit and bewilder it; for though they may be collated sufficiently for their conflict to be felt, they will be impossible to synthesize or fuse morally into a single vision, or a whole-hearted aspiration. The spirit will be torn by a divided personality and kindled now in one self and now in another, yet conscious in each that the other exists. A mad world of quarrelling demons will have been hatched in the proud intelligence that thought it beneath its dignity to obey the atoms or the stars.

Extreme forms of such distraction we now call insanity; but the same incubus oppresses the ordinary rebellious mind, producing sullenness and hypocrisy, or perhaps issuing in some fana- tical heresy or crime.   This, as well as frank madness, was once attributed to being pos- sessed by a devil; but I will confine my notion of bedevilment to forms of mental distraction compatible with conventional behaviour and plausible reasoning in words.   I conceive the devil after the manner of modern poets as a civilized tempter, intellectually in- bred, and perhaps secretly ravaged by some beastly or insane force. He is aggressive and revolutionary, scornful of nature and custom, not merely whimsical and helplessly odd; much less is he to be identified with a genuinely original mind, tending to establish new standards in logic or morals.   This might honestly mark the inception of a new type of human nature, perhaps as admissible as the old.   The nerve of be- devilment is that it renders *any* harmony impossible either within a man or between man and nature.   It is a rebellion of spirit against the sources of spirit; an attempt to be intelligent without docility, spiritual without piety, and victorious without self-surrender. There is nothing devilish in the formation of moral psyches, even if they seem grotesque to our human eyes; nature is full of that sort of monsters, and might be said to be composed of nothing else.   The devilishness of a Caliban or an Iago, of a Lucifer or a Mephistopheles, presupposes a normal psyche deranged, the higher facul- ties having reversed their function and become syco- phants to the lower, or else having declared themselves independent in an insane ambition to live by themselves.

The first of these bedevilments merely accepts the natural seductions of the flesh and the world, abdicating

His secon- dary and perverse character.

any spiritual right to control or reject them; and we see
sometimes how an undisciplined spirit, at the end of
its rope and corrupted by despair, reverts to this
natural servitude with a cynical scorn.   This is the
servility of Mephistopheles.   But normally spiritual
experience, as it grows clearer, seems to widen the gulf
between the transcendental witness and the spectacle,
between the victim and his predicaments; until the
innate claims and dignity of the spirit assert themselves
as rights, against an even infinite pressure of facts and
circumstances.   This is the rebellion of Lucifer.

There would be no rebellion but only analysis in
noting the transcendental status of spirit, and in seeing
that things cannot prove their existence save *Dilemma of*
by coming within its range, nor trouble it *solipsism.*
save by modifying its moral temperature.   Spirit is
everywhere the first person, the only speaker of all the
parts.   Here is a vital necessity, at once a quasi-divine
privilege and a fatal animal limitation, a blessing to the
humble and a snare to the proud.   Shall I wonder and
give thanks that in my little mirror such great things
can be reflected?   Or shall I proclaim myself the
universal protagonist, the indispensable Proteus, out of
whom all things are formed?   And yet is not this a
sad omnipotence, or rather a profound impotence,
never to have a neighbour, never to find a friend, but
always to dream unchallengeably and helplessly of some
vapid universe?   The spirit, enthroned in the animal
heart as in an audience-chamber, may fancy itself a
monarch.   Can any messenger reach it that it does not
admit into its presence?   Can any event alarm it, that
it does not choose to care about?   Can anything but its
own will dictate the commands that it shall issue?
And as these commands are often obeyed instantly by
its own thoughts, the privy counsellors in its presence,
ought not all things always to obey likewise?   Is it
perhaps only irresolution in the spirit, its want of faith

and courage, that allows events to fluctuate, to surprise, or to seem disastrous?   Might not a spirit that obeyed its own orders give orders to the universe?

Magic is a childlike belief and practice in which the pride of spirit remains instinctive and subordinate The pose of to some natural action or desire.   A mock omnipotence. art arises, a semblance of accomplishing something mechanically; but the method is capricious, playful, symbolic, out of all natural relation to the intended effect; and the mind jumps to that result, and names it or invokes it mentally, expecting thereby to help the sham operation to bring the result about. But as direct invocation, in prayers or curses, probably fails, a great elaboration is introduced into the magic ceremony, with scrupulous prescription of gestures and words, to see if nature cannot be at last compelled to obey the spirit.   Soon these prescribed magical methods form a new code of compulsions, a second mechanical world in which spirit is imprisoned.   Instruments here, as in genuine physical arts, still absorb attention and obscure or defeat their supposed purpose, so that nothing will be gained by magic towards liberating the spirit.   An experimental study of nature would have served better; because while this too subjects the spirit to a forced discipline, it secures genuine results, genuine wealth, genuine powers over matter, and above all it yields cogent and steady images of things, and methods of thought; whereas magic is as vain as it is pretentious, confused, and idiotic.

Magic and madness, battling with the non-existent, find a check at last in the existent, because they waste Experience energy and in the end are self-destructive; tends to dis- yet this control of life by death is loose credit magic and eventual, and much wild ceremony and but psychic mad thinking flourish always in the world, life to although in changing forms.   Dreams, con- renew it. tagious ambitions, arts, and religions sweep over the imagination, and fatigue it. These things have a spiritual air; they are spontaneous, they suspend meaner human entanglements, and show us how easy it is, if we have a little courage, to flout the whole mirage of worldly, legal, scientific conventions. Yet in freeing us from that vast public net these enthusiasms catch us in little private spiders' webs even more strangling. By giving way to mystic or religious passion we do not correct the folly only too natural to all life; we merely exchange many excusable vanities for a single in-excusable one. At least common life in its drudgery has its kindly, comforting and humorous sides, whereas consecrated wretchedness is wretchedness indeed; and we might say of the spirit what Aristotle says of the State, that of bad governments democracy is the least pernicious. In serving many masters that inspire no respect and are always contradicting and replacing one another, at least the spirit may snatch some moments of laughter and freedom.

The sense of omnipotence, though it flatters the ignorant spirit, is only a borrowed pride. The psyche, not the spirit, exerts power and would exert it, if possible, without limits; and even the inner pride of life, the joy of progression and achievement, though only the spirit feels it, is hatched in the growing and conquering psyche. It merely develops the radical animal Will to feed, swallow, clutch, and beget; a Will extended into all sorts of tentative playful actions and contacts, with which the young spirit is greatly entertained. Yet the growth and freedom of spirit are not properly of that kind. They are not prehensile, but self-diffusing; not migratory, but dominating. For spirit the ultimate object is always the same object—the total of events, the truth, the reality. This is an object impossible to appropriate, since it is always more than the given, and also impossible to disown. There is no willing or

All power physical and the lust for it psychical.

final surrender of any part in order to pass to something else; there is a perpetually self-confirming and self-enriching possession of the same treasure, viewed in different lights, traced to new extensions, and kindling varied emotions. The more spirit discovers, the more firmly it anchors itself. Psychic progression on the contrary loses at every step as fast as it gains; strives to gain more, and ends by losing all. The freedom, the initiative, the creative effort inherent in life is psychic, not spiritual. Spirit is stirred and borne along by that movement, but distracted by it, because everything remains inchoate, half ruined before it is completed, half forgotten before it is understood. For this reason the visible works of nature or art are dearer to the spirit than the dark processes of creation, which are necessarily tentative, laborious, often misled, always ultimately abandoned. But a full-blown flower is beautiful, lasts for a while, can be found almost identically blooming again season after season; and when the flowering psyche bursts into words or actions that are memorable, the spirit is not only excited but satisfied. Something has been achieved. The potential has revealed its secret, and time has enriched eternity. There can be no final victory in existence, except in the comment that spirit may make on it.

The dream of spiritual omnipotence is doubly shallow ontologically, because spirit cannot claim any power, not to speak of all power, without misunderstanding its spiritual essence and true dignity, and imagining it might quit its own field for the realm of matter. And the same dream is shallow morally, because omnipotence, if we had it, would merely stimulate our will to try every folly, not recognizing any limits or character to our human nature, or to the vocation of spirit in its very special ideal infinity and peace. We should be more distracted than ever, thinking we might do anything and become everything; as magicians actually are distracted by their nostrums and shams, and as wealth and science are distracted in their worldly triumphs.   What could be more vulgar than a Faust with a Mephistopheles to pander to his unsatisfied cravings?   What could be flimsier than the philosophies evoked by magic?   But Faust has nobler aspirations when he stands alone, when spirit speaks invisibly to him as spirit and not as a tempter exhibiting all the shabby kingdoms of the earth.   Science has a side that is not alchemy or spirit-raising; and even despair of science and of philosophy may enlarge the prospect, knock down the barriers, and reveal to us how omnilingual is the truth.

Omnipotence once exploded, the devil may tempt us with omniscience.   This is an aspiration far more deeply rooted in the spirit than the childish illusion of power.   When the eyes open they open on all reality; what happens to turn up is an accident, and spirit is always ready for more.   Indeed the accidental appearance cannot be fully accepted without inquiry about its origin, its background, its promise; so that every perception launches us upon an infinite voyage of discovery.

Less physical is the thirst for experience.

Now the love of knowledge belongs to the essence of spirit.   Far from being, as Baconian pragmatism would have it, a love of power, it is a love of imagination; only that imagination needs to be fed by contact with external things and by widening vital rhythms.   When the great explorers sailed in search of gold and of spices, imagination within them was dreaming of the wonders they might find, and of the splendours they might display at home after their return. The voyage too would be something glorious, to be described in fabulous books and woven into tapestries. This is a healthy love of knowledge, grounded on

Experience generates spirit when freely synthesized into images and thoughts.

animal quests, but issuing in spiritual entertainment.
Had the world turned out to be very small and handy,
and the science of it as simple as it seemed to Descartes,
spirit would have suffered no disappointment; there
would have been more than matter enough for all the
wit of man.   Perhaps the environing blank would have
positively helped to frame in the picture, and make it
easier for a religion of the heart to understand and
envelop existence.

There is a snare, however, in the very essence
of knowledge in that it has to be a form of faith,
But true and faith is something psychic rather than
knowledge is spiritual: an expectation and hope addressed
imperfect
and demands to things not seen, because they would match
humility. potentialities in the soul.   Actual belief (the
expectation or affirmation in it) is a state of the spirit;
but spirit could never fall into that state or maintain
that assertiveness by a purely spiritual insight, since
intuition is of the given and spirit is pure actuality.
In knowledge, as distinguished from intuition, there is
therefore a postulating element, an element of hunger
unsatisfied; the datum hangs in the air, not being
accepted for what it is, but taken as an index to a
dynamic object that is perhaps non-existent.   This
adventurous intent, this sense of the ulterior and
potential, strains the spirit, spoils intuition, and opens
the door to doubt, argument, error, and presumption.
Faith belongs to earth and to purgatory: in heaven it
would be a lapse into distraction.

Art for this reason is more spiritual than dogma
and freer than action.   It retains the image of action,
and the history of faith without the risk involved
in either.   Avowed illusion rescues it from illusion
unavowed.   Now spirit is essentially free, and always
an artist and a poet; and intuition, even in the thick
of action, where animal faith rules supreme and
unchallenged, turns that action into a spectacle and that

faith into science or prophetic vision. Time itself, though physically lapsing without arrest or recall in the process of thinking, becomes specious time for the intuition involved, which extends without sharp boundaries over the past, and virtually dominates the future; all ages forming for spirit a single panorama, always reviewable, and traversed by cross-lights, now from this point and now from that.

Omniscience is thus not only an ultimate goal of spirit, but in miniature an inescapable pose. We always profess to know everything, in the sense that nothing can be taken into account by us unless we somehow perceive or imagine or suspect it. This is the two-edged sword with which transcendentalism, or the cognitive sovereignty of spirit, cuts off its own head. Either we can know nothing, because confined to our passing dream, or we can know nothing because there is nothing but our passing dream to be known. In the first case, spirit is tempted to commit intellectual suicide, in despair at its own essential vanity and madness; in the second case, it is tempted to claim absoluteness and establish anarchy, both in living and knowing, spirit at each moment being declared free to take what direction and nurse what notions it chooses. This does not happen, says the devil, as animal faith assumes, under the influence of circumstances, so that both action and thought might have controlling objects, amid which they might steer a true or a fatal course. It happens, he says, groundlessly, without criterion, and without consequences. Spirit, by virtue of its actuality, is absolutely free and absolutely creative; the counterpart of which is, that spirit must be absolutely solitary and cognitively impotent or vain; since in creating its object at each moment it exhausts its powers, and has no environment that it can refer to or perceive.

In its desperation this solipsism is not without a

profound joy.   It is wreaking a metaphysical vengeance
on the great tyrant, on fate, nature, and circumstance.
It is even flouting the alleged authority of
one thought over another, the foolish desire of the talking mind to be consecutive,
consistent, conclusive.   Why should the living obey
the dead?   Why should the present fear the future?
Let me fear nothing, the mad spirit says to itself, let
me remember nothing, let me believe nothing.   Let me
love now what I love now, and call it the love of liberty.

*Emancipa-
tion by
delirium.*

Here we see spirit denying its source and divorcing
itself from piety.   Piety would attach spirit to nature
and to the ancestral order; something contrary to the essential openness of spirit.
Even, if need be, in madness, spirit will assert
its essential infinity.   Is not matter, too, in essence,
infinitely plastic?   Nature and law are never logically
safe.   Their antiquity is mere old age, their respect-
ability limitation.   Contingency signed their death-
warrant at their birth.   The sentence may be indefinitely postponed, the time may never seem to come
for execution; yet the guillotine is always ready to drop.
Free spirit laughs best and laughs last.

*Spirituality
defying
piety.*

Speculatively, this Satanic philosophy has been very
little developed, because both the Indian and the
Christian tradition are religious; so that, for instance,
Fichte or Nietzsche or Dostoievsky takes the spirit to
be a soul with a historic or personal career; and the
Indians never get rid of their primitive myth about
transmigration or inherited Karma.   These are psychic
speculations involving the realm of matter, since without material documents and conventional naturalistic
assumptions about the course of life, neither history nor
psychology could begin to be.   And if mystical insight
or romantic chaotic poetry ever breaks the spell of
animal faith, and actually lets the raving spirit hold the
stage for a moment, tradition and rationality imme-

diately seize upon the inspired nonsense, as upon an
oracle, turn it into some sort of meaning, and infuse
into it all those assumptions of common sense which,
in its wild sincerity, it had dared to drop. Perhaps the
future may explore the immediate more attentively,
and give the devil his due. Like dreams, absolute
intuition may open into perspectives of any depths and
show any degree of complexity; but the complexity is
all patent and the depth painted on a surface; because
when intelligence and faith are suspended objects collapse into essences, and nothing means more than what
it obviously is.

Such is the nemesis that overtakes the pride of
knowledge when this retreats into intuition and proclaims itself absolute.   How should I (the spirit argues)
refer to an object without knowing what it is?   Therefore the least suggestion of an object not present to
me, and not existing purely in the act of being present
to me, is absurd and self-contradictory.   Therefore I
know everything that exists and I create the world and
God and myself by thinking of them. Very well: that
is a proof internal to reflection, moving by logical
implication from therefore to therefore; but it ends by
proving that there is nothing to know, and that every
thought is simply about itself. "Knowledge" would
be pure intuition tied to the datum, chained in its
kennel, condemned to bark for ever at the moon and
never bite anything. All the radical irrationality and
vanity of the realm of matter would have passed into
that of spirit, abolishing in it all detachment, all elevation, all indicative and satiric force; for it would be
itself a substance in flux, the helpless and groundless
precipitation of existence.

Moreover, this scrupulous scepticism itself covers a
hidden animal vice. Pure logic does not argue; it is a
labyrinth of paths eternally open, urging nobody to
tread them, much less to tread one rather than

another. Pure spirit also is selfless. Separation, judgment, scope, while they are essential to a witness that is not an actor, involve no arrogance, so long as this superiority remains spiritual only, impartial, docile to every possibility, respectful to every power, and charitable

Spirit thereby caught in the trap of egotism.

towards every feeling. Far from posing as creative, incarnate spirit, tossed amid accidents, is humble and a little sad, and such as we find it pictured in Christ; because the divine prerogatives and insights in it render it unearthly, and half kill the natural passions which it understands and yet transcends by understanding. But this transcendence is no denial, no condemnation, either of natural passions or natural beliefs; if it were, it would have abolished the world to be transcended and lost its own function and sublime vocation. Scepticism, insolence, and cognitive paralysis appear only when the natural self, which is an actor in the world and a part of the world, usurps those divine prerogatives proper to pure spirit. The assumption of jurisdiction, of centrality, of comprehensiveness then becomes an insult to the rest of nature. Spirituality has become egotism; and the ego, full of natural pride and jealousy, begins to assert itself defiantly, arguing the absolute freedom of some natural impulse in the self, not because this impulse is natural (as all impulses must be) nor because it is rational (as probably it is not) but because this impulse is *mine*, because it *exists*, because nothing else can abolish its *right to be as it is*. But in reality this self, this psyche, is a natural and precarious growth in the heart of nature, the creature and sport of circumstances; any separation or superiority assumed by it is a lie. And this lie will displace and corrupt those spiritual prerogatives which belong to consciousness, when spirit awakes in the animal soul and begins to *conceive* the world in which it has come to live.

Such is the odious parody and corruption of divinity
which we see in all wilful egotism, be it in a man,
in a nation, or in a philosophy. Then spirit, instead
of being a deity in swaddling clothes, born helpless and
despised, to suffer in all who suffer, and rejoice in all
who rejoice, becomes the voice of an animality that
has taken to praising itself, unnecessarily and wickedly
confirming itself, in the name of heaven, in all its partiality, delusion, injustice, and hate. Universal Will is
inevitably self-contradictory and criminal, because it
pursues anything and everything for which there is the
least opening; and this in a seething and limited realm
of matter where hardly any impulse can be followed
without running up against another impulse, and in the
collision defeating them both. But this blind self-
contradiction in Nature is unconscious, and in that
sense innocent. By contradiction it advances, until it
begins to see; and when it has created spirit, it contradicts itself again. For the Will in spirit is precisely
not to will, but to understand the lure and the sorrow
in all willing. Therefore this specific Will in the spirit
becomes in turn distracted whenever spirit identifies
itself with any one creature or any one impulse rather
than with another, and thus lends a blasphemously
divine authority to a bestial preference.

Lucifer, or spirit posing as the champion of spirit,
cannot take refuge, like the worldly mind, in being
conventional and finding excitement if not Even Lucifer
happiness in distraction. Honour compels self-enslaved.
him to digest the truth. At the same time, being spirit
in rebellion, he is not willing to accept the moral of
his true story. He refuses to admit humbly that spirit
may be content with the tortuous but fruitful evolutions
of matter. Nothing remains for him but to skulk in
his tent, like Achilles, and there eat out his heart in
vain protests against vanity.

Moodiness, however, is something grossly psychic

and utterly opposed to the native sprightliness of spirit. How should this pure light dancing on the waves of mutation ever think of posing as a champion of itself against contingency or change or insecurity? That its own gift is to bridge and to transcend the flux of nature ideally, while sharing it existentially, does not authorize it to condemn all other realms of being. On the contrary, pure fidelity to its own vocation would intelligently salute and respect those realms in their several characters, and thereby would achieve its own liberation. We have already seen how mutability feeds intuition, and makes the very life and form of its most interesting objects; there being no greater triumph of unity and eternity, than the synthesis of movement in the truth of movement. And contingency or irrationality in things is no less proper to them and acceptable to a disciplined spirit. In analysing and comparing essences intuition certainly finds necessity; but this very necessity involves that the vast majority of possibles should be excluded from any given universe. This is in no way derogatory either to that particular universe or to the essences it excludes. Will you blame matter for being indefinitely plastic? Will you blame fortune for having shaped this plastic substance into a series of selected forms? Are you displeased at the abstract necessity of being something specific, if you are to exist at all? Are you offended for that reason at any existence? But what could be a more contingent prejudice, or a plainer mark of a particular vital bias, than such insistence on deducing essence from essence, and subjecting the universe to dialectic? I am afraid, when the spirit mopes at the irrationality of things, it is not this inevitable irrationality or contingency in them that troubles it. Intuition is innocently happy in the simplest visions or motions or novelties; it does not first ask that light and beauty should be deducible from something else. These murmurs have an animal

source. Things seem questionable when they are by
chance unwelcome to a chance disposition in the
psyche; and Lucifer is prompted to blame them only
by a vital impatience at their inconvenience, and by a
private rage.

That things are imperfect, that everywhere, as
in the spirit itself, universal Will confuses its own
endeavours, and spoils with the right hand
what it is making with the left, certainly
touches the heart with a hopeless sorrow,
generous because it is a sigh at all frustration, and genuine, because it is a sigh at one's own.
Yet even here, the purer the spirit becomes and the
more successful in its proper task, the less absolute
that universal imperfection will seem. The criterion
of perfection must not be imposed from outside. On
the path towards some goal which, if missed, was
perhaps never really proposed, a thousand minor things
may be achieved. The path of failure is strewn with
little successes, no less real to a free spirit than the
alleged end. And beyond, as well as within, there
may be perfections discernible to a plastic intuition.
Nor does nature, taken as a whole, *natura naturata*,
fail in the least to realize the form or the process
selected. The failures, as the Stoics said, are not
failures to her: she is victorious in all the defeats of
her children. Undoubtedly that is cold comfort to
the victims: the victims are free to struggle and curse
as much as they like and as long as they can. But
spirit is here supposed to have liberated itself from
that form of vitality. Even the successes of the psyche
now interest us not as prizes gained but as harmonies
achieved, as ideas defined, illuminated, made to shine
before the spirit in all their perfection. The failures
(besides falling into other harmonies in reflection,
romantic, comic, pathetic, tragic, scientific) imply
and reveal the beauties missed; and for the spirit

Inevitable
sadness of
imperfec-
tion.

N

these suggested perfections are no less estimable than
the others that happening to be realized in some
psyche, have attained a greater dynamic definition and
emphasis. And all can bide their time. They are
eternal; and perhaps a day awaits them when the spirit
may not only salute them with respect from a distance, but gaze on them at will, touch, embrace, and
espouse them, as perfect companions in some other
journey.

To upbraid creation for its imperfections is therefore a piece of insolence in Lucifer. Creation has a
perfection of its own; and the imperfection
of the creatures, taken each in its broken
career, is relative to their special wills, the
inevitable risk and eventual punishment involved in
finitude. It is an incurable pity, the inherent pathos
of existence, that special will should so often have to
be disappointed; but that is an argument for charity,
not for rage. Spirit too suffers from checks in its
scattered instances, yet with this resource, which other
forms of Will have not: that it may discern and worship
many a harmony not vital to its particular psyche, but
contained in some other trope, larger or more abstract
or otherwise concrete, such as poetry and music and
the plastic arts present to the senses, or as pure thought
may trace in the realm of essence. Nor is such intuition at all cold. When the theme is non-human, it
has a formal perfection capable sometimes of entranc-
ing; and when the theme is human or moral, charity
vivifies it in a chastened mind with feelings perhaps
deeper, if calmer, than those endured by the persons
concerned, as if by our own past selves. It would be
sheer perversity and doggedness to scorn this recon-
ciliation in reflection with things that may have been
intolerable in experience. The horror of them is
neither denied nor justified, but it is surmounted.
The psyche, which is itself a physical episode, cannot

*This imper-
fection itself
inevitable.*

help being absorbed in passing events, in things to be done or enjoyed here and now at all costs, with absolute rebellion against denial; but the spirit in turn rebels against that distraction, contemplates that necessity, and masters both as far as it can.

CHAPTER VIII

LIBERATION

FROM what does distraction distract the spirit? If the flesh, the world, and the devil impede the proper movement of life, they must impinge upon something deeper than themselves or degrade something better. But what is this deeper or better thing? Those who regard spirit as a separate substance, and spiritual life as essentially another life in another world, seem to solve the problem clearly; but I fear they would find it still on their hands if they actually passed into that other world. The moral adventure of existence would simply have been extended; and if that life were really life and that world really a world, the spirit would find itself there as much entangled and beset, if not as much tormented, as it ever was in the human body. So too if we suppose spirit to have first inhabited some celestial sphere, according to the Platonic myth. Evidently even in that sphere, if we take the myth literally, the spirit must have been subject to distraction. How else were its incarnations determined, or how else was it tempted to quit heaven at all? From the beginning those two ill-matched horses gave the charioteer no end of trouble. And if we choose a milder fable, and conceive a Garden of Eden where all was health, safety, and abundance, we invoke only an animal placidity, into which spiritual joy might break perhaps at rare intervals and (I should think) wistfully; because animal peace, to spirit, is half cloying, half pathetic, except as some

No escape possible from nature.

182

fleeting posture or aspect of it may be caught up and turned into a lyric note or a charming picture.

And why are such pictures or notes momentarily satisfying to the spirit, when the life from which they are drawn, in its monotony and decay, seems so gross and melancholy? Because spirit is essentially a culmination, and perfect happiness a quality to be attained occasionally by natural life, not another nonnatural life existing beyond. To say that we are distracted here because we belong by nature to a different region is simply contrary to fact. Nothing could bloom more naturally or tremble and sing more congruously than spirit does on earth; and the myths about a paradise, past or future, are transparent parables, expressing the rare, transporting, ecstatic quality that distinguishes the culminating moments of natural life from its endless difficulties, hardships, and embroiled hopes. These moments are sometimes the gift of a happy change in circumstances, as when agony ends and lovers are reunited; but sometimes, more spiritually, the supreme moment liberates us from circumstances altogether, and we feel withdrawn into an inner citadel of insight and exaltation. Let us consider how this can be.

Apocalypses and Last Judgments and cosmological wonders interest our moral or political passions: they give us a foretaste—conceivably not false— of catastrophes and triumphs awaiting the human race. They need not be inspired by a narrow partisanship, but may contain spontaneous insights into the genesis and fate of life in a thousand non-human or superhuman forms: dreams of angels and Titans, of Gods and devils. Like inspiration of any kind, such revelations may bring to light and may fortify the rebellion of the psyche against oppression and hopeless routine. So far, the thunders of prophecy, political or cosmic, will give voice to the spirit, and may promise to emancipate it. They may

Liberation does not turn on changes in the facts.

awaken it when perhaps it was sleeping; but they are
not needed and not satisfying. Not needed, because
clear and varied notes enough of the spiritual gamut
are struck spontaneously at every turn in daily life,
even if drowned in the hubbub; and not satisfying,
because those lurid transformations of the scene into
hells and heavens, or into marches and counter-
marches of reforming hosts, only redouble the pressure
of circumstances upon the spirit, and browbeat it into
being joyful or revengeful. All this may involve
fevers and nightmares of singular violence, but short-
lived: nothing can be more dead than dead prophecies.
The shouts of triumph in one camp cannot render the
spirit, which is universal, deaf to the groans of the
other; and by the indefinite prospect of fresh revolutions
and fresh catastrophes, far from being redeemed, the
spirit is tied more excruciatingly than ever to the wheel
of fortune.

The Indians, who gave themselves time to unravel
this question without private prejudices, saw that
salvation could come only by *not* being born
again: not because another life was not
possible and might not be more splendid,
but because, being life, it would be subject
to accident, confusion, and responsibility. It would
be essentially distracted. But not being born again
is a negative solution, and personal. The very
notion of being born again confuses the psyche with
the spirit; for the spirit is inevitably born again so
long as there is consciousness anywhere, whereas the
psyche might perhaps be restored to life by the resurrection or re-creation of a corresponding body, but
would lose its identity in proportion to the transformations suffered by this body and by its habitat. If the
moral heritage or Will of any soul were extinguished
by discipline and penance, so much of the transmissible
energy or burden of existence would be destroyed and

*Indian testi-
mony re-
garding
salvation.*

the universe would continue to live somewhat diminished in volume. I have not read anywhere that the universe was at last to be totally extinguished by this process, the last man being a saint by whose salvation existence came to an end altogether; nor would such a prospect make any difference in the moral issue. Under the form of eternity that finished history would remain a fact, with all the beauties and horrors that it may have contained; and the spirit said to have quitted it would still be faced by that fact, and be condemned to digest it for ever, if by poetic licence we conceive the spirit to survive disembodied. Salvation, then, must not be the beginning of a new life, which would make salvation again urgent; nor can it be existence without life, which except for dead matter would be a contradiction in terms.

When each sage reaches Nirvana or reverts to perfect identity with Brahma, who then is it that is saved? Certainly not the man, for he has abandoned and disallowed his personal being, even to the extreme of assuring us that *he* never existed at all, but that there was never anything but Brahma existing in him. Not the world; for this, even if with some diminution of potency or debt, continues to wag. And surely not Brahma, or the trance of Nirvana itself, for this has never been and never can be troubled. How then is spirit ever liberated, when in its proper nature it was always free, and in every phase of vital illusion it is still captive?

I think the Indians themselves give us the key to this enigma when they tell us that, in reality, the departed or finite being never existed, but only the One or the Absolute existed in him. This assertion, taken historically or physically, is indeed self-contradictory and contrary to fact: for only the finite and transitory property *exists*. But two genuine insights are conveyed by that mystic

It is an inward transformation.

formula.   In the first place, there is one plane, that of matter, or physical energy, on which the universe forms a single dynamic system and is presumably of one substance; so that all other realities, not being possessed of any substance, force, or permanence of their own, are called unrealities by the impulsive realist.   On this analogy, mind in its turn may be reduced to an alleged spiritual substance.   As the dissolution of bodies or worlds turns them all into water or ether or electricity or dust, so the dissolution of ideas and emotions is conceived to leave pure spirit, deep sleep, Brahma or Nirvana standing.   Thus as matter was, in a dynamic sense, the only "reality" in this variegated world, so pure and calm spirit may seem to have been the only lasting "reality" in our distracted consciousness.

Modern philosophy has enabled us to dismiss this notion of an underlying substantial spirit.   There is something substantial underlying our feelings and thoughts, but it is the psyche, or the organic life of the body, the substance of which, in its turn, is the common matter of the whole universe.   Spirit is as far as possible from being a substance: it is at the other end of the scale, the very flower of appearance, actuality, light and evanescence.

But in the second place the Indians, in telling us that Brahma was always the only reality in our lives, summon us to turn from that physical problem about the one substance in the cosmos to the moral problem of finding the quintessence of peace and joy in ourselves.   Their philosophy here takes the same turn that Greek philosophy took in Socrates, and substitutes morals for physics.   Now, morally considered, the only "reality" is the good.   To say that Brahma is the only reality in our souls will then amount to saying that the only *good* in our thoughts and feelings, and in our

The light which lighteth every man that cometh into the world.

whole existence, comes of pure spirit being alive in us. In fact spirit in our thoughts and feelings is terribly distracted; but it can be more or less so; and the nearer we come, at any moment, to spontaneous, disinterested, pure intuition, so much more nearly has spirit within us been freed from ourselves, and so much more completely have we become, in that act, identical with Brahma. There was something in us always, since consciousness awoke, that saw our persons as part of the world. From the beginning there was a moral ambiguity in our souls. We might identify ourselves with the self which we found existing and at work; we might adopt its passions and limits; we might almost forget that there might be other selves or other passions morally as real as our own. Yet such egotism is naturally unstable and perverse, because in seeing our persons as part of the world and at work there, spirit in us cannot help assimilating our action and fate to that of the other creatures visible in the same world; and sincerity then compels us either to admit the other wills as equally important and legitimate with our own (which would undermine our fighting morality) or else to detach our genuine allegiance from ourselves also, regard our passions as follies, our views as illusions, and identify ourselves not with ourselves, but with the spirit within us. This spirit will be qualitatively the same as exists, or may exist, in other creatures also: not in so far as each accepts and pursues his animal or political impulses, but only in so far as, like spirit in us, he detaches himself from those impulses, regards them as pathetic accidents, and equates them with our contrasting impulses, and those of all other creatures.

Physically, existentially, historically, nothing will be changed by this second insight; but morally the whole natural world, with our own persons in it, will be removed to a distance. It will have become foreign. It will touch us, and exist morally for us, only as the scene of our strange exile, and as being the darkness, the cravings, the confusion in which the spirit finds itself plunged, and from which, with infinite difficulty and uncertainty, it hopes to be delivered.

Thus when the Indians tell us that only ignorance makes us suppose that a world exists or that we have a natural self living in that world, I would understand them to speak of *moral* ignorance only; for they themselves heartily believe, for instance, in the transmigration of souls or (what is morally the same thing) in Karma.

Distraction is called ignorance in that it obscures the true good.

Spirit therefore has a long variegated experience of this ignorance, which is at the same time knowledge of the world, and of the path to salvation; and the created selves that obscure and distract spirit in this process are parts of the vast realm of genesis, with all its earths and heavens. It is not scientific or natural ignorance to discover and understand this too real machinery; but it is ignorance in the heart, ignorance of its spiritual vocation, to attach itself absolutely to anything relative. Those sufferings and triumphs weigh upon spirit only because they arouse spirit; otherwise they would be indifferent and morally null; and they are good rather than evil, true monitors rather than false, only in so far as they liberate spirit and pass into it, as oil shines only when consumed and turned into flame. Once lighted, this flame turns back upon all that it illuminates and upon its own fuel, as upon alien if not hostile facts. Being light, it thinks it shines of itself; but this is only the most inward and subtlest form of its distraction, when it torments itself about its own existence, perpetuity, and prerogatives, instead of simply shining upon all that there may be to shine upon, and consuming all its gross substance in that spiritual office. It is from the fumes of untoward matter obscuring the flame that liberation is needed, not from the fit occasion of this burning.

The burning forms the flame that is to be saved; to be saved from its own impurities, from its obstructions and vacillations, so that it may neither suffer in shining nor fear not to shine.

That it should cease to shine here, upon these circumstances from this odd animal centre, follows from the natural instability of existence, and The domin- of the world in which spirit is kindled. To ance of spirit have lighted those things once is enough, if cannot re- deem the not too much. In any case they cannot whole soul. lapse from the purview of spirit, which is addressed to all truth; they cannot lose their pertinence to that spiritual life which they once diversified; much less can their passing prevent other occasions and other objects from arousing spirit afresh. Frankly, this irrepressible vitality of that fire which by its very essence is continually consuming itself and ceasing to be, devours rather than sustains the animal soul; and those elegiac sentiments which gather round death, loss, old age, and mutation are not in the least modified by the assurance that truth is eternal and that life and beauty may be perpetually renewed in other shapes. On the contrary, both the eternity of truth and the vitality of nature merely perpetuate the reign of death and of sorrow; and far from promising an escape from destruction; they overwhelm the natural soul with a sense of how thorough that destruction is, how pervasive, minute, and hopeless. To be told that spirit may be inwardly emancipated from fortune, and that in innumerable other creatures it may live through endless adventures, sounds like bitter mockery to the poor wight mourning the loss of all his treasures, and shuddering horribly before his open grave. The soul so much concerned about its immortality is not spirit, but is an animal psyche, a principle of natural impulsive life. As thunderbolts, floods, famines and wars, sickness and blindness fill this human soul with horror, and as social obloquy torments it morally, so when by a sudden ray of intuition it foresees its own end, it is appalled and sometimes the thought of resurrection in the flesh, sometimes that of immortality for the soul only, arises in reflection to mitigate that despair.

Both these thoughts spring from the same intelligence that brought the knowledge of death.   Life is

Ambiguous
resurrection
and immor-
tality. a perpetual resurrection; and spirit too is continually being born again.   In essence it is incapable of growing old or weary or embarrassed by past errors.   Wherever there is existence there is youth; and death at every stroke by intercepting memory restores spontaneity.   In another direction all that perishes in time is in truth and for spirit raised to immortality.   Life moves on, but the achievement of life remains undeniable, even if forgotten.   Here are two honest counterparts to death, not adventitious hopes or hypotheses, but implications inherent in the fact of death from the first.   Resurrection is involved naturally, though not logically, in death, because life is a self-repeating trope, a rhythm in which death is the cæsura; and ideal immortality is implied logically in the truth of any finished life, which death rounds and frames in its wholeness.   The Phœnix that continually rises again, however, is no individual psyche, but mere spirit: not impersonal, since it can exist only in some person, yet not the past personality of any dead man; only the same rational light breaking out anew in some fresh creature. Such a resurrection of the spirit does not liberate it: on the contrary, in this new incarnation it must begin its redemption again, or at least continue it, if by a moral heredity the new psyche takes up the task where the old psyche left off.   This is not only the Indian and Platonic doctrine but in principle also the Christian. The number of incarnations is reduced to two (or to three, if we admit Purgatory), but spirit awakes in the second life with that degree of moral virtue which it had achieved in the first. This rank it now retains in each soul for ever, either in hell or in heaven; or else, according to Origen and some modern Protestants, it continues its moral adventures in circumstances perhaps more favourable than those it lived in on earth. We are not told whether the test of progress in either case would be an approach to liberation from existence altogether, as the Indians and other mystics aver. Probably not: the picture is rather that of an endless process, monotonous or varied, but essentially quite empirical and naturalistic.

Resurrection is the good old Hebraic hope. Such a prophecy satisfies the moral or political enthusiasm of the prophets and promises relief and compensation to Job. It does not profess to disengage the spirit from accidental bonds. Suppose the prophecy came true and we began to live in the Millennium or in the New Jerusalem. As we walked those golden streets and gazed at those crowned and white-robed phantoms that discoursed music in eternal peace, the still solitary spirit within us might well ask whether all this was not a dream, whether the heart was not deceived and disappointed by it, and whether reality possessed no other dimensions. Spirit would still need to do what it does on earth, what it is the nature of spirit to do everywhere, namely by its own intellectual insight to introduce us into the spheres of truth or of essence, detaching us from each thing with humility and humour, and attaching us to all things with justice, charity and pure joy. Is this what, after all, we should understand by heaven? In that case the heavenly kingdom is already come, and exists potentially within us; and there would be no occasion for spiritual pride to turn its back on heaven, since heaven would open wherever spiritual humility happened to look.

No dramatic eschatology would be involved in such inward salvation. We should simply return to innocence as before nature in us was distracted; or we should achieve natural perfection in some particular faculty, for the moment predominant, say in poetic intuition or in universal sympathy. It is an error to identify spirit with cold intelligence, or to think even intelligence primarily cold; however impartial our inspection of truth might become—and it never is wholly impartial —that very impartiality and scope, that very perception of contrary movements crossing or ignoring one another, and all issuing in the least expected or desired of destinies, would excite a tremendous and exhilarating emotion in the heart. Spirit has its lyric triumphs in childhood and in the simple life: wedding-days and moonlight nights and victories in war and soft music and pious trust. It breaks out momentarily in the shabbiest surroundings, in laughter, understanding, and small surrenders of folly to reason. Such moments are far from permanently lifting the soul they visit into a high spiritual sphere; often they come to ne'er-do-wells, poets, actors, or rakes. The spark dies in the burnt paper; yet it had the quality of a flame or a star. All the saint or the sage can add is constancy to that light, so that it colours all their thoughts and actions, turning the material circumstances into almost indifferent occasions. Yet the least disciplined or integrated of us sometimes feel something within us rising above ourselves, a culmination, a release, a transport beyond distraction. It was but summer lightning, and the sultriness continues unabated; yet that flash has given us a taste of liberty.

This is a spiritual gift, a gift of grace; it is not an earthly or even a moral benefit. Against circumstances and vices there are natural correctives; to apply them is the task of war, medicine, and labour; but easier

Common life has moments of spiritual freedom.

circumstances or healthier passions will not liberate the spirit from oppression by things not spiritual. Prosperity might even deaden and misguide it more completely than ever misfortune could. For instance, that erotic passion which moralists think of when the flesh is mentioned is a conspicuous source of inspiration and spiritual courage; before it entangles us in sordid complications, it liberates us from the drab world, where everything suddenly seems foreign and worthless. The snares and slavery that love prepares for mankind are like venereal diseases; surprises for the young lover, shocks to his confident emotions, emotions in which nature and spirit seemed at last to have flowed together into an intense harmony.

It is then the flesh as a power that liberates us from the flesh as an obsession. That which is liberated is still love. It may ignore the flesh that breeds it; it may turn its rays away from their source upon the most remote or ethereal objects; it may even consume its substance and exhaust its organ. But that would be the end, not merely of all possible relapses into fleshliness, but of love itself and the blessing of its ultimate visions. Love presupposes a creature addressed to objects naturally harmonious with its deepest needs: otherwise love (if it could be imagined still to subsist) would be a blind unsatisfiable longing, incapable of fixing upon any true object, or even distinguishing the predestined beauty for which it longed.

We find, then, that it was not the flesh in its simple animal functions that imprisoned the spirit, but the world and the mind, complicating those impulses or compelling them to hide, that overwhelmed the young Eros with all manner of extraneous reproaches, jealousies, sorrows, and cares. We should liberate the spirit quite enough from the flesh if we could liberate the flesh from all that, as flesh, distorts, starves, and degrades it.

Spirit is freed by the perfection of the body, not by its absence.

Nor is it liberation for the spirit to be removed from the world. This, too, is physically impossible: By under-standing the world, not by quitting it. but even in the sense in which a hermit or a lover of nature may flee from the world of men, liberation is problematical. It will not ensue if the hermit or poet still takes thought for what he shall eat or drink, what people will think of him, or how he may persuade them to reform their ways. As the flesh is the necessary organ of spirit, so the world is its inevitable environment, and its appointed theme when spirit is intelligent. Perhaps a purely sensuous, musical, or conceptual life might never discern a material or social world beyond the sphere of linked images; but when images are acted upon and understood, when objects, events, possibilities and certainties loom before the mind, then spirit, by becoming intelligent, becomes a conscious and absorbed inhabitant of nature. It lives by finding itself in the world, by seeing how the world wags, by tracing with emotion the tragedies of history. The greater the range or deeper the insight of spirit the more inextricably will it live the life of the world, though not as the world lives it. Ignorance is not liberation; and for that reason the world is such a slave to itself, not in the least understanding its own mechanism or foreseeing its destiny. But spirit, in the measure in which, by attentive study and sympathy, it may have understood the world, will be liberated from it, that is, from distraction by it.

And as for the devil—all that mesh of deceit, which language, imagination, reasoning and self-consciousness By natural faith not by pure reason. weave round the spirit out of its own creations—the devil needs indeed to be exorcised, but cannot be destroyed so long as spirit endures, because in their substance the two are one. We have seen how the distraction of the spirit by the devil reaches its height in insanity and suicide:

on the way to which there are many stages and devious
paths of sophistication, obsession, delusion, and fan-
atical pride. We need only follow the thread backward through that diabolical labyrinth to find the gate
to freedom: not always, or perhaps often, a gate by
which we entered or which we recognize as opening
upon fields native to our souls; because we are born in
original sin, hatched within the labyrinth, and accustomed from childhood to be little spitfires and little
devils rather than innocent clear minds. Yet, though
probably never experienced, perfect health and simple
knowledge would have awakened and filled full within
any animal a spirit free from distraction, and so attuned
to its successive intuitions as to find the devil's whisper-
ings inane and utterly repulsive. To this innocence,
armed with the strength of unclouded spiritual wisdom,
we may penitentially return; but only a long discipline
can avail in most cases to smooth out all sophistry and
banish all pride, so that undisturbed by the devil,
spirit may deploy all its notes and all its tints in a new
springtime of inspiration.

Health and knowledge: essentially nothing more is
requisite for liberation from distraction by the flesh,
the world, and the devil. Negatively we *Treacherous*
may observe this liberation in placid sleep. *primitive paradise of*
A sleeping child is not distracted, yet he is *indistinction*
alive. Nature has given him health; fortune *and peace.*
has not yet taxed his powers unduly; and while consciousness is in abeyance, the feelings and images ready
to appear, and forming his latent store of knowledge,
will serve perfectly to express his simple contacts with
the world. But spirit in the sleeping child is in what
Aristotle would call its first entelechy: it is ready, it is
perfect, but not employed. It must awake before all
that brimming potentiality can pass into action. And
then, after a first phase of confidence and eager experiment, trouble will begin. Foreseeing this, must we

o

say with the Indians that liberation can come only by reverting to that deep sleep in which all things are alike and nothing ever happens? It would be foolish to deny both the physical and the moral insight enveloped in this doctrine, but discrimination is needed. There is, let us allow, a universal substance to which we all return and which was always the real force and agent within us; and a worshipper of mere force, permanence, or existence may see in all that is evanescent (that is, in all that is in any honest sense *spiritual*) a vain delusion from which it is blessed to relapse into unconsciousness. This unconsciousness will not be death, because unconscious substance retains all its energy and potentiality, and will still breed, very likely, endless worlds out of itself. But in a spiritual sense is this liberation? Is it even liberation from life, if you are tired of thinking, loving, hating, and hoping, and wish for eternal rest? It would be death indeed to *you*, if that is what you long for: but the unconsciousness of universal substance is immensely alive (else we should not be here, with our troubled phenomenal world) and the end of spiritual troubles in you will not dry up the fountain of spirit or of endless distraction in the universe. The liberation, if you call death a liberation, will therefore be personal only, material and unspiritual. The spirit will not have learned how to live; and to speak of freedom where there is no life, of freedom in non-existence, would surely be an abuse of language.

No: liberation cannot be liberation from spirit itself; and therefore not from those natural circum-
Problem of being emancipated without being starved or uprooted. stances which make spirit possible. On the other hand, these circumstances plunge the spirit, as we have seen, into all sorts of dis-traction, since the organ of spirit, not by chance but essentially, forms a particular and specific nucleus in the organization of nature. Were not the psyche a special nucleus, subject to

external interference and needing external support, it could never have become the organ of spirit, that is, of an intellectual and moral self-transcendence. Living suspended upon circumstances the psyche felt this suspense, reached and covered those circumstances by its concern, and thereby became spirit. Individual life must subsist, with a station from which to survey the world, a set of organs and interests to canalize that survey, to render it graphic, lyrical, tragic, and moral, if ever spirit is to arise or to endure or if in any positive sense it is to be liberated. Yet how shall it be liberated if it must continue, while it exists, to face a world of circumstances not only alien in themselves but often inimical? Between extinction on the one hand, and endless distraction on the other, it might seem that for spirit there were no salvation at all.

Perhaps a surer and more positive idea of liberation may be drawn from observing what spiritual men are than by discussing what they say. They are not all alike. Some are initially spiritual and free, not needing liberation, but birdlike and gay like children, or bovine and steady *Appeal to actual types of spirituality.* like peasants. Others who are more sophisticated represent all degrees of regeneration, from comfortable worldly wisdom to the extreme of asceticism. Even frankly mundane sages, like Goethe, while blandly smiling on the world, the flesh and the devil, seem to disinfect those influences by the breadth of their knowledge and sympathy, being too mature to run amok with any one folly. But such equilibrium seems rather the gift of a sound temperament than of a renovating philosophy. Nature at a certain distance and on a large scale looks sublimely calm, as if God lived there; but all is strain, torment, and disaster in the parts, if we take them on the scale of their inner effort and animation. So an Olympian naturalism lives at peace with all the vices, and is more selfish than sympathetic, thinking that inevitableness and beauty justify nature as they justify woman, no matter how much she may entangle or how much she may suffer.

In such pantheistic allegiance and respect for nature as a whole, spirit may be philosophical, absorbed in curiosity and wonder, impressed by the size, force, complexity, and harmony of the universe; the eyes are open, but the mind is still in leading strings. So it should be in natural science; so it was in that happy childhood of philosophy represented by the Ionian cosmologers. Yet at two points the existence of spirit, with its transcendental rights, is bound to assert itself. The naturalist, being a man, must also be a moralist; and he must find himself dividing this seamless garment of nature, by a sort of optical iridescence, into the shifting colours of good and evil; and he will probably turn his reflection from pure science to giving counsel to his soul and to his country about the wiser way of life. At the same time, within his natural philosophy, he must ultimately notice the existence of sensation and emotion in animals, with his own moral philosophy crowning that immaterial and invisible experience; he must discover the witnessing and judging spirit. This is the adolescence of philosophy, and has its sentimental dangers. Only in the most home-keeping, industrious, unheroic souls will spirit be content, when self-conscious, to accept reality uncritically, and to run every errand of instinct or opportunity with the alacrity of a trained dog. Either overwhelmed by the disproportion between outer and inner forces, they will turn against themselves in the hope of suppressing all moral distinction or rebellion; or they will reserve the moral sphere as a private retreat, a humorous or sarcastic or poetical oasis for the spirit in the environing desert.

Worldly wisdom involves a judgment on the world and a choice among the natural virtues.

This last was, at heart, the path chosen by Socrates and his less metaphysical followers, who were not also followers of Plato. Cynics and Cyrenaics, like Confucians and sceptics elsewhere, summoned the spirit to live on its own Feeble glow of satire and abstention. resources, in studious or domestic peace, dominating the world only intellectually, describing it sometimes scientifically, sometimes satirically, and cultivating abstention from passion and war, and from excessive confidence in fortune or in human virtue. The spirit, as these men saw, was invulnerable in its idyllic modesty, and far more divine than the thundering gods; yet the authority of this spirit over the rest of the human soul remained precarious, and philosophy when honest had to be composed in a minor key. Minor, that is, in its philosophical pretensions, yet often merry and running into *scherzo*; for in fact this homely strain in Socratic wisdom has flowed ever since through all the pleasant fields of literature and worldly wisdom, while religion and science, not always more spiritually, frowned from the heights. For can it be regarded as a triumph of spirit to live, artificially exalted, on its own illusions? The zeal, the trembling anxiety, the fanaticism with which these illusions are sometimes defended betray their non-spiritual source. They represent psychic and political forces struggling to maintain a particular form of life, and dragging the spirit into their vortex, which is by no means identical with the free and natural organ of spirit.

No doubt the metaphysical side of Socratic philosophy, the hypostasis of language and morals into cosmic powers, expressed spiritual enthusiasm, and seemed to support it; yet in the end we find that it contaminated and betrayed the spirit. Earthly warfare against the world is an earthly and worldly business; it impoverishes its own side by condemning too large a part of nature and of human nature, which might also have served the spirit; and it constrains such spirit as it fosters into a false alliance with particular opinions and moralities. Spirit soon has to cry aloud to be saved from such salvation. Plato, who had the soul of a poet, knew perfectly how much he was sacrificing to the desperate enterprise of maintaining an impregnable and incorruptible city on earth; and the Church afterwards acknowledged that on earth it was but a Church militant; triumph, liberation, happiness could come only in heaven. Mankind were to remain an enlisted army, heavily armed, narrowly hedged, covered with blood and mire; spirit was to visit them only in the weariness of the twilight, and to rise heavenward in the smoke of their camp-fires.

A dogged allegiance to a particular temperament or country or religion, though it be an animal virtue, More sub-   is heroic; it keys the whole man up to stance yields sacrifice and to integrity; so that persons more fire.   devoted to such a specific allegiance attain a high degree of spirituality more often, perhaps, than sceptics or original philosophers. Yet pantheism, or joyful allegiance to nature as a whole, also has its saints; it too, in one sense, is a special allegiance, since it excludes every irreconcilable passion. Indeed what essential difference can it make to the liberation of spirit from what world or what passions it is liberated? To be liberated, let me repeat, is not to lose or destroy the positive possessions to which the spirit was attached. It is merely to disinfect them, to view them as accidents, to enjoy them without claiming them, to transcend without despising them. So we find the pantheists, when they are spiritual, retreating from this infinitely deployed universe into an inner silence and simplicity that holds infinity, as it were, in suspense; and we also find the disciples of particular religions interpreting their tenets as symbols or occasions for an inward revelation that renders those tenets indifferent.

When St. John of the Cross, for instance, who knew that the accepted facts of religion did not prevent the spirit from passing into the darkest night, tells us that the one guide out of that darkness must be *faith*, what does he understand by this word? The dogmas of the Catholic Church? But those he never seems to have questioned or lost sight of. Any partial heresy seemed to him perverse, and he had no intellectual or historical lights to show him the whole system of Christianity from the outside, as one figment of imagination among many. Faith in that system, as a materially true account of the facts, had not prevented his spiritual desolation. How should it save him from it? The faith to invoke would seem to be rather faith in salvation itself, allegiance to the whole enterprise of the religious life, *Fides caritate formata*, trust that beyond that blank negation and inner death which utter self-surrender involved there would come in the end a positive liberty, a clear vision, a living flame of love. And it could come, it did come; although even the most exquisite poetic inspiration could not avail to express its nature in adequate images. The verses of St. John of the Cross have the lyric brevity, simplicity, and passion that anonymous popular ditties in Spain borrow, perhaps, from the East; there is something so entire, frank and ultimate about such effusions, that they are not unspiritual even when merely amorous or witty. The man who sings them, and perhaps improvises them, sees himself and his feelings from above, as did Catullus when he wrote: *Odi et amo*. Here is a torment that, in seeing how animal it is, has become spiritual. At least it has become awareness of a double life; you are perishing in the sea of fortune and passion, and you are making a philosophy or a poem out of your shipwreck. Or while the whole world is asleep you are slipping out invisibly into the night on the secret errands of your love.

Living flame and traditional fuel in St. John of the Cross.

It was a godsend to Christian mystics that the Song of Solomon was canonical. It countenanced False erotic allegories that otherwise might have seemed symbols. scandalous. The flesh as we have seen is naturally a breeder of spirit; even vulgar infatuation often touches ultimate insights, defiance of the world, self-surrender. And spontaneous sublimation here may well be used as types of sublimation for all the passions. Yet I find two defects in erotic symbolism, even in the delicate hands of St. John of the Cross, in which it was comparatively safe; because he seems to have had a less erotic temperament, or a more manly control over it, than many other mystics. One defect is that (as in the Song of Solomon itself) the images overpower the thought, if indeed the thought ever existed; and we are charmed by a lascivious picture or a poetic sigh, when we ought to be transported into a perfectly spiritual, entirely sacrificial bliss. The Indians, with their metaphysical intensity, are better guides here. The other defect is that lovers asleep in each other's arms on a bed of roses represent a pleasant death rather than a sublime life. Appeasement of a sensual instinct makes a bad symbol for attainment of intellectual light. The true spiritual sublimation of love is charity, not inebriation, or blind transports, or happy sleep. So that if in its imagery I find erotic mysticism less instructive than Indian concentration on pure spirit, in their issue I find both schools alike too negative, too drowsy, too unintellectual. Blank ecstasy is a form of intoxication, not of disintoxication. Instead of cleansing the lamp, it puts out the light.

St. John of the Cross is now in great favour even Appeal to among the merely curious in spiritual the person matters, because he is the most poetical of Christ as conceived by and psychologically expert of mystics; but the Church. neither in speculation nor in heroism was his genius of the first order. What the essence of liberation

is might be more readily gathered from St. Francis of
Assisi, or from Buddha: one would teach us the cheeri-
ness of utter renunciation, and the other its infinite
peace.   But I am not writing a history, and will jump
at once to the supreme instance obvious to all natives
of Christendom.   Obvious to believers, because where
could spirit be freer or less tainted than in God made
man?   Obvious also to unbelievers, if they have any
discernment; because at the moment when ancient
civilization touched the summit of its greatness and of
its misery the Hellenized Jews were exiles in the midst
of that world; they learned from it without loving it,
and were weaned from their own national ambition and
bigotry, sublimating these into a purely religious zeal,
still filled with prophetic grandeur and fire: and, to be
the heart of this new religion, they composed the legend
and maxims of Christ.   Christ was supreme spirit
incarnate in a human creature, suffering and dying
guiltlessly in that creature, and immediately rising
again and carrying with him into eternity his earthly
body strangely transfigured, and thus opening the
way of salvation for the spirit in all flesh.

What is this salvation, not as the Christian myth
describes it (we have settled our accounts with myth)
but as the adored person of Christ exhibits it, and as
his followers would experience it if they shared his
passion and his resurrection?

Christ in the Gospels continually tells us that he
is subject to "the Father", who has "sent" him into
this world.   Liberation as a Christian should He is the
desire it, cannot be liberation from fortune Son, accept-
or domination over it.   Spirit is *sent* into ing his being
this world: it does not command this world, from the
much less create it.   It may work miracles Father.
here, when it feels the silent consent or monition of
the Father prompting it to invoke them; but they are
secondary, and the fuss the world makes about them is

disheartening. "The Father" represents the realm of matter, where the sun shines on the just and the unjust, where to him that hath shall be given, where the lilies of the field flourish and the sparrows fall, where the house built on a rock will stand (for a season), where the poor are always with us, and where there shall be weeping and gnashing of teeth. Miracles belong to that natural sphere, and manifest the hidden sympathies and harmonies between its parts. The spirit notes them, but does not dwell upon them, or value them except as evidences of the unfathomable fatherly power on which spirit itself depends.

Jewish tradition unhesitatingly identified this universal power with Jehovah, conceived at once as a national patron and as the divine vindicator prophetically invoked by an aggressive conscience; but these strains are separable and not spiritual. "The Father" we hear of in the Gospels bears a more intimate and a more universal relation to the spirit. He generates and inspires it, and at the same time subjects it to the chances and cruelties of an impartial natural economy. To this economy the spirit submits painfully yet gladly; because the beauty and terror of that impartiality liberate the spirit itself from its accidental bonds. Family, race, religion, human conceit, human hypocrisy are transfixed by the clear spirit in Christ with a terrible detachment; but where love is refused, this is not because it does not exist; it exists overpoweringly for everything that the Father has created, that is simple, that is young, that suffers and is mangled in the hideous madhouse of this world.

Is universally detached and universally compassionate.

Thus we see by the example of Christ that spirit, even when conceived to have been originally disembodied and voluntarily incarnate, is neither contaminated by its descent nor made proud by its intrinsic elevation. In Christ spirit did not need to

be saved, it was free initially; yet it was inspired to
love and willing to suffer; neither tempted, like the
gods of Greece, to become an accomplice to human
passions, nor like Lucifer to shut itself up in solitary
pride. It was humble towards universal power, wisely
respectful towards the realm of matter. Salvation
could not consist in pretending to be independent, that
is, in becoming mad. It could not consist in correcting
the divine economy, and becoming creative, that is,
in becoming guilty. Humility, piety, is a prerequisite
to spirituality. It is much more than a prudential
virtue, good for those who wish to prosper in the
world. It enables spirit to recognize the truth and
to be inwardly steady, clear, fearless, and without
reproach.

Spirit is not the whole of life, only a child of the
family. The others, the uninspired, cry out even more
urgently and need to be helped first. The
good Samaritan is more spiritual than the
Pharisee. Learning and science and art
scarcely deserve to be mentioned, or only
ironically, in that they refute and stultify
themselves. Spirit, being at once vital and disinterested, cannot but be merciful. Wounds, weakness,
conflicts are the immediate evils; when these are healed,
we may turn to higher things. Nor is this last possible
or necessary to everybody; the parting word rather is:
"Sin no more." Enough, to strike at the source of
each grief, to staunch this wound, stop this pain,
banish this care. Why force anybody to be greater
than he naturally is? There is nothing enlightened
in moral snobbery; and spirit feels more at home amid
simple things, if they are perfect, than in ambitious
minds. Its own perfection consists in charity, in the
perception and love of possible perfections in all other
things.

Thus the innate humility of spirit is turned not only

*Proud to-
wards the
proud, and
humble to-
wards the
humble.*

towards the realm of matter, the universal power on which spirit depends, but also towards the realm of spirit itself, towards all the lives, languages, and loves into which spirit can enter. To corporal works of mercy Christ adds spiritual charities: patience, forgiveness, understanding, defence of the heart against cant, hypocrisy, isolation, and the insanities of conscience. Spirit, that suffers distraction by the disorder of its instruments, rejoices in the salvation and perfectness of all creatures and all aspirations, as in so many preludes or approaches to its own happiness. It is not spirit that sins, but the terrible cross-pressure of a thousand motions in nature that stifle and confuse it, when they allow it to open its lips at all.

St. Paul tells us that Christ liberates us from the law, and therefore from sin, saving us by faith and an infusion of the spirit. This might be (and has been) interpreted so as to countenance moral licence; as the charity of Jesus in the Gospels has been interpreted by sentimental or romantic moderns as an invitation to indulge all their corrupt inclinations. But health and morality are not based on spirit, spirit is based on them; and no spiritual insight can abolish or weaken the difference between what nature allows and rewards and what she punishes and condemns to everlasting torments. The point is that spirit, caught in this vice, suffers guiltlessly for that natural disease and corruption; and to rescue that guiltlessness, to extricate spirit from inner madness as well as from outward oppression, is the double work of mercy proper to Christian charity. The moral economy of the universe is not destroyed or suspended: rewards and punishments, saving miraculous exemptions, take their natural course; but sins are forgiven because they *ought* to be forgiven, because the suffering they bring to the spirit, *the spirit* never deserved.

Sins rightly forgiven because it is always nature that sins and spirit that suffers.

Is it too bold an interpretation of Christian dogma
to say that this inevitable innocence of the spirit, in
all it suffers, is symbolized by the passion Its continual
and death of Christ, and by his resurrection? passion and
The possible liberation of the spirit is not a death.
liberation from suffering or death, but through suffering
and death.   This suffering and death need not be
bloody; often some silent spirit is overwhelmed like a
modest brook grown brackish and lost in a tidal river.
Suffering and death come from the contrariety of
motions in nature and, among these, from the way in
which life rises into spirit and sinks away from it.   Yet
this spirit, however cruelly circumstances may play
with it, remains congenitally positive, self-justified,
heroic; it has been sent into the world by the very
power by which the world was created; and it aspires
to live, and to find a good and beautiful world to live
in.   It loves, and although it suffers only because it
loves, it wills to love and to suffer.   Our sufferings will
chasten and transfigure our attachment to the circumstances and passions that caused those sufferings.
Death will soon annul the ignominy that confined spirit
in us to our private views and private interests.   Even
now, by accepting that death in advance, we may
identify ourselves dramatically with the spirit in us
that endures and surmounts those accidents and laugh
at that death, since apart from those accidents spirit in
us is identical with spirit everywhere, a divine witness,
a divine sufferer, immortal, and only temporarily
and involuntarily incarnate in a myriad distracted
lives.

So the Cross is a symbol for the true liberation, the
ultimate dominion, possible to the spirit in man.[1]
Salvation comes by shifting the centre of apprecia-

[1] "L'Esprit saura se priver de puissance, de toute espèce de puissance;
tel est le plus haut règne.   Or, le calvaire annonce cela même, de si éloquente
et de si violente façon, que je n'ajouterai aucun commentaire." Alain, Les
Dieux (the last words of the book).

tion from the human psyche to the divine spirit.
It is a shift within the psyche, otherwise it would
not enter at all into our lives; but in each
human soul some spark of divine spirit
cohabits with the animal nature of the
rest; and shifting the living centre from
some other faculty to this spark, which is the focus
of intellect, by no means abolishes the remaining
faculties; these merely become, for appreciation, peripheral.   This means a change of heart, a conversion,
momentarily real, but relapsing and becoming more
or less nominal and merely intended as life goes
on.   For genetically and substantially those non-
spiritual faculties were not peripheral but primary,
and the nucleus from which intelligence and spirit
were put forth.   So that man is irremediably a
human person assuming and adopting a divine nature,
and not, like the Christ of theology, a divine person
assuming a human nature added to and subordinate
to his native divinity.   This religious image is
formed in worship, it expresses an unattainable limit
of aspiration, it is hyperbolic.   It represents as a
descent from heaven that inward darkness which is
in fact a presupposition to the idea of heaven.   It
would be heaven to shed all these backsliding inclinations and distracting cares, and to live only in the
spirit; but spirit would have nothing to live with and
nothing to live for, if it had begun and ended by being
a spirit.   For us to wish to become divine persons
like Christ would be chimerical and, for the pious
Christian, blasphemous; but Christ may come and
dwell within us, transfusing our human nature with
divine light, so that our natural functions, while
continuing to be performed, and performed perhaps
more healthily and beautifully than before, will now
be performed with detachment and humility and an
eye seeing what lies beyond.

The soul redeemed by grace remains human.

The fact that spirit is grafted on the animal psyche and is a continual hypostasis of natural life prevents the sacrifices imposed by spirit from being unrewarded, and the spiritual life from being merely negative. Calvary is not the end: there is the Resurrection. And this post-mortal life has two stages, or two dimensions. One is a rebirth by expansion and re-incarnation in all those phases of spirit in which the spirit is free, and therefore self-forgetful. Selflessness can see no difference in value between what is enjoyed here and what is enjoyed there, by one man or by another. Envy is abolished; the very limits of sense and imagination seem virtually to break down; you feel all you have not felt, know all you have not known, live in every one who has ever lived. Yet with a happy partiality; because the endless evils and sufferings which fill actual lives fill them precisely because the will in those creatures has not been liberated. There the spirit cares for what does not concern it, wills things contrary to itself and to one another, and in a word is subject to distraction. This we are now supposed to have overcome: and surely the passions and illusions that are dead in ourselves are not to be replaced in us by adopting the passions and illusions alive in others. Only the clear spirit in each can be identified with the clear spirit in all the rest. The distracted spirit in the world will be succoured with charity, and not hated even in its madness; but only the liberated spirit will be embraced with joy. For this reason hell does not poison heaven. The modern sentiment that heaven could not help being poisoned by the mere existence of such an eternal contradiction to its bliss, though generous, is not intelligent. As all truths fall together into the truth and are perfectly welcome to the intellect, all errors being understood and rejected, so all sane joys add themselves together uncontaminated in the

Spirit may be liberated, first historically, by re-surrection or reincarnation.

heart, when the heart is pure; while the sorrows and hatreds, though perceived, cannot be shared. Pain is itself a kind of hatred, and however intense it may be elsewhere, it cannot find its way into a free spirit. But this very freedom lifts the spirit, in its outlook and virtual attainment, into the presence of all good, wherever this good may be realized; so that it now clings to the earth, and to its native soil, only by the hidden roots of which it is unconscious, while its head flowers out and drinks the light from every quarter of the heavens. Self, so turned into a mere pedestal, ceases to intercept intuition, yet continues to make intuition a possible temporal and local fact, and determines its point of view, language, and perspectives. Spirit continues to live, and to inhabit persons; but it feels no drag in this attachment, can carry away and transform its body as it will, and rise into any heaven to which it has a natural bent.

This I seem to see symbolized in the risen Christ appearing unannounced, unrecognized, in various disguises; a real body, yet not as it was; the same person, and yet escaped from his trammels, having finished his mission, transmitting his work, without regret or anxiety, into other hands. There remain a few relics of the man, but the spirit has passed untraceably into new mansions. If we come sorrowfully at dawn to the grave where we thought he was laid yesterday, we behold young men, strangers, sitting by the stone that has been rolled away, and saying: "He is not here, he is risen. Why seek ye the living among the dead? He goeth before you into Galilee. There shall ye see him."

Such is the escape or migration, or resurrection of spirit horizontally, in the direction of further instances and developments. But there is also, and simultaneously, a possible liberation ideally, in the vertical direction, when at any moment, or habitually, the spirit in a man recalls its universality, its merely momentary lodgment here, or preoccupation with this trouble, and expands intuitively into the equilibrium of *In the* all moments, and the convergence of all in- *second place* sights, under the intense firmament of truth. *mystically, by identifica-* Here there is no longer any pang of loss, any *tion with* dubiousness in re-union, any groping in *pure spirit.* the twilight of birth and death. Birth and death have become integral to life, like the outburst and the close of a phrase in music: there are no winding-sheets or sepulchres or embalmings; we have been initiated into the mystery of the divinity of Christ. In Adam, in the human psyche, the spirit is secondary, dependent, intermittent, only a point of view occasionally taken histrionically, by transcending animal egotism only the better to serve it; but in Christ, in the spirit that then enters into us, the opposite happens. There the centre is divine, and what is put on like a garment or a dramatic mask is human nature. And though this assumption of humanity be voluntary, the very fact that it is voluntary makes it incomplete. The humanity that can coexist with divinity in the same person must be a singularly chastened, subordinated humanity. Such in fact is the humanity depicted in Christ and admitted by Christians into their ideal of life.

A divine person coming down into the world to redeem it could not adopt its errors or its vices. He could not even adopt its passions, however *Liberated* legitimate or inevitable in the natural man. *spirit accepts* He could not marry and have a family *life asceti-* claiming his special affection in contrast to *cally.* mankind at large. He could not possess a home or a country that should tether his heart and compel him to defend them. He could not become a national hero, like Joshua or Solomon or Ezra. He might speak figuratively, and with great pity in his heart, of the kingdom to come: but it was not one in which his disciples should sit on thrones, like Cæsar, judging the nations. The first condition was that they should leave their nets by the seashore, take up their cross, and follow him. Nor was this a temporary repentance, because the end of the world was at hand, and it was not worth while making earthly provision. The end of the world is always at hand. The world is transitory, not only because our lives in it are short, but because it is unstable and contradictory and self-devouring essentially. In the true kingdom to come, in the soul transformed into spirit, there would be no anxiety about place or person, no marriage or giving in marriage, no pride of knowledge or power, no rebellion against suffering. These things are in the order of nature. The Father has ordained them. There can be no thought of abolishing them in their sphere. Christ himself came eating and drinking, living with the poor, and even feasting with the rich. Why not, when these things were profoundly indifferent in themselves, and the spirit could strengthen itself and pray in the midst of them whatever they might be?

Christianity was thus a fundamentally new religion, a religion of the spirit. It completely reversed the inspiration of the Jews in their frank original hopes, and rather resembled Neo-Platonism and Buddhism. The Jews did well, from their point of view, to reject it, and the Protestants, from theirs, to reform it so as to revert to the cultus of marriage, thrift, science, and nationality. Nevertheless a religion or philosophy without repentance, without disillusion or asceticism, reckons without its host. The Jews themselves produced Christianity, and the Greeks helped them to do it. After all, it is the spirit that makes human nature human; and in the confused, tormented, corrupt life of Christendom, not only do we find many a bright focus of mercy, sanctity, poetry, speculation, and love, but even the tone and

And also clarifies it emotionally.

habit of the common mind seem shot through with
more wit and insight, more merriment and kindness,
than in ages and nations that have never asked to be
saved. Salvation is demanded, and in one sense is
possible, because by virtue of his intelligence man
already has one foot in eternity. Each passion, each
period of life, each political enterprise, after its heats
are over (or even in the midst of them, when spirit
shines through) enacts a tragedy which though vain
materially need not be vain morally. Error and
suffering, by the very change of heart that they provoke,
may be offered up as a holocaust; affections lost as joys
may be preserved as allegiances; and all experience may
be accepted for the insights which it brings. Brings,
that is to the spirit and for the spirit; because if after
stumbling we merely plodded on, and if after dying we
were merely made flesh again, the wheel of nature
would go on grinding brutally for ever, no music would
be heard in those spheres, and the soul would have
sinned and suffered only to go on sinning and suffering
unredeemed.

CHAPTER IX

UNION

LIBERATION is something negative, as freedom itself is; yet the soul feels confident of finding great things Having free-
dom to what
shall we
devote it? to do, if only the enemy would let it alone. This is an illusion, because the soul could not live for a moment without the support and suggestions of the environment; and even if, by an unnatural abstraction, we imagine the soul living on by itself, as in a dream, then, when once the vestiges of its old dependence on the flesh and the world were erased, it would be reduced to feeling itself lingering on in a void, watching the flow of sheer duration, and wishing it might go to sleep. The illusion of a fertile freedom comes of not distinguishing dependence from distraction. The sources of life and Will flow into us, and become ourselves; and so long as we move in harmony with the part of them that remains outside, we think we are our own masters, and even masters over all other things. It is only when there is conflict, and our spontaneity is not only fed and guided by circumstances, but also thwarted by them, that we protest against them, and wish to be free. Liberation, however, would bring no positive benefit, but at best the peace of death, unless it were a mere preliminary to Union.

This, though not always understood by politicians, has always been understood by mystics. Union, even identification, is their constant watchword; and words fail them to describe the fullness and rapture of that consummation. I trust their sincerity, but I doubt their self-knowledge; and in any case we must ask ourselves, since they fail to tell us, *with what* they are united, and *in what sense* union with such a thing may be possible.

To union with what, and to what sort of union?

It would be useless to recite the names given to this supreme object: God, Brahma, the One, the Absolute. The question is what these words stand for; and as a beginning I will take the name given to this ultimate object by Plato and his followers, who are comparatively articulate, and the origin of whose doctrines we are able partly to trace. This name is the Good: it is with the Good that a liberated soul should be united.

Classic reply: To union with the Good.

Socrates, in whose mouth Plato puts his views on this subject, was an austere moralist, what we should call a reactionary and a man of the Right, inveighing against the sophistry and luxury of the age, and idealizing the principles of simpler, harsher, and more religious times. But like all reactionaries that found a new order he was a man of the people, with the tone and manners of that corrupt society which he condemned; and though occasionally he seems to have reached extremes of asceticism and mystic abstraction, which made him the precursor of the Cynics and the monks, he ordinarily passed his days eating and drinking, reasoning and joking, and pushing a plebeian utilitarianism to its most comical consequences. Thus he maintained that his own pop-eyes, upturned nostrils, and voluminous gross mouth were better and more beautiful than regular features, because they served and expressed better the uses of those organs. Such paradoxes, in raising a laugh, were meant to awaken the conscience. Away, they suggested, with all prejudices, all whims, all empty pleasures. There is a true, a perfect, a sublime Good within reach, to which it would

The Socratic Good both utilitarian and spiritual.

be a joy and a deliverance to sacrifice everything else.

This Good, as we learn ultimately, is harmony, to be established by the perfect definition and mutual adjustment of all natural functions, both in the individual and in the State. Nothing could be soberer, more hygienic, more politic. Here is the ancient Greek sage, chosen to legislate for his city in earlier times, but now condemned to legislate only for his own thoughts. Othello's occupation's gone; yet this enforced futility, if it favours exaggeration in the moralist, also favours freedom of mind and tongue, and poetic aspiration. Playfully on a small scale, solemnly in prophetic moments, we find the homely Socrates harping on love. That harmony, that rational Good, which seemed so abstract a conception in argument and so cold and repressive a Utopia in political philosophy, appeals visibly to the heart in everything young and beautiful and positively transports the soul in moments of religious rapture. The Good, then, is not merely a harmony to be established or approached in the economy of nature; it is an influence to be felt, an inner transformation to be experienced, a beatific vision and union with God.

The harmony of natural goods becomes a spiritual good called the beautiful.

Are we then in the presence of two Goods, and will union with one of them mean something entirely different from union with the other? Not altogether: for dissimilar as the two Goods are in description, they are one in origin and may converge in attainment. Erotic feeling permeates all mysticism; but erotic feeling belongs to the machinery of reproduction, that is to say, to one of the most elaborate and therefore precarious harmonies established by nature in the institution of animal life. No doubt it is precisely when this animal harmony is suspended or deranged that the feeling belonging to it overflows or is sublimated into

ideal enthusiasms; but we need not conclude that the
ideal enthusiasms cling now to no other, perhaps wider,
harmonies and are wholly hectic and diseased. The
boys with whom Socrates pretended to be in love were
for the most part nonentities and the notion of breeding
philosophy out of them was preposterous: yet Plato
was among them, and a legitimate Socratic philosophy
was begotten in him, and propagated to our own minds.
So too those beautiful institutions, which were to be
the stepping stones to the highest Good, though never
realized as conceived, were missed instances of social
harmony that, in other forms, may be often realized;
they may actually enlist vivid devotion, and may
support materially the happiness found in maintaining
them. Even that union with God, more often talked
of than experienced, need not be an illusion; because
the universe has, at each moment, and in its total career,
a particular form, with which everything that exists
must needs be in an actual harmony: and nothing
forbids some sense of this harmony to resound occasionally in a particular soul, and to overcome it.

I say advisedly, to *overcome* it: because in a union,
even if called a union with the Good, some sacrifice is
involved. In embracing the greater good, Any intense
the soul abandons some, or all, of its former love involves
affections; it therefore abandons some forms exclusion and
of the Good; and the notion that *all* good sacrifice.
can be found in one moment or in one object is merely
rhetorical. Often, and not only in an ultimate mystic
trance, all other goods may be forgotten; they may
cease to be desired; but this exclusiveness of itself
suffices to prove that a psyche in a special phase is
pronouncing that judgment, and that this judgment, if
made dogmatic, is egotistical. The other goods remain
good for the other phases of the psyche; and the
determination and discipline that fix allegiance and
love on a single good, are sacrificial. For that very

reason they are healthy, noble, and if achieved deliberately, even sublime; since this willingness to surrender true goods, admitted and felt to be good, for the sake of one good only, offers to the beloved a supreme proof of love, and to the world a supreme example of wisdom and humility.

Commonly the word union is understood eulogistically, as signifying a new strength and range for the elements united, so that the gain overbalances any losses involved. Yet in marriage and other social partnerships the living unit remains the individual person, and the union is likely to be partly a disunion and a latent war. Therefore union, in the eulogistic sense, must be carefully distinguished from interdependence. Interdependence, whether logical or physical, may be like the interdependence of the man hanged and the hangman. Now spirit has no occasion to aspire to interdependence with the universe with the truth or with the residual life of the psyche, because it is allied with these already, genetically, totally, and compulsorily. This biological bond is worth mentioning, in view of the confused pantheistic sentiment that professes to see a marvellous consummation in this necessary cosmic unity or equilibrium. Conformity with fate or with the will of God (which cannot be defeated) is a needful though partial factor in spiritual peace; yet brings peace only when the spirit conforms spontaneously, in that the order of nature seems to us magnificent as well as irresistible, and the intuition of that order becomes our happiest employment. Such epic or stoic sentiments are included, as occasional events, in the same universal order that includes every actual crime, folly, and torment; yet this fact by no means involves logically that spirit should aspire to nothing in its own life except this helpless acknowledgment and deadly resignation.

Physical interdependence or identity of substance involves no moral union.

Spirit can aspire to union in a eulogistic sense, only with the object of its congenital love, in union with which its own life would be perfected. Virtual knowledge of the truth, in so far as relevant, and conformity with it, are indeed involved in such a union, because spirit is natively intelligent; but much else is involved also, because spirit is not, as Aristotle supposed, a disembodied act of thinking about thinking, or a hypostasis of general ideas, but is the passionate and delicate flowering of some animal soul, to whom much that exists in the world is inimical, and much would be lovely that does not exist.

Socrates and Plato were therefore true spokesmen and great liberators of the spirit when they made the Good, and not the universe or even the truth, the goal of life, attainment of which was happiness. They thereby placed the object of union in the moral sphere, which

Fusion with the universe is not union but death.

is that of spirit; because in material union with the universe, or fusion with the Absolute, no spirit is required or even permitted to survive. There can be no union where there are not at least two things to be united. If one is suppressed, the other may remain, but not the union between them; and if the two are merged in a single thought or feeling this feeling or thought is a new fact, a material resultant, perhaps, of the two previous existents, but not a union between them, since both now have ceased to exist. Union in prayer or in love requires the persistent physical separateness of the two beings united; and their union can be only spiritual, a union in intent, a perfect unanimity. If it were more than that, it would not be a moral union at all, but a material fusion in the dark, with a total extinction of spirit. Everybody achieves that substantial union by dying and being dissolved into cosmic energy and the flux of change. It is a consummation, in some cases, devoutly to be wished; we may thereby turn into the potentiality of many a better thing than ever we were actually. Yet that better thing in its day, and spirit in any of its instances, can exist only by distinction; not only by distinguishing one essence from another in intuition but by distinguishing one object or eventuality from another in appetition, aspiration, and love. The truth and the universe will enter into this union only under the form of the good; that is to say, in so far as they contribute, by support and by denial, to define both the adored and the attainable good, both religion and politics. But it is with the Good only that union is good; and only with the Good that it is spiritually possible. Union with anything less, or with anything more, kills the hope that was to be brought to perfection and damns the soul that was to be saved.

One point, a fundamental point, is thus settled in our inquiry: The union sought by a liberated spirit is no fusion of its substance with any other substance, but a moral unanimity or fellowship with the life of all substances in so far as they support or enlarge its own life.

This first conclusion also arms us with a thread of spiritual security in our wandering through the laby-

The Good also a saving thread through the labyrinth of philosophies.

rinth of religions and philosophies. Are our steps turned towards discovering the real or articulating the possible, with no reference to the good? Then in our philosophic dream we may accompany great naturalists and subtle logicians through unending windings; the eye may range over prospects vastly discursive or intensely concentrated; we may summon spirits and work magic; but the Will in us will never swerve from its first animal direction, from blind craving or idle play. We shall be studying matter or essence, but not harmony. In these reaches we shall find the peripatetic Aristotle, the reasoning Parmenides, the Stoics, Spinoza, and Hegel: all naturalists and historians in their ultimate allegiance,

and never more so than when they raise pure intelli-
gibles or sheer substance or infinite existence into a
supreme idol. They may call it God, but it is still
fact or truth that they are worshipping, not excellence.
Or, weary of that pursuit, we may turn down other
paths, less stately and trodden, but more fragrant,
where the poets walk. At the end, not far distant
(since repentance follows close upon love) we may find
some saint in his hermitage or some cynic in his den,
or perhaps Epicurus in his little walled garden. Here
every alley will be blind, with no thoroughfare. We
must turn back into the maze, or stay with these
solitaries for ever.

But the thread in our hands may not be broken, and
may encourage us to look further; and finally we shall
not fail to reach the very centre of the laby-   Moralistic
rinth, where there is a great marvel: Nature   systems of
replanned and twisted into a green temple   nature.
for the mind. Here dignified priests officiate—Pytha-
goras, Plato, Plotinus—while in a rival sanctuary the
Fathers of the Church vehemently preach and gesticu-
late. Apart, in wider spaces, the Indian teachers sit
cross-legged and sleepy, each in his little shrine, and
Buddha under his Bo-tree. But the thread we hold
fast, the pledge of our safety and sanity, while it suffers
us to approach all these arbours, grottoes, and artificial
rockeries, will not allow us to enter any of them; if
we attempt to step nearer, it pulls us back. Pure Good
is not worshipped here. Actual good, which can only
be a consummation, a smile suddenly breaking out on
the face of nature, or some great gift of fortune to the
heart, here is magically materialized into a fantastic
monument, not a good realized but a new set of conditions imposed upon the spirit. The Good, falsely
petrified, is inverted into a power, limiting the possibilities of the Good; a power here bribing us to accept
something not perfect, there forbidding us to love and

to praise the inalienably beautiful. But fortunately, we were only dreaming. This inverted universe is in fact undiscoverable and non-existent; those revealed histories were but fables, contrived for the sake of their moral. Inspiration no doubt invented them well, and they in turn may have inspired many a holy life; but, the spell once broken, those deceived passions become mere pantomime and those doctrines dead words. It remains for us to pluck the secret out of that dream, and to trace our guiding thread back to the living Ariadne who spun it.

This Ariadne is the human soul. It is only the psyche that can conceive a good or can love it, or can uphold or misguide the spirit in the pursuit of that good. An original theologian is but a poetizing moralist, and the mystic who thinks he is becoming one with the deity is simply purifying himself and learning to see all things from the point of view of the spirit. For that reason those pious philosophers do not altogether waste their time studying their fabulous universes: for they are but reversed images of the spiritual life, and the deeper the devotee penetrates into their magic economy, the better he learns to know his own heart. He becomes very much wiser, in spite of his fables, than the positivist who rails at them as invented physics, without understanding the moral secret of those inventions.

They are fables expressing human aspirations.

Yet truth conveyed by a fiction is an ambiguous good, and if it deepens our insight in one direction, it is in danger of misleading us in another. The bigoted positivist, who ignores the existence of his own spirit, is unwittingly doing the spirit a clearer service. He does not endeavour to be edifying; yet his views, in their externality and darkness, may serve staunchly for edification, by leading the spirit to a more complete disillusion, a simpler hope, and a greater liberty. The spirit does not need

Hard facts the better counsellors.

a universe composed of pure spirits. It needs a world that will suffer spirit to live in it.

Now, with gods conceived as powers, or with the real powers that they personify, a spirit seeking the Good may make alliances and compromises; it may offer propitiation and undertake service with a hope of reward. These are the normal expedients of primitive religion: the calculation is prudential, the aim preliminary, and the alliance political. There is no moral union involved, and the powers addressed are respected as much for being dangerous as for being friendly. Therefore when loyalty is merely political it remains conditional and essentially unstable. It is an accidental method of securing our personal ends. Yet since the psyche is plastic, an imposed subjection to some constant calculable power may grow into an easy habit and a happy allegiance. The servants of a great king at once annex pride to their servitude and ambition to their loyalty. The power, the kingdom, and the glory of their master become indistinguishable in their minds from their own safety, profit, and eminence. Nature in this way sometimes overflows calculation and restores spontaneity where there was at first some ungenerous artifice. So polite language turns to wit, labour to art, superstition to religious devotion; and the ultimate goal is touched unexpectedly in the midst of a tedious journey. The journey continues, but now free from haste and from despair, since the goal is known to be always at hand, not before us, but within.

Facts, in closing one gate to the spirit, may open another.

In fine, a spiritual good does not cease to be spiritual because matter supplies it, or a humble occasion. We may eat and drink to the glory of God; but when, and in what sense? And when may the arts and sacrifices imposed on us by external forces become free arts and fresh vocations? I reply: when the psyche has undergone

Provided that the psyche achieves a new unity.

a radical readaptation to the facts, so that in living in harmony with them, it can live in harmony with itself. This is genuine conversion or *metanoia*, a true education and discipline, that in trimming away all excrescences and parasitic growths allows the plant to shoot up straight to its predestined flower.   We see signs of this when asceticism is joyful, limitation avowed, labour interested in its function and excellence, with the heart detached from the issue and set on no particular event. And we see signs of the opposite when the will is merely cowed and suppressed provisionally, the original passions remaining alive under banked fires, and watching for some partial or mock satisfaction.   Overt life, social life, then becomes one vast hypocrisy, all duties forced, all virtues conscious, all work sullen and unwilling and bargained for in terms of some irrelevant reward.   Something of this ugly lining is visible even in the pursuit of spiritual perfection, when that pursuit is systematic, since conversion is seldom so thorough as wholly to purify the unregenerate will; and some strictly virtuous people are so artificially good that it is only in their lighter and unguarded moments that they are at all tolerable or at all spiritual.   The two meanings of the English word *light*, in this respect, seem not wholly divergent, because in order that spirit may be wholly *luminous* it must be also *imponderable*.   The creaking of a motor must not be heard in its flight.

Union cannot be attained by sacrificing integrity. With inner integrity a spirit might live in moral harmony with chaos, as the romantic spirit thinks it can live; the only trouble being that chaos could never breed a firm spirit, or any spirit at all; so that your romantic hero draws all his strength from the natural order that he despises, and dreams of a congenial chaos only because his own integrity is shaky and diseased. But admitting, in a myth, that a perfect spirit could exist

Inner integrity the first condition of unity with anything else.

facing a chaotic world, that spirit would make no further claims on that world and would find no fault with it. It would positively love that disorderly order, no matter how many torments and mutual hatreds might be involved. And this tragic exultation, like that of the Stoics, Calvinists and Hegelians, would not become cruel or egotistical, unless, in view of his own Olympian peace, the philosopher denied that the world was a great evil to the world, and tolerable only to a spirit that had overcome and renounced it; a solution easy enough for the fabulous Olympians, but almost unattainable to actual spirit, incarnate in that very world.

Thus we see that it is easier for a free spirit to live in charity and peace with an evil society, than for a distracted spirit to tolerate the most perfect universe. Solitude is morally the most social of states, since it knows no enemies; and the concentration it allows equalizes distances, *It makes range and insight possible in thought.* material and moral, and places the spirit at its own source, from which flow all the radiating varieties of moral life, none of which then seem unnatural or alien. Inwardness makes moral scope possible, the experience obtainable externally being a mere annexation of casual views, without insight or moral understanding. Moving time and endless evolution cannot survey themselves; they straggle and grope along from moment to moment, ignorant of what they were or are going to be, and incapable at each point of conceiving the burden of any other. They can be surveyed only by virtue of a quickened sensibility lodged in particular places within that flux, where long-range organs play upon long-range instincts and unused potentialities in the psyche. Every affection of the organism may then become a perspective for the spirit.

There might seem to be a paradox in the love of truth, and in being spiritually exalted by the spectacle of an evil world. If spirit were a power, its first concern would indeed be to reform this world, and (lest it should falter in that endless task) to sharpen and stiffen its own demands, so that the existence of any evil in the world should never pass as a matter of course, and excusable; much less that evil should come to seem an entertaining and pleasant thing, or a necessary shadow and relief to the high-lights of virtue. The least blot should then fill the spirit, to all eternity, with an irreconcilable horror. But spirit is not responsible for the world; it is the world that is responsible for the spirit, and guilty of often tormenting it to no purpose. Yet this happens, so to speak, only by mistake, since consciousness, by its very existence, marks a vital if imperfect harmony already achieved in nature; and the imperfection of this harmony could not be perceived unless the potentiality and need of harmony were at work, impatient to make it perfect. Partial failure is inevitable, because the life of spirit is only a small part of the world's life, and not synchronous with those wider vibrations. Spirit cannot *be* the world; it can only *think* the world; and this function of thinking has conditions that are local and specific: there must be integrity and clear sensibility in some animal psyche. Such perfection of function brings an inner light and happiness. Truth, in the appropriate terms and relevant measure, has been discovered and defined: and this truth is a pure good for the spirit, no matter what disorder, conflict, or dangers in regard to spirit itself the discovery may reveal. Storms are not appalling to the spirit, nor even death; what is appalling is only inner contradiction, delusion, and madness hugging its own torments. Integrity banishes all that; and it renders the truth life-giving and refreshing, like pure air and the solid earth.

This spiritual love of the truth is not love of what the world loves, and therefore not hatred of what the world hates; but is understanding of

Union with the truth not connivance with what the truth reveals.

both those passions. It is therefore a kind of love
for the world, a pitying and forgiving insight into
its loves, such as the fratricidal world is incapable of
feeling towards itself, but such as we might imagine
that God would feel for it. He would not *adopt* the
passions of his creatures; he would be like a perfectly
wise and infinitely sensitive tragic poet, holding all
those passions in suspense, as possible sentiments,
and seeing their interplay and their moral issue: things
to which they themselves, except in some ultimate
moment, would remain blind.

Many an old philosopher and theologian has denied
that God, if conceived to be pure spirit, could love the
world or could have created it. It could   How spirit
only be some Demiurgos, himself a natural   may love
wild being full of fatal passions and limita-   the world.
tions, that could have contrived so many ingenious
ways of using or circumventing the forces of matter,
and could have nursed a fatherly fondness for his work
and a tendency to pull his too hapless creatures out of
the traps that he had covertly laid for them. That
seems speculatively correct; yet the notion of God as
pure spirit is religiously inadequate. The God of
religion must be also a power, the fundamental power
in the universe, controlling our destiny: and he must
also be the truth or the Logos, that specific contingent
pattern which this power imposes on existence. I will
return to this point later; here, taking spirit as we find
it in ourselves, we may readily see in what sense it
cannot help loving the world: cannot help at once
enjoying it, and pitying it, and wishing to save the
spirits that inhabit it from the troubles they endure.

In the first place, is not spirit an emanation of
animal life? How then should it not enjoy breathing
and eating and fighting and loving? How   By vital
should it not enjoy the sights and sounds that   sympathy.
arouse it and stimulate it to fix the terms in which all

Q

its thinking will flow?   Here then, inseparable from the
movement of the world, we find the pleasures of
emotion and of perception, pleasures intrinsically
spiritual.   The vital dependence of spirit on nature
involves a responsive affection towards nature on the
part of spirit.   And this affection (as just now ex-
plained) will survive all the buffets of fortune, so long
as the power to think, to observe, or even to protest,
remains in the spirit, the very badness of the world
being a fountain of eloquence in a free mind.

Yet, in the second place, love is an exacting passion,
and we cannot willingly allow the object of it to be
less than perfect.   When imperfection, folly,
or shame invade that object, love turns into
suffering.   Shall we deny the facts?   Shall
we excuse and adopt them, betraying our own honour
and conscience rather than forsake our darlings?   Yet
what would these darlings be without the charms that
we found in them?   Shall we detach our love altogether
from existing beings and platonically worship only
universal Ideas of the Beautiful and the Good?   This
might be wisdom or spiritual insight, but is it love?
And can such sublimation really be professed without
hypocrisy?   Could it be realized without a mortal chill
benumbing the heart?   If ever we have ceased to suffer,
have we not ceased to love?

Whence it follows that a pure spirit that loved all
Good would necessarily suffer with all sufferers, since
they suffer only because they are deprived of something
that has become for them a need and a good.   Union
with the Good might then seem impossible and self-
contradictory, since it involves participation in all evil,
and in all loss of the Good.   And it is very true that
union with the Good, with all Good freed from all evil,
becomes possible only by the prior renunciation of all
impossible or contradicted desires.   We must first let
the sorrow involved in love correct the love that is

vowed to sorrow, not by denying the natural charm of
those contradicted sweets, but by not pursuing them or
demanding them wherever the natural Will does, or
where, at a later moment, it would curse itself for
having obtained them. This necessity establishes the
double level of moral life, here natural, there spiritual;
and it is only at the spiritual level that perfect union
with the Good is possible, union with it at the natural
level being precarious, blind, and almost always infected
with suffering, remorse, and injustice. These two
levels are not to be conceived as separated like heaven
and earth, or lived in by different persons: they are
moral levels within each life, often within one moment,
when we partly tremble at our predicament or that of
our friends and partly accept our fate and admire their
virtues. Our love of the world is natural in so far as it
rests on kinship and contagion; it becomes spiritual in
so far as it grows disinterested, looks before and after,
and discriminates the dead loss from the clear gain.

When sympathy with the world reaches the spiritual
level it receives a Christian name and is called charity.
This charity is seldom pure or universal, but *By trans-*
touches home sentiments with more or less *muting both*
sympathy
spiritual light. We see this in the slowness *and pity*
and hesitation with which the notion of *into charity.*
charity was first distinguished. In later Judaism and
early Christianity, there was a fervent spirituality of the
heart, but the intellect had not discerned the nature of
spirit and looked for a miraculous transformation of
this world into a celestial society. It was the speedy
coming of this mythical revolution that inspired the
quite unworldly and ascetic practice of charity that we
find praised in the First Epistle to the Corinthians.
There was prudence, there was speculative joy, in
renouncing this world when this world was dissolving,
and in making ready for the next, where only the con-
verted would be admitted. Being forgiven, it was easy

to forgive, to be patient, to succour all, and to think evil of none.   But such charity was unawares an inner initiation into that new spiritual order which was expected to burst so dramatically into public existence; it involved detachment from all that made the glory of earth, not only from the glories of the heathen or of the natural man, but even from those of the saints, when they were filled with gifts such as prophecy, working miracles, or speaking with tongues, which though called gifts of the spirit were grossly psychical or demonic faculties. These were worthless spiritually without charity, without the insight that renders love universal and the humility that accepts all homely cares, forgives all injuries and, without disclaiming eminence where there is eminence, knows that it is no private possession but a gift of grace.   Spirit is not essentially seated more in one man than in another, and in all suffers semi-darkness and tribulation.   In all it has an equal need of salvation and an equal capacity for it.   Respect for persons and their gifts is worldly; so is enthusiasm for their ambitions.   These are seductions for the spirit, blinding it to the simplicity of the Good and of the true love of it.

If thus charity is sympathy with universal Will, it is a sympathy doubly chastened, first by understanding Rationality and then by renunciation.   The world is of charity. seen to be in one sense innocent; its great sin is original sin, the sin of being a spontaneous world, self-contradicting and ignorant of its destiny.   And this predicament runs deep, to the very centre of the heart.   There is no spark of Will anywhere that circumstances might not blow up into the greatest crimes, and the world falls into no error the roots of which might not be found in any soul: so that charity implies repentance, not for this or that slip, but radically for willing otherwise than as God wills.   Therefore the true saint unaffectedly thinks himself the greatest of sinners, because he finds in himself, in so far as he is himself and not pure spirit, the potentiality of all sins. Yet this sinfulness calls for grace and deserves it, because there is still spirit in it, and hunger for the Good.

To blame nature uncharitably is not to understand the circumstantial origin of evil. Law and morality must needs punish and suppress natural Will whenever it transgresses the prevalent order of society; and they can trace this *It sees victims in sinners.* transgression no further back than to the voluntary acts or thoughts of particular persons who may be fined, imprisoned, executed, or at least banished from good company. But these are stopping-places conceived on a gross human scale. Responsibility and freedom no doubt lodge in persons as they do in every contingent unit arising in this contingent world; but for a speculative eye the obliquity of those initiatives is not inherent, nor the evil absolute and all on one side. The world is as evil for the natural Will as the natural Will is evil for the world. The true sin is cosmic and constitutional; it is the heritage of Chaos. This is the sin of which spirit is the innocent victim, which it expiates with undeserved sufferings, and from which it is redeemed if those sufferings and its own insight avail to detach it from the natural Will altogether, not by abolishing that Will (since then spirit would be abolished) but by understanding it and its self-contradictions.

To have passed in this way to the spiritual level is the first prerequisite of charity. Love here walks hand in hand with renunciation: not followed by renunciation after love has been disappointed but clarified by renunciation at its very dawn. *Its transcendental point of view.* Not having any stake in the contest, the Will expressed in spirit can rehearse all the other passions, which are not this *intelletto d'amore*, this understanding and this lesson of passion. Love, when so universalized and so disentangled, can forgive all injuries, endure all injustice, malice, or madness, and this not by an affected meekness, as if one begged to be trodden upon, but intelligently, justly, in the light of truth. The initial aspiration of life is everywhere innocent, the perfection of it would everywhere be beautiful; and everything is disfigured only by confusion, inopportuneness, and a hostile fate. That which is here and now impossible, impossible for ever *for me*, must be renounced; but it remains a good and cannot be detested without blindness. It may have its day in eternity. Charity is a love that outlives defeat and foresees it, that embraces death and is immortal; a love not demanding the impossible nor imagining the false, but knowing the intentions of the heart in each instance, disregarding the rest, and not despising the least spark of spirit in the cinders.

Charity comes to assist or modify some work already afoot, or one that the natural Will might prompt or Its spiritual   might welcome: but the motive is different. quality.   Animal passions are claims to possession, or extensions of self-love to wife, children, kindred, or party. The psyche expands and operates in a wider field, but remains an animal psyche. Love remains a pursuit, a need, a demand, and is represented in the spirit, if at all, by desire or anxiety, that is, by some form of distraction. Only if at some moment that natural Will is fulfilled, is the spirit liberated and does love attain to union. But union for the spirit cannot lie in physical possession or in material expansion of its domain, things which impose more problems than they solve. Union for the spirit can be nothing but *presence*; nor need this presence be uninterrupted. Presence to it anywhere, full presence, is virtual presence to it everywhere else; its treasure is laid up in heaven, that is to say, in its own depths. Spiritual

love is therefore not anxious and is entirely free from
desire; it lives in the virtual presence of all the fulfil-
ments and all the possibilities that the natural Will
pursues.

The world appreciates charity, and finds it co-
operative, when remedial action is requisite and the
Will is trying to recuperate from its follies. *False esteem
and con-*
Yet morally a spiritual temperament has its *tamination*
pros and cons, like any other temperament. *of charity in*
Some monarchs who have been spiritual men *the world.*
—Marcus Aurelius, Saint Louis, Henry VI—have been
unfortunate politically. Their heart was not in the
conduct of affairs, yet they were not strong enough to
recognize their true vocation. A greatly inspired prophet like Buddha would have at once renounced his
throne and his family. Even this might not have
sufficed. The professed and professional prophet is
sometimes entangled in a worse net than a king. He
may be led into self-assertion, into denunciations, into
controversy; he may find himself working reputed
miracles and inspiring fables that he must wink at; he
will probably be utterly misunderstood; a sect betraying
his thought if not his person will follow at his heels.
Martyrdom, in such a case, would not be an escape;
it would turn him into a myth, into an idol. His
spirit would be dead, and more solitary in the other
world than it had been in this; while here his bones
would be encrusted in jewels. Books, laws, and traditional religions, supposed to embody the spirit, are
parts of the world; their effect is compounded of a
thousand influences alien to one another. Undoubtedly, even in their midst, as anywhere in the midst of
nature spirit may be reborn; perhaps a docile intelligent spirit that can avail itself of all symbols without
worshipping any fetich, but more probably a spirit
soured and made wrathful by those very fossils of
spirit. The world then takes sides in spiritual

quarrels, or rather introduces quarrels of its own into
that spiritual life which in itself would be free from all
human partiality.

If charity be a universal spiritual sympathy with
the world how does it seem so contrary to more than
half the impulses that flourish there?   Only
because intelligent sympathy halts wherever
one good conflicts with another: and this
arrest is a consequence of universal sympathy, not a
contradiction to it.   As in a complex psyche or a
complex world almost all passions are competitive and
hostile to one another, charity is reduced to befriending
them rather when they are down than when they are
up; because when wounded and helpless and already
suffering for its rashness, a creature ceases to be
aggressive, and its enemies would be vindictive and
fiendish if they still continued to assail it.   They can
afford to leave it alone to its involuntary penance;
and charity can then step in with its double work of
mercy, corporal in alleviating suffering, spiritual in
rendering suffering a means of salvation.

Why charity is chiefly remedial.

This is the rationale of that check which a superstitious moralism would impose on all natural Will.
To check any living being for the sake of checking it
would be diabolical: the hypertrophy of egotism, when
one movement of Will not only asserts itself absolutely
against all others, but declares that all others are wicked
and ought never to have existed.   Moral passion shouts
about right and wrong; applying to ends terms proper
only to means: that is the feminine eloquence of the
psyche, blind to everything but her home interests.
To reason and to charity this prejudice is nonsense; it
amounts to saying that some goods are good and other
goods are bad.   All are good, but not all are compatible in the same family.

Good-will on the contrary is the disinterested
sympathy of one Will with another; a natural sympathy

in kindred beings, where there is affinity in their Wills,
but requiring spiritual insight before it can turn into
sympathy with aliens and enemies. The
infusion of this insight into natural good-will
has observable stages. A mother will defend
her young with ferocity; their bodies are
extensions of her own; their psyches are colonies of her
psyche; and she will passionately forget herself in
serving them, as the hand forgets itself in defending
the eyes. But as the young grow older, they become
less a part of the mother's life; she will scold, beat,
and enslave them. She will grow jealous and sarcastic
about their separate interests; if she were not human,
and bound to them by economic and legal ties, she
might even lose them in the crowd of young ruffians,
and not know them for her children. Nor is it otherwise in friendship, where there seems to be no material
bond. Friendship is a union in play, in adventure,
in war. It is essentially exclusive, clannish, founded
on sympathies that are common antipathies to all that
is different, a comradeship prized for being segregation,
cut off by special tastes and powers from the rest of
the world. Manly friendship is based on physical
affinity, as brotherhood is, only that instead of being
passive, hereditary, and often annoying, it is freely
chosen and tested in common action and adventure
and in community of thought. It flourishes on sympathy (not confluence) in matters of love and honour.
Personal reserve and idiosyncrasy are accepted tacitly
and always respected; they make no difference in the
common field, and are gladly felt to exist beyond it.
A friend is not the keeper of his friends' souls; mutual
liability is limited, but within the field of their common
life and *virtù*, they feel sure of one another; and this
confidence, when well tried, may be not untouched
with admiration. And here a spiritual element may
supervene. Friends may club together in cultivating

Gradual clarification of good-will into charity.

music or philosophy as they might in mountain climbing: yet if the common ideal object predominates over the social occasions, with their incidental humours, the original personal atmosphere gradually becomes transparent, indifferent, and finally disturbing. Friendship is at an end, and each must tread the winepress alone. Even in the mountain climbing the supreme moments are solitary; the comradeship reigns in the projects, the dangers, and the irrelevant human incidents.

Exclusiveness and pugnacity appear also in all intellectual, political, and religious bodies—called bodies not without unconscious wit. They glow with local affections, with privilege, with scorn and hatred of the damnable outsider. If ever some ray of speculative spirit or universal charity pierces those enclosures, friendship is saddened, party is transcended, religion can be endured only as a human convention and nationality as a physical accident. Whatever measure of truth, beauty, or happiness there may have been in those associations is not denied or diminished; but the heart has travelled beyond; and it is only in an infinite landscape transfiguring their values that they continue to be prized. What was before lived is now understood, and this understanding is a second life in another sphere.

For this reason personal friendships and cliques are discouraged in the cloister. They are distracting and equivocal. Charity should extend equally to all the brethren, without favouritism or attachment. Not that affection is anything but natural and generous; but in the spiritual life it is accidental, as are also the particular doctrines and cults of any religion. They are to be accepted as we have to accept ourselves, not as goals but as points of departure. When we come to a spiritual communion of poets, philosophers, or saints, it is avowedly the divine grace, truth, or beauty flowing through those human channels, and not the human

Union through all channels is interior and only with the Good.

channels, that we profit by and embrace: so much so
that all important spiritual figures necessarily become
mythical, even when they were originally historical.
If they resist this transformation, they become
irrelevant to their spiritual mission, as Shakespeare
the man is irrelevant to the poetic world that we find
in his plays. The creation of mythical heroes seems
deceptive only to the pedant who insists on proving
them historical or proving them unhistorical. To the
spirit those *numina* are true, as the gods are; since the
real source of influence in both cases is some diffuse
cosmic power at work in the dark, and exciting these
graphic images in the mind. We therefore conceive
plastically and love as kindred beings and charitable
powers the powers that actually liberate spirit in ourselves. They make for the Good; or, as we say, the
Good works through them. This last, if pressed too
literally, becomes not thinkable, since the Good is a
result, a harmony in the workings of power; yet this
power often serves the Good, which therefore may
dramatically be called its master, commanding its own
realization.

There is a school of theology that would clip the
wings of love, so as to prevent it from ascending and
make it always descend. Love of the Good, *Charity*
they say, is self-centred and erotic; by it we *versus*
aspire greedily to something that we might *Eros.*
enjoy, to the perfection of our own being, in the
possession or presence of something that, for us, is the
Good. Charity, on the contrary, searches out the
victims of evil, like divine grace poured out regardless
of merit, and dedicates itself to their service. Forgetting self, it labours to relieve and instruct others.
In a word, these moralists see charity in Martha, a
hard-working Evangelical Christian; but in Mary they
see only a corrupt enthusiast of the Greek decadence,
absorbed in the passions of her own battered soul.

In one sense unselfish love is not only possible but primitive. The Will is directed upon its objects by nature, without any calculation of satisfactions to accrue or torments to be avoided. But it is perfectly impossible that any love should exist not rooted in a psyche and not directed upon an object chosen and pursued by spontaneous Will. There is therefore no love not directed upon the Good, not directed upon something that makes for the fulfilment of the lover's nature. This good may be the good of others, but doing good to others will to that extent be a good for oneself. Or shall we say that a social life, involving friendliness and a sense of duty, is in itself nobler than self-help? If the monkeys agreed always to pick the vermin from one another's skins and never from their own, the operation would indeed have become social but the benefit would remain private. Amiable as the impulse may be to benefit others, this impulse would be cruelly stultified if no benefit could be really conferred; and it is only because Will is already directed upon life, health, food, and liberty that the ministrations of intelligent charity are a benefit and not a nuisance. If to pursue the Good be pronounced selfish the most unselfish charity would be openly serving the selfishness of our neighbours, and secretly serving our own.

Perhaps, however, the good that charity aims to bestow might be no other than charity itself. "The greatest thing in the world" being love, by diffusing love, without any other benefit, we should be saving the world. But should we? Flattered as everyone would be by the idea of being loved and full of ready love in return, yet if it were impossible to benefit anybody, the whole world would be tormented by a perpetual desire to do good and a hopeless inability to do it. But perhaps we may here be the victims of an ambiguity in the word love. Love

Folly of love for love's sake.

may mean loving actions or it may mean the emotion of love. Now the *emotion* of love might be diffused universally, even if no positive natural goods could be secured for society. But then love, love, love would be a vapid sentiment; yet this is the happiness that the sentimental saviours of the world seem to be pursuing. Thinking themselves disciples of St. Paul, or even of Christ, they have removed all disillusion and asceticism from their notion of charity, all austerity from their love, and have become in reality disciples of Rousseau.

The position becomes even more precarious if we extend it to theology. That God is love is an orthodox saying; and even if God were essentially power rather than love, in one sense love would be involved in his being: for power selects what it shall do and this selection *Possible meanings of "God is love."* marks a preference and a kind of love. When the Creator said, *Let there be light*, he exerted power; yet the direction in which he exerted it betrayed an innate affection and proved that he loved light. The Book of Genesis represents God as an artist, loving the world in idea before he had brought it into existence. But a world, like a child, has a life of its own and may soon begin to wander from the parental intention. The parent may even be tempted to disown his offspring; yet the artist, even if disappointed in his work, remembers the Platonic Idea that first inspired him, and still feels its magic. He will be inclined to preserve the erring thing to be revised and corrected. So we learn that God has resumed his labours, this time not to create the world but to redeem it. The absolute artist has been softened into a forgiving father, a miraculous physician, a patient teacher, even a propitiatory victim. God's love of the world has become charity.

Arabian subtlety has known how to refine on these intuitions and to maintain that creation itself was a work of charity. Allah is continually called the Merciful

and the Compassionate, even when his decrees are
most severe; and there might seem to be a voluntary
Was it a   one-sidedness in these epithets, seeing that
mercy to be   Moslem theology makes Allah absolutely
created?   omnificent.   How should universal Will be
moved by charity, when there can be nothing outside
to succour or to love?   The psyche is not moved by
charity to fashion the body, or to react with a healing
power on diseases and wounds.   Nor is spontaneous
unanimity between various psyches an instance of
charity: it is not charity that leads a crew to pull together
in a race or in a storm.   Nevertheless we are told that
charity moved the Creator to make the world, because
non-existence is the worst of metaphysical evils and
the most necessitous.   Allah therefore took pity on the
unwedded essences of things and entirely without any
claims or merits on their part married them to existence.
The worst of monsters and of torments has this to be
thankful for, that at least it exists.   We may smile at
such an ambiguous mercy; yet the principle that *giving*
is blessing, whether the gift were needed or not, has
a great vogue in religion and in society; and even when
the gift is needed, the question remains whether the
need itself was not an evil.   The Prayer Book thanks
God for our creation; yet in being created we received
nothing but needs with no assurance that they would
be satisfied; for what is our organic Will, our psyche,
but a vast concourse of needs, some urgent, others
latent but brewing and rendering us fundamentally
unhappy?   Common sense is blunted to such unremit-
ting perceptions, and takes for granted our existence,
our needs, and our desire to satisfy them; and on this
basis we may unfeignedly thank Providence or Fortune
or the charity of mankind for any aid in satisfying them,
however inadequate.

Charity has more insight into nature than conscience
or self-interest can have; it understands the innocence

of contrary wills and the goodness of contrary goods.
For this reason charity seems unnatural or supernatural to the conventional mind. It re-
bukes in assisting. But if no will can be unreservedly abetted by charity, this happens
only because natural wills are in conflict; for
although some of them involve worse consequences
than others, even the best involve consequences that
are unfortunate in some direction. Human wisdom
cannot consider everything or really look to the end;
and charity must begin at home and never lose its
moorings there. Therefore it is always quick to relieve
bodily distress. To relieve suffering in anyone's body
is an immediate mercy to the spirit there, and can
hardly bring an immediate injury to the spirit in anyone
else. For the same reason charity gives alms, even
when rational economy might hold back; because the
benefit is clear, even if undeserved, and the detachment
just, even if ill-timed. Thus charity is a second birth
of love, aware of many wills and many troubles. It
is not creative or constructive of anything positive,
unless it be hospitals and almshouses. Institutions
produce rival ambitions, rights, and contentions.
About all plans and projects charity is disenchanted
and sure only of the ever-present propriety of charity
itself.

    If in saying that God is love we understand that
God is charity, we are led to certain consequences
perhaps unwelcome to theology. For if the
whole essence of deity were bounty, evidently
the creator could not exist without the
creation; and if the whole essence of deity were mercy,
God would depend for his existence on the existence
of suffering and sin. These implications are pantheistic; they are incompatible with Christianity, the
religion of charity. But a more insidious consequence
follows. If the impulse to give and to help were the

*Charity is
humane,
with roots
in nature.*

*To deify it
involves
atheism.*

very spirit of God (the occasion and demand for such charity being presupposed naturalistically) what would God be but goodness in ourselves, in so far as we are good?   This insight may rather satisfy a moralistic and mystical piety, as the pantheistic insight satisfies dialectical wit: but if we say that God is nothing but the brotherly love that we feel for one another, it is clear that we are atheists.

Neither the animal psyche nor the Good to which the psyche aspires can ever be banished from morals. It is natural The psyche introduces the element of pre-
Eros en- ference, the distinction between good and
lightened. evil, success and failure; and the Good is thus set in its ideal place, as the goal and perfection of a natural life.   If we call this vital aspiration Eros, which is its ancient poetic name, we may say that charity is a form of Eros, and thoroughly erotic; for if it were not erotic it would not be a psychic force nor a passion of the spirit.   What turns Eros into charity is reason, recollection, comparison, justice. The great tragedy of Eros is its blindness: remove the blindness produced by a too narrow and intense light, remove the bandage that turned vision into dreams, and Eros is charity itself: the pursuit of all Good, guided by all knowledge.

Now sympathy with all good and attention to all knowledge are not possible to an animal psyche in its physical action; they enter the field only as ideals of the spirit, evoked by the psyche in the act of becoming sensitive to *some* sympathy and to *some* knowledge. Correcting a first impulse in consequence, the psyche creates the principle of a rational conscience or of universal justice.   The universality of both sympathy and knowledge is posited initially but never attained in act; yet charity (as also science) lives in the light of that ideal.   Truth far outruns actual knowledge, or any experience possible to any individual or any species of living beings; and charity far outruns any actual code of politics or morality. Charity extends to all animals and, as the Indians tell us, to all gods, whatever gods there may be; because existence of every type involves difficulty and imperfection, defeat, and essential impermanence, so that everywhere existence deserves compassion and demands transmutation into eternal terms. This the spirit performs instinctively, wherever it can, clearing the gold everywhere from the dross, and laying it up for an eternal treasure.

How is this possible? How shall we be united, even in spirit, with a good that is absent, how recognize a truth inexpressible in our language, or be at peace with a power that is perhaps destroying us? There is a way: it is prayer. Prayer seems sheer foolishness to the world, and rather a puzzle to the materially pious. Why pray, an indoctrinated child may ask, when God loves us, when he knows everything, and when he has already decided what he will do? And the only answer might seem to be the one given in my first Spanish catechism to any hard question: "The Church has doctors that will know how to explain it." We may smile; but in this case the explanation is really at hand if, whether doctors or not, we can distinguish the spirit from the psyche, or in Christian language, the other world from this world. In this world, or for the psyche, prayer is an instrumentality, and it could not be efficacious except magically if incantations, or the unspoken desires of the heart, could compel the powers of nature to obey our commands. This is what superstition expects and asserts, even in the most modern psychology. But for a spiritual religion the idea of compelling God or compelling matter, by magic words or by tears, to do as we wish, is sacrilegious. Magic does not begin to be prayer until it leaves the issue in God's hands, and reconciles itself beforehand to a denial of the need or

Union with all good is possible only in prayer.

R

the hope expressed. It is not expressed for the preposterous purpose of changing the will of God, or
causing nature to revise the contingency of things,
which seen from within is freedom and seen from
above is fate. It flows out spontaneously from the
fullness of the heart, in confession, in reflection, in
prophetic vistas, in resigned and transmuting union
with the truth and with a different infinite Good at
first hidden from the eyes.

In his life-long prayer the reflective man need not
be especially inclined to address petitions to heaven;
rational prayer is not a means but an end.
Petitions enter into prayer inevitably, because
its language is a social language; and the
spirit has a direction in which it wishes to
move, so that it lives in a perpetual alternative between
I would and *I would not*. It therefore can hardly
conceive anything without gladness or aversion; and
this vital bias comes to clearness, as all things come to
clearness, in prayer. Yet in prayer all these wishes and
sorrows are uttered in the felt presence of omnificent
power and eternal truth; so that all preferences are, as
it were, suspended and neutralized by the sense of
dependence and by the virtual acceptance of the perhaps
contrary fact. The very expression *Thy will be done*
which breathes resignation also defines a hope. The
will of God on the one hand means whatsoever happens;
on the other hand it means that which ought to happen.
In the latter sense it seems as yet not to be done on
earth as it is in heaven; and the Kingdom of God seems
not yet to have come. But this postponement too must
be according to God's will in the first sense; and if it
were not we should not implore him to shorten the
interval and to deliver us from evil. If the will of
God be not conceived as omnificent (that being too
pantheistic for a political religion) and if events are
determined in part by the free-will of other agents, the

Double interpretation of the divine will.

ultimate union to be attained in prayer would not be union with God, but with the entire moral society of the universe. With this totality we should have to settle our ultimate accounts, dynamic and ideal, since it would be this conjunction of free agencies, with our own included, that would determine the total destiny and truth of things. A moral theism, in denying that God is omnificent, would still have left omnificence the ultimate court of appeal; and this court would not be composed merely of the sundry free agents visible within it, but also and most importantly of the manner and time of their conjunction, and its effects. Now these conjunctions and effects of various free wills are contingent to any one of them and a primary fatality for them all; yet these unintended conjunctions and results are conceived in orthodox theology to have been foreseen and accepted by God at the creation of the world; so that his will seems to be double. As the designer and ultimate sanction of destiny, God wills whatsoever happens; but as lawgiver, merciful saviour, and moral judge, he wills us, for instance, to do not those things which we do but those which we ought to have done; so that his moral and redeeming will is only one strand in his total handiwork.

But the language of prayer should not be pressed as if, when we are living the life of spirit in its full freedom and transcendence, we were still *The langu-* bargaining and plotting in a social and *age of prayer* diplomatic world. In expressing our needs *is poetical.* and our sorrows we do not ask ourselves whether we are calling on the Almighty to will what he does not will, or whether we are calling on ourselves to contradict our moral aspirations and to think our evil good. We are probably doing neither. We are recollecting, digesting, purifying our conscience. Essentially, we are addressing nobody; the names and forms of the gods are as mutable as our necessities. Even when we are expressing a wish, we are doing so in the face of the truth, or of fate impersonally, considering how excellent it would be if fortune came to our assistance. We pray as spontaneously as we curse, and cry *Would to God!* without any theory of divine government. The same exclamation, *¡ojalá!* is even more familiar in Spain, meaning *May Allah will it!* If the Moslems, the most prayerful and most manly of men, sometimes abstained from petitions as irreverent, they could not abstain from desire; and their most unfeigned prayer was not to God, but concerning God. They could not suppress the feeling how beautiful the beautiful would be, if it came true. And among us now there are good people who pray that there may be a God to pray to.

Moreover, sincere prayer need not affect that hushed tone and demure attitude which we associate

Need not be timorous or cringing.

with religious devotion in modern times. The spirit may often be sorrowful, but when it thinks, when it dominates, it cannot be afraid. Prayer is essentially *oratio*, the eloquence of destiny; it contains the whole free comment, lament, and jubilation of the spirit, challenging its fate: a continual contrite reconsideration of all things, for which memory and hope supply the materials; so that prayer, as a sincere spirit may utter it, abounds in regrets, praises, aspirations, laughter, and curses, but all transposed from the plane of action to that of reflection and prophecy. Omnificent power and eternal truth mightily sustain this contemplation, rendering it, in so far as it conforms to them, victorious and full of light. Action is not excluded, as it is not in the drama. Prayer may easily glow with an assurance of the direction in which omnificent power, perhaps through our own agency, is carrying the world. We may be fighting with the big battalions, or even leading them; yet in the midst of action that which is proper to spirit is only observation, wonder, comparison, judgment. What has happened, what is happening, and what is bound to happen fall into a dramatic vista, which the prophet or psalmist develops eloquently in his prayer; and he judges nothing and promises himself nothing except as the agent and messenger of God.

Thus, strange as it may sound to the rationalist who thinks prayer ridiculous, the only perfectly rational form of life for a spirit that has attained self-knowledge is the life of prayer.

To this we must come morally in the end, accepting all inevitable evils for the sake of the good still possible; but there is a partial union that the spirit *Transition to* may reach vitally at any moment, as in *laughter.* laughter. Here there is no acceptance of ultimates, only merriment at present absurdities and deceptions. The Olympians did not pray to Fate, they did not *care* enough for that; but being free and happy, they laughed at existence.

There are moments in childhood when spirit breaks through in a clear triumph. Children laugh, they laugh easily, whole-heartedly, at all sorts of *The pure* things. In laughter there is a release of ten- *laughter of* sions, as in play; but the tensions released *children and* in play are vital only, and inarticulate, while *the impure.* laughter is provoked by release from little obsessions about things already familiar. Things and persons are imposing objects to a child; they seem stolidly committed to be and to remain themselves; but they grow more engaging when they change, and still more when they make faces and pretend not to be what they are. Yet the circle of their tricks and of their stories is soon run, and they become prosaic. In things and persons this commitment to remain as they were may make their individuality and force, but for the spirit it is a restriction. In reality that solemnity and dullness in things and persons is a false pretence. Things are not the essences they put forward; they are configurations of a matter that has indefinite potentialities, just as the spirit has. Any day some unforeseen accident will disclose their inside, or their miscalculation of their powers. The gods have always been laughing at them, and now the spirit in us may laugh too. Even in the silliest fun, when a word meant in one sense is taken in another, there is some release from a false restriction, a little flight from one perch to another; but a pun disappoints if it merely drops us at another chance station. Had it been true wit, it would have kept us on the wing.

Laughter loses this innocence when children lose theirs and become rancorous. In their boasts and jeers we see the difference. These grimaces of egotism are forced, cruel, essentially unhappy. Pure laughter is not malicious, not scornful; it is not a triumph of one self over another, but of the spirit over all selves. It is a joyous form of union with our defeats, in which the spirit is victorious. The bubble once pricked, everybody stands on homelier and firmer ground. In passing, there is exultation at having rung the dirge of something unreal. This pleasure is dear to children, even if a little shrill. They, poor creatures, are being cheated so regularly by their elders, by one another, and by their own fancies, that it is sweet to turn the tables for once and to mock the solemn fools in return. But the enlightenment of children is apt to be a fresh delusion, destined to end not in laughter, but in tears; and tears are not enlightening. They water the roots of passion in the psyche and pile up the fruits of Karma for the world. It is laughter that liberates once for all from error, without taking a new pledge. It therefore unites us freely with whatsoever may truly deserve our troth. Laughter rings the recess-bell in school hours; and then perhaps some ugly little seeds of learning, sown in us against our will, spring up beautiful, free and unrecognized in the playground of the mind.

In after years laughter becomes bitter; we have laughed enough to no purpose and can no longer laugh merrily at the old comedy of things. One *The seamy* half of us has despaired and smiles sadly at *side of* the other half for not having been able to do *cynicism.* so. Meantime, at all ages, laughter can sink into ribaldry and become the by-play of vice, when vice throws off the mask, or wins a trick against its demure enemies. But cynicism is not itself inwardly free; its professed wit (as in the Roman satirists) is not very witty, being tarnished sometimes by savage zeal and sometimes by a base relish for scandal. Nevertheless true merriment may anywhere break in unofficially at the shams of vice as at those of virtue, lifting us out of both to the happy level of understanding.

Sometimes, however, this music changes its stops, and grows solemn. Laughter, for all its innocent spontaneity, is too bodily an affection to be *The victory* wholly satisfying. It lapses sadly into a *of mind.* blank; the next thing is irrelevant and mutes the impulse. When the elevation can be sustained on a wider view, we no longer laugh, but grow speculative, commemorative, even liturgical. The catharsis found in tragedy is only a solemn universalized form of the solution that unravels some comic knot, and leaves us, for a moment, contented with the world. Elegy also leaves us content, not with some gain but with all losses. The *bourgeois* endeavours to explain his love of scandal, of reported crimes, horrors, and ruin, by throwing pleasing considerations into the balance, such as his own safety, or the incidental merits of the report, diction, images, or moral lessons. But this is all beside the point. The nature of spirit and the divine allegiances of spirit have not been discerned. Why is the diction poetical or the imagery sublime or the moral edifying? Because in those intuitions the spirit triumphs over the triumphs of limitation, error, and death. It is not a question of sugaring the pill, but of drinking the fatal cup to the dregs, and being reborn into another life. We should be only lying to ourselves if we pretended that troubles had ceased or that death was not ultimate; but by being ultimate death frames all troubles in, completes the picture, removes it to the plane of historic accidents, and renders it an object fit for intuition to rest in. *Memento mori* may suggest only worms and ghastly corruption; but we might say just as well, *Memento vixisse*, remember that you will have lived. Such is the eternity intrinsically native to spirit and visible from each of its moments, be they few or many. The judgment then passed on the spectacle may be favourable or unfavourable; but it is always a sublime judgment, a true last judgment. David and the Sibyl sing for ever of the Day of Wrath and of the world sunk in ashes, and they are deeply happy.

Spirit could never *see* the truth or conceive it in an actual thought if spirit were not a function of life; and the intuition of eternity must always be a passing or repeated intuition. Now life is a trope in matter, proper to an organism that can restore and reproduce itself. Such life cannot help being precarious. It is inwardly continuous with material processes that outrun it, so that some of its developments will be disruptive and contrary to one another. Life may be killed by life, as it may be stifled by lifeless forces. Therefore the good that a liberated spirit may embrace cannot be the truth, but at best some conception of the truth. This will be more than the truth, in being living and emotional and having an internal movement from potentiality to act; and it will be immensely less than the truth in being always partial, intermittent, and subjectively directed. For it is life, raised to the scintillating light of spirit, that notices this rather than that, sets problems, and finds

Union not with unvarnished truth.

solutions, which are privately exciting scents followed
to ends privately gratifying; whereas the truth displays
the whole eternal labyrinth of real relations through
which question and answer miss their way a thousand
times, for once that they find it.

The triumph that inwardly raises spirit to its height
is intuition, not knowledge; for when fact and truth
have to be regarded, spirit has mortgaged its *The value of*
freedom, and is as often depressed as exalted. *knowledge is*
Therefore before the truth, or behind it, and *moral.*
intercepting knowledge in a thousand ways, arises a
ghost of that which is not but might have been: something better than the truth, or worse than the truth,
and evoked by fear of what the truth may be. And
this play of heated imagination, which the truth if it
could speak might call impertinent, flows from the
sources of spirit more directly, and prophesies the Good
more truly, than knowledge could ever do. The function of such free intuition is by no means superseded
by eventual knowledge; it persists to enlighten the
spirit morally about the truth that may have enlightened
it intellectually. Truth is contingent; but spirit, being
addressed to essence, can rest only in what is necessary:
in the form that a form has, and in the inevitable relation
of that form to all others. More deeply, therefore, than
with the truth, spirit is concerned with conceiving,
loving, or hating what might have been true. Spirit
speaks not for the truth or for the intellect alone by
which truth is discovered, but speaks for all life, in so
far as life has been perfected and harmonized. Even
the intellect is an exercise of this spontaneous or poetic
faculty that rebels against the intellect; because the
categories of the intellect are variable and vital, like
those of language, and knowledge, like any other art,
trembles between a good and an evil fate.

The fine arts and the traditional religions are vast
instruments in the realm of matter, that seem to serve

the spirit directly, apart from utility or truth; yet even
they carry an immense load of impedimenta. All the

So is the   technical, scientific, historical, social, local,
value of   and temporal side of art and religion, that
imagination. absorbs so much blood and ink, has
nothing to say to the spirit about the Good.   At best,
the ground may be thereby cleared for a free spiritual
life, which will begin where those distractions end.   I
do not mean where they end historically, for they can
never end while life in this world continues.   I mean
where they culminate morally and provisionally and
yield their spiritual fruits.   These fruits are gathered
in moments of insight, recollection, and prayer.   They
are not probably novel fruits historically, but they are
always fresh and spontaneous for the spirit that develops
them.   They are not discoveries of facts in another
world, such as religious dogmas seem to a simple mind
to report, or such as the arts of fiction add to common
reality as it were in a dream.   We are not divorced
from the facts of this world in order to be subjected to
the facts of another world, expected to be better: that
is an illusion of the animal Will, unteachable and bent
on trying its luck for the second time.   We are divorced
by a revelation about the old and familiar facts, and
remarried to them by a new charity that understands
their hidden virtues and forgives their vices; a revelation
about our own lives and affections transfiguring them
in a superhuman light that robs us of ourselves and of
our world, only to return our world and ourselves to us
drenched in a truer Lethe, not of forgetfulness but of
eternity.

Might not the union to which we aspire be a union

Union with   with other spirits?   Might there not be
other spirits   a supreme spirit, or perfect form of spiritual
only inci-   life, to which all spirits were inwardly
dental.   directed?   At bottom, this suggestion introduces nothing new: if any spirit inwardly aspired to a

specific form of life, that form of life would be its good; and if all spirits aspired to the same form of life, that form of life would be the Good, absolute because universally relative. A supreme spirit that should actualize that ideal, as for instance by being omniscient, would possess the Good; and all lovers of the Good would be united with him morally, but not existentially, since the other spirits that aspired to omniscience without possessing it would *ipso facto* not be that supreme spirit itself, and could embrace that good only in prayer. If, on the other hand, we conceive the supreme spirit not as simply actualizing the good pursued by each spirit, but as a power with which all must reckon, union with the supreme spirit could never be wholly spiritual but would remain in some measure political, and such as pious souls without spiritual insight seek to establish in their religion. In seeking union with any other spirit we are therefore seeking either the Good, in that this other spirit realizes the perfection to which we are inwardly addressed; or else we are seeking such conformity with power and with truth as is necessary to the attainment of our proper good.

So the matter seems to end, if we take spirits existentially, and conceive union with them materially, as union in a tug-of-war. But a tug-of-war, and social union generally, does produce spiritual union; not because the spirits pull, as an absurd moral materialism supposes, but because when bodies pull well together, and psyches are akin, spirits for the time being become unanimous. Each has the very purpose, the very hope, that animates each of the others; and this actual spiritual unison is not unconscious. Spirit is divided into spirits by its organs, and into intuitions by its occasions; but we have seen that spiritually it is homogeneous and everywhere transcendental and potentially infinite. When, therefore, in two souls it thinks the same thought or

Spirits can be united only by thinking alike.

254 THE REALM OF SPIRIT

sees the same fact, while the intuitions remain two,
their object is identical: else we could never think twice
of the same thing privately, or ever think of the same
thing together. Yet we know that we do so, because
we are deeply aware of our animal separateness and
cohabitation. The presence of the friend or enemy
resets the whole soul, and there is nothing of which
we are more quickly conscious than of thinking alike
or of thinking differently. This feeling often leads to
rash alliances in the world, rash because real coopera-
tion does not depend on spiritual union but on
confluence of functions and interests, often more
harmonious and cooperative for being diverse: and the
spes animi credula mutui, in this world, is an *ignis fatuus*.
Yet not so in the other world, in the realm of spirit;
for there we are not looking for fidelity or active
support or common ascendancy over opinion, but for
the miraculous rhyming of mind with mind, when a
thought, we know not whence or why, re-echoes our
thought, confirms and clarifies it, setting it apart from
the flux of irrevocable sensation. This spiritual bond
is enough: the occasions when it is discovered may or
may not recur; the happiness lies in the sense of an
intuition once shared, a thought once anchored and
become domiciled in history. Then the clearness of
the light that had once shone upon us ceases to seem
barren: as if a star, burning alone, had news of another
star alive with the same fire.

Such unanimity would be a fact in the realm
of truth prior to being discovered: and when the
discovery brought a sense of spiritual fellowship, the
comfort of this added intuition would not make union
less spiritual. For we suppose material contact to
be absent or impossible, as when our unknown friend
is dead or not yet born or perhaps non-human; and
what we gain is only fellowship in worship, reduplicat-
ing the light that falls, within each of us, upon the

realm of ideas. The repetition of insights, though it may fortify an uncertain mind, is not spiritually important, and each angel, according to St. Thomas Aquinas, is the only individual of his species. In fact, the consideration of instances of spirit as events in nature is external to their spiritual import. Their occasions distribute them through physical space and time; but internally, though they are living acts, and in that sense events, they are distributed only by the relations of their subject-matter and individuated only by the ideas that they light up. Intellectually, two exactly similar intuitions make but one idea, being intuitions of the same essence. The multitude of witnesses, therefore, though it has animal weight, adds nothing to the truth or beauty of any revelation. It adds nothing to the happiness of pure life in the spirit.

That no spirit can absorb any other is evident, since spirit (as I use the word) is an act, not a transferable or transformable substance. Therefore any spiritual union actually experienced is necessarily specious and a pure datum of intuition. Not that a real union between spirits may not exist, in that separate minds may be unanimous; but this unanimity would be a fact external to their experience of it, a truth about them, which they might conceive and credit, but which could not in itself be a condition or ecstasy attained by either of them. Yet the union that mystics speak of seems to be emphatically a state into which they pass, internal, certain, and overwhelmingly actual. It has the surprising and all-solving character of a datum: and the character of a datum, by definition, is exactly the same whether it happens to be true or merely imaginary. Therefore the only spiritual union that can be certain, obvious, and intrinsically blissful, must be not a union between two spirits but the unity of a spirit within itself.

Actual union an experience of inner unity.

This conclusion is a corollary from the general critical principle that nothing given exists. That which certainly exists in such a case is only the intuition of that datum, not the datum in its own specious field, which is that of essence. So mystic union resides in intuition; it is not a union of objects or with objects, but a synthesis reached in life and expressed in a given quality of feeling. This is a feeling of union and bliss; but the given union does not exist (it would abolish the universe if it did), only the feeling of union exists; and if the bliss exists for a moment (not without a certain deceptiveness as to its absolute volume and finality) this is only because, in the case of inarticulate feelings, we give the same name to the intuition and to the quality revealed to that intuition. The feeling of bliss exists; the bliss, if taken for a secret reality revealed or for the truth of the universe, certainly does not exist. For the world continues to be just as divided, just as obscure, and just as little blissful as it was before.

It is an essence given, not a fact discovered.

Spiritual union with the Good does not, then, alter the general facts or discover any general truth. It is a new dawn within: where the sky was clouded, it is clear, namely, in the mind. The currents that confused and abolished one another before join now in one harmonious deliverance with an all-solving force. And we must not infer that there must be ignorance of the world or a pious monotony involved in this spiritual symphony. On the contrary, the whole torrent and violence of things swells within it and exalts it. There is nothing too painful or too audacious to be included, only it cannot be included as it would exist outside in separation and wilful blindness. The union into which it now enters transmutes it, and is a fact in another realm of being, a creation of the witnessing and recording spirit. Experience cannot

contain bodily any of its posited objects, or even its
own past, in its past existence; it can contain only the
thought of them. It obviously cannot make identical
the contradictory beliefs and desires afloat in the
universe; but it can compose, in thought, a single
drama out of their conflict, where the spectacle of their
folly turns into wisdom, and their ruin into salvation.

There might seem to be æsthetic cruelty and
intellectual selfishness in such an enjoyment of evil
at a speculative distance; and this would Is spiritual
indeed be the case, if spirit were a power happiness
and either produced or did not wish to selfish?
abolish the horrors of this world, in order to gloat on
them from a private heaven. But spirit has no power;
and the Will that supports and evokes spirit (and exerts
power to that extent) is entirely secondary and sympathetic, being the Will to understand all Will, and to
love all the goods that Will anywhere aspires to create.
Spirit therefore would not be expressing its own Will
if it condoned any evil or was dead to any good; but
its nature forbids it to *repeat* within itself the efforts,
sufferings, or pleasures that it understands; for it could
not then understand or transcend them. Such repetition would be ignominious, and would reduce spirit
again to utter captivity, while its vocation is precisely
dominion, spiritual dominion, without distraction, responsibility, or power. Not, however, without joy,
such as the full exercise of Will necessarily brings
when it is conscious.

Thus it is at once a sad, a comic and a glorious
spectacle that existence presents to spirit. Spirit would
never have *commanded* this performance, like a Nero,
if that had been within its power; it understands and
feels the inwardness of the matter far too well for that.
Yet it watches and records the whole with avidity,
though not without tears. How far this liberation of
spirit from all it finds afoot differs from selfishness

appears in this: that the evils spirit transcends are its
own sufferings, since no catastrophe in nature would
involve any evil if nature had remained unconscious.
Spirit captive has endured whatsoever spirit free may
turn into glowing tragedies; and it would contradict
its own Will if it did not rejoice in its final freedom.
Yet even this tragic wisdom and tearful rapture are
imposed on the spirit by a power above it. Had it
the choice, perhaps it would renounce this victory also,
and humbly prefer silence and peace; but choosing is
not its office; it cannot exist before it exists and decide
whether or not to bring itself into existence; and if
it thinks it can kill itself, that is a psychic illusion, for
it cannot prevent its rebirth. Nor is it asked to decide
how much is worth enduring in order that something
may be enjoyed.

Accepting that which is offered as, be it pious or
rebellious, spirit cannot help doing, it may distinguish
the direction in which its Good lies. It
lies in the direction of harmony; harmony
between the Will and its fortunes, and harmony within the subject-matter open to
apprehension. A world without evil in it,
that is, without contradiction in the Wills
animating the various parts, would be better than a
world in conflict. And if this seems to wash the field
of experience somewhat too clean, and to diminish too
much the risks and excitements of living, this feeling
must be pronounced vicious, and a remnant of perfectly
mad cruelty and masochism. There are creatures that
might, for a moment, find nothing interesting to do,
if evils ceased to torment them; yet if they had eyes
and hands they might soon find work without torment
and images without stain. The thunder of chaos
receding would render audible "the music of the
spheres": the life of a universe where the Good was
not posited but realized.

Evil, though it may be transmuted in reflection, is not there- by rendered desirable.

If we imagine this harmony hypostasized into an actual intuition, we conceive the mind of God in its omniscience and glory. It is therefore perfectly legitimate to say that the union craved is union with God, and that when we have experience of such union we are merged in God indistinguishably and feel that we become God. *If the Good were hypostasized the union with it could be only political.* Yet this can be true only of the essence that we have hypostasized into a divine person; and nothing proves that such a God exists or that we have been really united with him, or ceased to be our separate physical selves. On the contrary, if a true union of this kind is to take place between two existing spirits, it must be more than the experience of union, and God must be more than ourselves thinking we have become God. Our experience must be derived from its object and God must be a power infusing that experience into us by an act of grace, as is evidently the case in human love or mutual understanding. There would be no union and no society if our friends were all personages in our own novels; instead of being united with others we should only be deploying ourselves. This inner dialogue is indeed what the life of spirit terminates in at any given point or in any given person: it is all that *experience* can contain. Yet intelligence, which is the cream of experience, transcends experience by revealing to it its own secondary nature, and the existence of its thousand causes and companions; and union with these ambient realities, harmony between these free and independent facts, makes the surprise and the joy of friendship.

Here lies the human advantage that popular positive religion has over mystical insight: it brings us into communion with the gods, and socializes our inner comforts and aspiration by ascribing them to friendly intercessions and divine favours. The myth is deeply true and salu- *Advantage and disadvantage of religious impersonations.*

tary. We are not self-created spirits, but everything, including our best inspirations, comes to us from beyond ourselves, from the primeval fountains of matter. But the *dramatis personæ* of popular religion are fabulous and grow more and more novelesque as we make them more and more human. Intercourse with these invisible persons is not, even in fancy, an ideal union between spirits, but only social intercourse between psychic agents interacting under common conditions in a natural world. Even miracles, when they are admitted, obey the proprieties and conventions of some divine economy. Rather than the Good hypostasized, God now seems a particular monarch against whom we might rebel or to whom we might swear allegiance. His existence becomes a question of cosmology and political history, to be established by rational evidence.

The point would be important morally, inasmuch as, being a natural psyche with a Will shown in sporadic action, an existing deity might greatly influence the fortunes of other souls. He might be a great friend to some, but others would surely find him an enemy, because action in a particular world cannot possibly pursue or secure all particular goods, and the lovers of the goods sacrificed would cry to heaven against God for vengeance. "Heaven" would there signify all Good, unrealizable at any point in an existing world but inviolate in its essential authority and goodness. "God", on the other hand, would signify the power dominant over us for the time being. Job felt the conflict between these two claims to allegiance, that of the Good and that of the Lord; and the Whirlwind enforced the claims of power with a deafening eloquence, utterly unconvincing to the spirit. Many a pagan god might be blameless and perfect, and might point with pride to his mighty works, or even,

In society the greatest good is only the least of evils.

like Apollo and the Muses, to his inspiring or healing
influence. He might, in a sense, be holy, in that he
realized his chosen good absolutely, and remained
steadfast, whatever monstrous growths chaos might
vomit around him. But before a god of power could
speak persuasively to the spirit he would need in his
own person to be spiritual and religious. He would
need to be inspired by a perfect understanding and
love of all goods. In his action, however powerful
he might be, he could never bring all these goods at
once into existence. Probably, as no power can assure
itself against the intrusion of some other power, he
would be incapable of bringing even some goods into
existence in perfect order and uncontaminated; so
that his choice of the greatest possible good at each
moment would really be a choice of the least of evils.
To such a patient and merciful power spirit might
well cry, *Though thou slay me, yet will I trust in thee*;
and there would be a spiritual union possible with
the antecedent Will of God, addressed to universal
Good, as well as political submission and piety towards
his consequent Will, determining actual events.

Essentially, however, it is not with the gods of
popular religion that spiritual union is possible: they
are not themselves at peace with mankind, Without
with one another, or with the universe. denying the
Mystics are normally believers in the ortho- gods, spirit
doxy of their day, not being curious about union within
facts nor thinking opinion very important; itself.
yet they cannot help piercing the reigning myths, not
critically but interpretatively, and reaching truths about
the spiritual life at once more abstruse than traditional
dogmas and more intimate. Why does the mystic keep
his vigils and fasts, if not to escape from subjection to
things external, and in the first place from the cravings
and illusions of his individual self, the most accidental
of seats for the spirit and, as he feels, the most unworthy?

It would be a sorry failure to relapse in the end into the worship of earthly prosperity or disputatious learning, or into subjection to new accidental passions and hypnotic powers; and what else are the benefits proposed by popular religions?   Paradises, as the Indians know, are fit rewards for active virtue, temporal rewards for occasional good conduct; but paradises are but stepping-stones for the spirit; and what does it matter whether the stepping-stone be a lump of gold or of granite, if only the foot neither slips nor sticks there, but leaps easily to safety and freedom?   And this safety and freedom cannot be found in union with any existing being.   If we say it is union with Brahma we must understand by Brahma pure spirit present in all its instances, not any one instance, however extraordinary; and if in order to avoid mythology we speak rather of Nirvana, we must understand by this no passive lapse from existence but a moral victory over it, occasionally possible, though never physically final. What is suspended is not existence but ignorance, and what is gained is not indifference but equilibrium.

That spirit should have its centre in itself, wherever and whenever it may exist, so that all its adventures must be ideal and all its symbols internal and specious, follows from its transcendental nature.   This nature was clearly if inadequately expressed by Aristotle when he called it *intellect in act*; an act being a spontaneous, transitional, momentary exercise of life, and intellect being such an act in an animal psyche that has become perfectly cognitive and conscious.   But intellect is only the side of spirit that is addressed to knowledge and system; and life may be perfectly actualized also in feeling and in imagination.   Everywhere, however, this actuality will be conscious light, the dawn of attention making something present: so that spirit can neither escape from itself nor be confined to any given

Spirit always a consummation, never a finality.

object or sentiment. For these are present only in act, by being felt or conceived; and they have no hold on spirit, to prevent it from living on, and being differently active. That which can hold spirit down to steady objects and fixed categories is only the power of matter, which also elicits spirit itself; and the healthy limitations of the psyche give to each special spirit its special circle of sane thoughts. But an act is necessarily self-limited and self-delivered: what it does or thinks it can never undo or unthink; and spirit may shine again in another act, similar or dissimilar to the last, according to psychic and physical occasions.

The idea of final union with anything specific, even with omniscience or with pure Being, therefore contradicts the very nature of spirit. In one sense there is always union with so much as the spirit has clearly felt or conceived, since it is the same act that makes the actuality of spirit and the actuality of the feeling or thought. But in another sense, there is never union, never completion or finality, since an absorbed datum dies with the actual absorption in it; and no act, dying as it must in the process of living, can abolish or prevent a further act.

A sustained act would be perfectly possible if there were, as Aristotle supposed, perfectly sustained celestial motions. But everlasting sameness is something non-natural and a fabulous materialization of ideal eternity. Eternity belongs properly only to essences and truths, and may be extended by assimilation to intuitions in their deliverance, but never in their existence. In their existence intuitions are events: they arise and vanish; and in the interval they illustrate a *nunc stans*, since they fill a natural moment and actualize some essence or truth, in itself eternal. But the duration of such an actual *nunc stans* is not to be measured astronomically in fractions of a second or in light-years. It is a unit, however long

The nunc stans *how possible.*

sustained or however fugitive, in the realm of spirit, spiritually individuated by its quality and deliverance, not by its station (which it borrows from its organ) in physical time and space. For although each intuition has a date and a home in the physical world, if viewed from the outside or historically, when viewed from within each always stands in the middle of the temporal and spatial universe, introducing a moral centre into a flux where probably no centre exists physically.

These moral centres are as many as they happen to be; so that the realm of spirit is intrinsically a democracy (as the realm of truth is not), spirit being everywhere sovereign in its own right. This sovereignty, however, is only spiritual, as human equality, when not a sham, is only spiritual; and the sovereignty of each at home expressly invites and rejoices in the home sovereignty of all the others. For spirit exists; it is not a tyrannical idea, to be imposed on spirit; and existence is intrinsically dispersed, tireless, inexhaustible in its youth, ready to die and to be reborn, to discover and to re-discover, to sing sometimes an old song and sometimes a new one. The only totality or finality is ideal, it is the truth; but no view of the truth can be final in the life of spirit. Even omniscience, if it were possible, would not be final there; it would be a single instance of spirit, a supremely complex intuition. Simpler and partly ignorant intuitions would remain possible, and perhaps better. The truth that is requisite for the honour and peace of spirit is not omniscience but the absence of delusions; and this, where humility exists, does not demand infinite information. So it happens also when a man surveys his personal history. There is no contribution of experience that need be excluded from recollection, but the new total at each moment forms a new object, caught in a new intuition. The various

The galaxy of spirit.

perspectives have arisen in the same world; they contain
errors and contradictions if turned into absolute dogmas
and made to debate every point face to face, as if they
stood or ought to stand in one another's shoes; but
seen in their origin and causes, they are always complementary, explicable naturally, and unified objectively
in the realm of truth. Yet actually, in the realm of
spirit, every intuition is a flying spark, private,
momentary, and saved from total death only by its
ideal bonds and its inner vision of eternity. Each
spark, by the radiation of its light, has revealed for a
moment one region of heaven; and in that heaven it
is united, with its friends by mutual confirmation,
with its enemies by the common risks of existence and
a common appeal to the jurisdiction of fact. Intent
on the same reality, material or ideal, and spreading
over different parts of it, all intuitions, the greatest
with the least, form the galaxy of spirit.

This is an unwitting conspiracy of free natural
beings, each springing from its own seed in its own
country, and growing into whatsoever may   Thoughts
flow from the potentialities of its substance   remain in-
and fortunes. The union is a fact in the   dividual.
realm of truth: the fact that many spirits or instances
of spirit exist in the same universe, partly similar, partly
dissimilar, sometimes unanimous, sometimes complementary in their insights. I say again, complementary
rather than contradictory; because although judgments
may be contradictory if expressed in words, they
become supplementary phases in the history of judgment, when this history is surveyed as a whole. They
may be judgments about different objects; or in regard
to the same object, they may express different fractions
of the relations between that object and different souls.
The Babel is but the totality of languages; and if each
seems gibberish to the others, there is always some
analogy in their logics, for they are languages, and some

identity in their object, since they exist in the same world. So the galaxy of spirits has a natural orderliness in its moral confusion, and each spirit, in its solitude, a great kinship to all the others. Even if some or all, at the Last Judgment, should discover this spiritual society, which they had always composed without knowing it, no mind would become another mind, or like another; for even their common discovery of their relations would present these relations, in each case, in a different perspective; and an omniscient mind, in holding all perspectives at once in suspense, would differ enormously from all the other minds held by one perspective exclusively. Were not these personal histories and feelings eternally distinct, they could never orchestrate their celestial symphony.

On the other hand, it is not persons in their personal limitations, that can enter into a spiritual union; for the limitations are transcended in being understood, one's own limitations as well as other people's. Persons become translucent, like the souls in Dante's *Paradise*, and what each sees in the others is only that part of the truth which they saw. It is in them that this part became visible, for the truth is not visible to itself; therefore this remains a union of spirits, of thoughts living and thinking each its special thought. But the rest of the man disappears; as in reading a book, the material book is forgotten, and the reader lives in rehearsing the author's thoughts without thinking of the author. At least this happens when the book is interesting and the author was himself lost in his subject; the realm of spirit is not to be entered by literary peacocks, or by bibliophiles that do not read, but hoard their books, pat them, and talk about them. So in communion between spirits, the man or the god is rendered invisible by the light he diffuses, and we are inwardly united only with so much of him as by his gifts or his grace can exist also beyond his

person and can become a part of ourselves. For
the spirit, therefore, the dead are still living, and
the living are present *numina*, like the remembered
dead.

This is not to say that the real existence of persons,
or that contact or friendship with them, has not a real
function, and one prior to the function of
ideas. Friends are important for the spirit,
as a man's own identity and fortunes are
important. Without such special occasions and attachments, spirit would have no foothold in nature
and could not exist. Occasions, we have said, distribute spirit among psyches and divide each spirit
into intuitions. Yet intuition itself is born out of
a synthesis, and the field it opens up embraces, in
conception, all that the flux of existence may have
diversified and separated. The world was not made
for the spirit, nor by the spirit, as the beautiful is; but
for this very reason the world and the truth about the
world have a tutelary function, and a guiding function,
in the life of spirit. They are the gates through which
the garden of the beautiful may be safely entered, the
walls by which that garden is circumscribed and
defended. The first step towards union with the Good
is to have settled one's accounts with the world and
with the truth. After that, truth and fiction may be
entertained together, and the difference between them
may be ignored. Yet this licence, which the world
takes for incompetence or madness in spiritual men,
would really be madness or incompetence if it were not
founded on health, on adjustment to universal power,
and on a deep ironical allegiance to the truth. When
such moral health is presupposed the perspectives of
truth and of fiction may be developed together, with
no spiritual fear of either, since the agile spirit can
digest both.

If union must be unity within the spirit, might we

The nest and the wings.

not say finally that the Good is the existence of spirit itself? Not at all. Spirit is evidently a prerequi-
Spirit not site to union within the spirit; but spirit is
itself the more often distracted than harmonious;
Good. and the attainment of harmony depends on
many other causes than those that suffice to evoke spirit. The causes and conditions of the Good are not themselves good: else matter and universal Will would be good, and more radically good than spirit, since they are needed to generate it. The Good lies not behind all this movement but before it; it is the end that life proposes to itself when conscious and rational. Each endeavour furnishes spirit, which is by nature sym-pathetic, with an initial criterion of values; whatsoever helps each flower to grow seems good to the dramatizing spirit, and whatsoever blights it, seems evil. But how shall the relative value of these endeavours be judged? The most considered judgment could only express some other instance of initial Will, a preference as contingent and groundless as those it criticizes. Shall the spirit succumb to this universal egotism and judge that whatsoever in the universe conduces to the free exercise of spirit shall be pronounced good, and what-soever hinders that exercise shall be pronounced evil?

Such a shamelessly egotistical judgment is in fact implicit in so much of unconscious Will as rushes
Understand- blindly to create spirit. But the peculiarity
ing and love of spirit, when once it exists, is not to be
must make blind, and to be eternally ashamed of egotism.
no claims
for them- Its Will is not to will, but to understand all
selves. Will; and so without willing any of the ends that universal Will pursues (not even the Will to create spirit) it sees the beauty of all those ends, including the beauty of its own impartial but enamoured vision. Spirit too is only an incident in the life of nature; the Will to be spiritual can as little be pronounced to be absolutely good as can any other natural impulse; yet

like any other natural impulse, when once launched into life, it inevitably becomes a criterion, by which all other things may be judged relatively.

Therefore the spirit, if free to criticize its enemies, is free also to judge its own aspirations tragically or satirically; and the higher flights of wisdom and self-knowledge have always done so. Never, however, when spirit is vigorous and free, can it judge any fate coldly or any aspiration unsympathetically; because to be sympathetic and warm towards all endeavours (though they may know nothing of themselves) is the very essence of spirit; and how then should it not be so towards its own endeavours? Yet this acceptance and pursuit of its specific aims will never be safe or pure until they are qualified by a prior complete renunciation of all illusions about them. The spirit can never be altogether spiritual, or morally other than a caprice of blind Will, until it has traversed the *Dark Night* described by Saint John of the Cross, and adopted his motto: *Nothing, Nothing, Nothing.* It is only on this understanding that all things may be understood without confusion, loved without disgrace, and touched without infection, or that a life of action, for the spirit, can be a life of prayer. Henceforth we are playing a part: we do not become kings because we may wear a crown upon this stage, nor fools because it is set down for us to talk nonsense. We may give commands, when they are in character, without arrogance, follow our fortunes without greed, and declare our affections without fear of disillusion. The disillusion has come already, and the affection flows out notwithstanding, without any claims. We know that the power that creates us and shapes our passions and prompts our acts is the Poet's, and not our own; that our knowledge is but faith moving in the dark, our joy a gift of grace, our immortality a subtle translation

The great witness is the great victim.

of time into eternity, where all that we have missed is ours, and where what we call ours is the least part of ourselves. We are not impatient of injustice. It is not the fate that overtakes us that makes our dignity but the detachment with which we suffer it. All belongs to the necessary passion and death of the spirit, that to-day rides upon an ass into its kingdom, to be crucified to-morrow between two thieves, and on the third day to rise again from the dead.

In the animal psyche the passions follow one another or battle for supremacy, and the distracted

Spirit con- spirit runs helter-skelter among them, im-
centrated is pressed by the sophistical arguments which
clarified. each of them offers for itself; but if the psyche grows integrated and rational, its centre, which is the organ of spirit, becomes dominant, and all those eloquent passions begin to be compared and judged, and their probable issue to be foreknown and discounted. The waves will not be stilled, but they will now beat against a rock. And with inner security comes a great inner clearness. We may now become aware of the world to any depth, in any degree of complexity. We shall have reduced our psychic centre to its precise function as a centre; and from this centre, in duly shaded perspectives, the spirit may spread its silent light over all nature and all essence.

By so fortifying the spirit we shall not have saved the world; all its titular saviours have left the world much as it was. But we can reconcile ourselves with the world by doing it justice. It is a natural process: why should it have been other than it happens to be? We shall also have reconciled ourselves with our own destiny. Materially, we could not be more than poor animal experiments, lame yet wonderful, defeated yet breaking out in places into a jubilant sympathy with all creation. Spirit may live in its universal affinities, forgiving itself its ignorant errors and childish woes.

It could not have suffered if it had not loved, and to
love is to have eyes for the beautiful. This privilege
is bought at a great price, but spirit speaks for a part
of universal Will, for that part which becomes conscious. It is therefore essentially brave, as it is
essentially enamoured; and the goal once seen, it
cannot count the cost.

Intermittence is intrinsic to life, to feeling, to
thought; so are partiality and finitude. Spirit cannot
achieve unity or perfection physically; the *And is*
living flame must dance. It suffices that its *united with*
light should fall on things steadfast and true, *all things,*
thinking
worthy to be discerned and returned to and *itself no-*
treasured; so that though spirit be every- *thing.*
where halting in achievement it may be always perfect
in allegiance. Its happiness must always remain volatile, and its union with the Good ideal. This union
is achieved not by physical possession or identity, but
by intellectual worship, in which spirit, forgetting itself,
becomes pure vision and pure love. Then to the spirit
that has renounced all things, all things are restored:
and having renounced itself also, it cannot resist any
inspiration or think evil of any good, but embraces them
all in the eternal object of its worship, not as they may
have existed in the world in passing and in conflict,
but as they lie ideally reconciled in the bosom of the
Good, at peace at last with themselves and with one
another.

CHAPTER X

GENERAL REVIEW OF *REALMS OF BEING*

HAVING, after sixteen years, brought this work at last to an end, let me look back and consider how far the performance has been true to the intention.

I said in the Preface to *Scepticism and Animal Faith*, "Here is one more system of philosophy"; and I pro-

The plan of
this work
and the
execution.

ceeded to warn the reader that this system would not aspire to be new or personal or metaphysical or a system of the universe. It would be a revision of the categories of common sense, faithful in spirit to orthodox human tradition, and endeavouring only to clarify those categories and disentangle the confusions that inevitably arise when spontaneous fancy comes up against an intricate inhuman world.

Unfortunately, as some of my readers think, my own fancy is too spontaneous, interfering with an accurate and orderly exposition of facts and arguments: so that, contrary to my promise, my system is personal and new-fangled, without being original, and is extravagantly metaphysical in places, as for example in regard to the realm of essence. Nor does it escape being, in effect, a system of the universe, since the realm of matter, conceived mechanically, here forms the groundwork of all existence, the realm of spirit being only a sort of invisible vegetation flourishing in some of the stars, and the realm of truth a history of those happenings; while the realm of essence is but an infinite void presupposed, a part of which is occupied by the other realities.

Is this a fair report?   I think it is, in the sense that such a photograph might be taken of my system in a bad light at a great distance. The impression would truly proceed from the object, but would not render its true characteristics. My philosophy neither is nor wishes to be scientific; not even in the sense in which, in temper and method, the *Summa* of St. Thomas might be called scientific. My philosophy is like that of the ancients a discipline of the mind and heart, a lay religion. In saying that I did not intend it to be personal, I meant that I was to rely on the common and notorious state of mankind, and to discount as much as possible the special circumstances and influences to which I might have been subject. I did not mean that my philosophy was not to spring from the inner man and not to embrace all my faculties and interests working together, but was to be a dry compilation of other men's theories and arguments, with judicial comments. I like theories and arguments when they are spontaneous and not used to refute one another; but they come to me as refinements or excursions. The large facts, the great interests by which theories and arguments are to be judged, are known to me, as to everyone else, in the daily process of living. My philosophy endeavours to enlighten this process morally, and to define its ultimate issues.

This philosophy is ordinary reflection systematized, or lay religion.

Philosophy so conceived, though it need not be new, ought certainly to be fresh. There must always be some variation in thinking the most orthodox thoughts, and I hardly know how much novelty of this kind may have crept into my ideas; but my happiness lay in understanding the ancients (or thinking I understood them) rather than

Not meant to found a new sect.

in contradicting them; and I should dislike to frame an unprecedented opinion, unless at least I thought it more congruous with common sense than what people repeat habitually, and better fitted to become conventional. I should prefer that something of me should subsist anonymously buried in the public mind, than that my name should remain attached for a few years to some technical curiosity.

That this system was to be frankly ontological, and not humanistic like my earlier writings, was obvious from the very title, *Realms of Being*, and was admitted from the beginning, since three of the four realms distinguished were non-material and two of them non-existential. The system is therefore quite properly called metaphysical, in the current literary sense of the word. But I was reserving the term metaphysics for a particular, though widespread, abuse of super-material categories; an abuse that occurs whenever logical, moral, or psychological figments are turned into substances or powers and placed beneath or behind the material world, to create, govern, or explain it. When I aver that my ontology is not metaphysics, I do not mean that I admit nothing but "data" or "sensations" into my philosophy. I mean that I regard all immaterial things, in so far as they exist or are true, as qualities, products, or ideal implications of the physical world. Nature certainly could not have existed or produced our minds, if it had adopted no form or method of existing; but this form or method is arbitrary, contingent, and essentially variable, so that in its ideal essence it has no power or prerogative to impose itself on existence. Physics, not metaphysics, therefore reveals to us, as far as it goes, the *foundations of things*; and ontology is a subsequent excursus of the mind, as in non-Euclidean geometry, over all that the facts may suggest to the fancy.

Ontological but naturalistic.

From this it appears how far my system is from
being a description of the universe. It is immensely
more, since it contains, or might contain, The place
everything that logic, poetry, or religion of science in
might invent; yet it is immensely less, since this system.
it remains absolutely passive and modest in respect to
the facts reported by natural science and by credible
history. My very flights into the supra-material render
me docile to the darkness and contingency of this
world. In respect to the facts I am ready to accept
anything that the experts may tell us for the moment,
to accept it as I do the weather, without cavil but
without excessive confidence. When I was younger
what was pompously called Science wore an imposing
aspect. There was a well-dressed Royal Family in
the intellectual world, expected to rule indefinitely:
sovereign axioms, immutable laws, and regent hypotheses. We had Newtonian space and time, the
conservation of energy, and Darwinian evolution.
Now there is a democracy of theories elected for short
terms of office, speaking shop-dialects, and hardly
presented or presentable to the public eye. The
investigator's technique takes the lead, not the exigences
of popularizing eloquence. The frontiers of this
science seem less secure, with vast claims to un-
discovered or undiscoverable regions; and first
principles at home are wobbly and vague. Yet this
looseness in thought goes with ingenuity in methods
and multiplicity of contacts; and it serves to dispel an
illusion that better-digested science might create: the
illusion that scientific ideas reveal the literal and
intimate essence of reality, as the images of sense
certainly do not. But the fact is that both sense and
science are relatively and virtually true, being appropriate to the organ employed and to the depth to which
this organ may penetrate into the structure of things
or may trace their movement. The senses do this well

enough, in their own terms, for the uses of animal and social life; but modern science approaches the dynamism of nature by means of artificial instruments and experiments: hence its astonishing mechnical applications, and its moral and pictorial blindness.   It studies methods rather than objects; it works indirectly if not directly in the service of industrialism, which needs to manipulate and not to understand; and if it succeeds in its manipulations it has done its duty.   But this is a very special development, perhaps temporary, and certainly not fundamental in human knowledge. The images of sense will be with us while the human race endures.   They will always yield our classical and personal view of nature.   The stars will remain the visible stars, no matter what science may tell us about them; earth, water, air, and fire will still confront the spirit, and survive the disintegration that chemistry may subject them to.   Ultimately the authority of science will always depend on the evidence of sense and on the analogy of familiar objects and events.

So too with the authority of history, which is much more closely bound up than physics with the life of The place   spirit.   History extends a man's dramatic of history.   view of his own life and of contemporary society into the past, by the aid of documents and monuments.   History is true or plausible fiction, such as we compose instinctively concerning one another's motives and mind and even concerning our own.   This current knowledge that we have of ourselves is most slippery and deceptive: our memories, expectations, and reading of other people's minds would run wild in a moment, if they were not controlled by well-certified physical facts; and it is the course of physical events, observed on the human scale, that guides psychological imagination in reconstructing the past, in so far as imagination can be guided at all.   Drop that thread, and you have passed at once into poetry and legend.

In general, it would avoid misunderstanding to remember that essence, matter, truth, and spirit are not, in my view, separate cosmological regions, The limits of separately substantial, and then juxtaposed. scepticism. They are summary categories of logic, meant to describe a single natural dynamic process, and to dismiss from organized reflection all unnecessary objects of faith. Essence is not an object of faith, but a least ultimate term in scepticism, showing how little evidence there can be for faith of any sort, since all data are in themselves dream-data, actual in that we evolve them, like a pain, but false in that they do not otherwise exist. And in regard to the realm of matter I propose no theories, but only ask a preliminary question, namely: What presuppositions do we make in pursuing knowledge of anything? And I reply: We presuppose that there is some real object or event to be known or reported, prior or subsequent to the report that reaches us. In other words, we presuppose existent facts about which our affirmations may be false or true. About these facts our knowledge will be true, as far as it goes, if we have access to them and discount the relativity and partiality of our perceptions and theories. To assert this principle of realism is no more than honesty. Such trust in animal faith is involved in action and in the impulse to look for, to describe, or to make anything. It is the first presupposition of intelligence and sanity, and any scepticism that denies it asserts it.

Similarly what I lay down about the realm of spirit involves no system of idealism, psychological or Platonic, no eschatology, no providential or magic philosophy of history. On this subject, too, I am as sceptical as it is possible for me to be with sincerity; but just as I would reject all hypostasized myths, so I would reject all affectation of disbelief where life and action render belief inevitable and perpetually renew it. I posit therefore that the realm of matter is

animated by spirit, as in myself, so in my fellow-
creatures, as far as my sympathies avail to conceive
that animation spontaneously, or my experience, reflectively, to confirm my divinations. Even in regard to
one's inner history one's notions are insecure, unless
they are controlled by external evidence, like that of
old actions or old letters; and self-knowledge grows less
out of memory than out of discipline and concentration
of thought, because spirit is not a phenomenology of
spirit but the act of witnessing, reviewing, and judging
natural facts. In regard to the extent and detail of the
realm of spirit, then, all must be hypothesis and literary
fiction, to be indulged in by poets, historians, and
critics as their genius may prompt or their prudence
allow. In reconstructing the *moral* history of spirit,
however, we are not left without guidance. There is
a traditional language, the language of poetry and
religion, in which the essential fortunes of spirit are
recorded, and these traditions impose themselves, like
other external facts, upon each new soul; yet they count
spiritually only in so far as they are confirmed or re-
discovered in each case. Spirit cannot live except alone.

  In regard to my intended allegiance to common
sense, I confess that in several important matters I
Divergences have not been able to maintain it. There
from com- are too many traditional equivocations and
mon sense. inconsistencies in human language, for instance in respect to spirit, which in current parlance
retains its original sense of breath or invisible force,
while also used, as I use it, for intellectual light.
There are also too many vestiges of myth and superstition in moral and religious convictions. And in
fact it was not common *opinion* that I respected or
wished to follow, especially not the common opinions
of my time, which I instinctively abhorred. It was
rather the common *intellect* that I wished to adopt and
to fortify in myself, after the manner of Aristotle; and

even this not from any absolute reverence for the intellect, as if it were infallible or universally competent, but because I felt myself to be inevitably an accomplice in that vital adventure. I must think humanly or I could not think at all. My allegiance to common sense is distinctly not religious but political or grammatical, and therefore from a spiritual point of view accidental: something particularly obvious to a man whose spiritual attachments lie in one quarter and his linguistic attachments in another.

To have drawn this distinction between the natural and the spiritual sphere I do not regard as itself a break from human orthodoxy. All intellectual nations have had prophets, poets, and mystics whom they have honoured as certainly wiser than the vulgar rationalist; and this because in every man there is an alternation and opposition between the outer and the inner life. While in the rush of action and talk he must rely on conventional assumptions, in repose, in sorrow, in art, in love, or in prayer he is aware of passing to another order of considerations, unreal to the world, but most important to himself. Perhaps he thinks there are two worlds, or two criteria of truth: but this is precisely one of the points where I part company with tradition. To double the world would unspiritualize the spiritual sphere: to double the truth would make both truths halting and false. There is only one world, the natural world, and only one truth about it; but this world has a spiritual life possible in it, which looks not to another world but to the beauty and perfection that this world suggests, approaches, and misses. On this point, although I am perfectly willing to stand alone, I rather expect that posterity may agree with me: not that mankind will ever accept or remember my philosophy, but that, by fellowship with what is perennial in their hearts, I shall have had a foretaste of their sentiments.

Matter and spirit not two worlds.

The primitive mind is inevitably superstitious; that is to say, it attributes power to appearances and turns accidents into laws. All that is requisite in order to transform such superstition into a critical philosophy is to trace back all power to the continuous transformation of physical forces, in other words, to matter; and at the same time, by the same insight, to recognize all appearances to be mere appearances, and all accidents mere accidents, sensible signs of power manifest to the spirit, but having no substance or power in themselves.

All four realms involved in the life of nature.

This simple dissolution of superstition yields three of my realms of being: matter, as the region and method of power; essence, as the proper nature of appearances and relations; and spirit as the witness or moral sensibility that is subject to the double assault of material events and of dramatic illusions. There remains the realm of truth, which is the total history and destiny of matter and spirit, or the enormously complex essence which they exemplify by existing.

This rejection of superstition preserves the original categories of the animal mind: power succumbed to, feared or exerted, and images distinguished. But the animal mind, and the psychologism that tends to revert to it, do not keep these two categories distinct, but employ them together; and this for a manifest reason. Man, as Aristotle would say, is a compound; he exists at once in the realm of matter and in that of spirit. It is as an individual animal, one person with two natures, that he is named, and finds himself acting and talking. He constantly exerts power, sometimes visibly by bodily acts; but often the physical sources of his power are hidden from his mind, or not attended to, and he attributes his action to his ideas. But his ideas have no place in the traceable sequence of material events; they brood over that flux like the invisible gods or the laws of nature. This

Superstitions root of psychologism.

magic of laws, images, and words he interpolates into the hidden continuities of matter; and as his thoughts are fed by passion more than by observation, his beliefs remain inveterately mythical. To be essentially poetical seems to me a virtue and not a vice in the mind; and the illusion involved when thought professes to be transparently cognitive may easily be corrected. It is corrected instinctively in poetry, which ceases to deceive without ceasing to be significant; and it might be corrected in science if data as well as theories were recognized to be only symbols, deceptive to the idolater, who takes them for substances, but true indications to the enlightened man, who takes them for signs. This recognition of the ideal character of the given seems to me to emancipate the spirit from a horrible net of contradictions in its cognitive pretensions and to restore it to its proper poetic and religious function.

The critics will tell the public that I run hopelessly away from common sense in denying the material efficacy of spirit. Yet this is a misunderstanding, because neither the critics nor the public take the word spirit in my sense. They understand by it the self, the soul, the psyche: and nothing could be farther from me than to deny the interaction of the psyche—that is, of bodily life—with surrounding events. The continuity of these motions, outside a man, in through his senses, out through his impulses, into his actions and influence, is perfectly obvious. His senses and impulses will not be aroused without arousing his spirit; so that it is quite true that if he had been unconscious most of his actions would have been different, or rather would not have occurred at all. He would have been asleep. In sleep, it is not spirit that departs or determines to close the eyes, but the eyes that close of themselves, and shut the world out from the spirit. With eyes closed, a man will certainly not act as if his eyes were open:

The inefficacy of spirit inherent in its nature.

and when the physical cause of his lethargy or gropings is so evident, it is sheer myth to suppose the cause to be the absence of light in his mind. That light is eclipsed, as everyone can prove experimentally at any moment, because the eyes are closed. Spirit is therefore a concomitant effect of physical causes and not a separate cause descending from another world.

To read actions in terms of spirit and to divine the thought that doubtless accompanied them

Knowledge of it is intensive but insecure. is perfectly legitimate in principle although often mistaken in practice. I call it literary psychology and believe that when the mind-reader and the mind read are genetically akin, it may be more literally true than any other kind of knowledge. Yet it is essentially divination, not science. Scientific psychology must be behaviouristic: it can discover, not what spirits feel or think, but what people are likely to say and do under specific conditions. This science cannot prevent people from being erratic; but if they are so, it will not be because spirit in them intervenes, but because there is or may be an indeterminable element in erratic psyches, as in erratic atoms or stars. Spirit in those cases will be erratic too, and may possibly go quite mad and dissolve into a chaos of shocks and images. I do not, then, deny either the efficacy or the indetermination of human action or Will, but only a miraculous interference of spirit or of visionary objects with the flux of matter.

The universe, however broken and inconsequential may be its course, is what it is as a whole; but

Psychic *versus* spiritual freedom. this totality is itself contingent; so that while I have not the least faith or hope in indeterminism, I see that all regularity is relative and factual, and by no means imposed on existence by any essence or law. The freedom that so many people, learned and unlearned, passionately wish to possess is a vital freedom, freedom to be themselves, and to bring to light the potentialities of their psyches, all knocking at the door of life. This freedom exists; and though variously modified by the acquired habits of the psyche, it belongs fundamentally to all life, if not to all change. Everything is what it is by its own initiative, not because some other thing was like it earlier, and compelled it to repeat that essence. Essences are all passive, and the flux of existence is as self-guided at every point as at the beginning.

As to the freedom proper to spirit, this is no power to move matter by magic, but the fact of being sometimes liberated from distraction and permitted to be pure spirit. Magic may be real enough, the magic of a word or an act, grafted upon the invisible influences that course through the material world; but no spiritual religion, in availing itself of magic and miracles, regards them as the measure of spirit. A spiritual man may say: "Take up thy bed and walk." That is the psyche speaking to the psyche. But when he says "Thy sins are forgiven thee," the spirit is speaking to the spirit.

That God is a spirit, though the text be orthodox, has never been the popular belief, nor have theologians taken it seriously. As a man seldom identifies himself with the spirit in him, but at best speaks of spirit as something higher than has descended upon him and possessed him, so in thinking of God the dominant *Universal power deserves reverence, but is not a spirit.* consideration is that God is a power at work in the world, as man is an agent there; and as man attributes his actions to his feelings, so he introduces feelings into the powers in nature, according to their operation. But this mythology, like his own psychology, is in the air, and criticism should lead him to attribute to his gods *only the powers which they exercise*; as to-day, if we speak of the Muses, we mean only the inspiration actual in artists, with its obscure natural sources, and not nine invisible young ladies whispering our thoughts to us. So God in Spinoza becomes identical with Nature, speculatively magnified; and if I retained the word God, as I do not in this connection, my result would be even more scandalous, since God, conceived merely as a power, would become identical with matter, the omnificent substance and force in everything. It should be remembered, however, that sunshine and rain, the stars and the harvests, justify many of the emotions and virtues cultivated by religion; and it is in the economy of nature that divine beneficence, justice, and wrath are manifested. If mankind had always lived without contact with open rural nature, as does the proletariat in large modern cities, mankind would have had no religion, but would have perished believing that it could be saved by its wishes and votes and the eloquence of politicians. Disrespect for matter, ignorance of the real seat and method of substance and power, therefore kills the belief in God at its roots.

By definition there is an *ens realissimum*, though this be but a blanket-name to cover all the radical, pervasive, and terrible influences to which the spirit is subject. When people ask, Does God exist? the question is really verbal. They are asking whether the reality signified by the notion of God, if we understood that reality better, could still bear the name of God, or had better be designated by some other word. This is at bottom the whole question in dispute between theists and atheists.

Now in this verbal sense, and in respect to popular religion that thinks of God as the creator of the world and the dispenser of fortune, my philosophy is atheistic. It puts all substance and power into the realm of matter; and although this realm presupposes essence, creates spirit, and involves truth, yet in its dynamic procedure it takes no account of those accompaniments, and excludes the spiritual and moral vitality implied in the word God.

Sense in which this system is atheistic.

God, at least for Jews, Christians, and Moslems, must be a power that is a spirit, and a spirit that is a sovereign power. As I place spirit and power at opposite ends of the ontological scale, and of cosmic evolution, making spirit the fruit and enjoyment of power, but no part of its radical energy, I must be pronounced an atheist in this company. I am not even a pantheist, as if I regarded the whole realm of matter as an organ of spirit; for then, even if the dynamic order were purely mechanical, the omnipresence of spirit and the pervasive ministration of matter to moral ends, would allow us to say that the universe was a divine body with a divine mind. But that, in my opinion, is a false extension of spirit, where the animal and moral conditions for perfection and for consciousness are absent; so that while I regard spirit as the culmination of life, at least in our planet, I am far from regarding all nature as directed upon spirit, or intelligible to it, or good in its eyes.

Still the question is not settled, since there are developments even in the Hebraic idea of God, that transcend the spheres of power and of con- *Truth and* sciousness; and there are also other religious *essence* traditions, Indian and Greek, in which I *identical* might seem less heretical. I have revived, *with the* in a form clearer than is customary, the *idea of God* perennial notions of truth and of pure Being, *able from it.* or as I call it, the realm of essence. I should not myself identify either of these notions with the idea of God. Truth is but the complete character of the universe seen under the form of eternity; and essence, in its infinity, is but the field of all the complementary characters that any given character excludes. Both this infinity and that eternity transcend mutation, transition, and local emphasis, and therefore transcend life. Neither can be a living God; yet unless the idea of God somehow included them it would remain a wholly mythical poetic idea without philosophic or rational warrant. And if the existence of divine forces were to be shown empirically, by miracles or historical evidences of design, we should have new but limited knowledge of nature, and not any inward, speculative, or religious revelation. Therefore it is not surprising that the most concentrated and speculative minds, if not the most religious, should have regarded sometimes truth and sometimes pure Being as the supreme reality.

That pure Being should be thought of as alone real and divine may seem strange, yet is explicable, because the sense of instability and vanity in all existing things, supervening upon animal love of life and of self, produces a spiritual longing for peace and security in a heaven where all that is possible shall be understood and nothing that is transitory shall be loved. Then pure Being, something neutral, infinite, and eternal, may become the focus of the prayerful mind. Dialectically too for its unity and omnipresence, and æsthetically for the clearness of all its modes, pure essence can fascinate the intellect, as we see in the Eleatics and Pythagoreans. In Spinoza the flight from contingency leads to the same goal; for although we perceive nothing of substance except agitated extension and agitated thought, yet, when he comes to define that substance ideally, what he defines is neither matter nor mind, but precisely the realm of essence, namely, infinite Being, deployed in an infinite number of attributes, each attribute again deployed in an infinite number of modes. It is true that, without the least shadow of evidence, he attributes existence to this enormously imaginary Being, and identifies it with his Nature-or-God; but that is a vestige of idolatry. As for me, partial as I am to the realm of essence, and happy in the presence of non-existent objects, when they are beautiful or significant, it would never occur to me to eulogize *all* essence. That would be treason to human nature and to the

Esoteric deification of pure Being.

Good; because even if much that to the human mind is tedious or horrible might be acceptable from some other point of view, animal or divine, that would be because some living psyche found its happiness in that object. For as Spinoza himself says,[1] the great advantage that the imaginary may have over the true is that free intuition evokes it; whereas in the perception or report of matters of fact, vital spontaneity cannot be perfect, but is constrained by the occasion, by the distribution and unhappy changes in its objects, and by irrelevant stimulation or lapses of attention. Perfection is better than truth; but perfection itself is relative to a definite existing nature and its spontaneous functions; so that to worship infinite Being as good or sublime, and to make a God of it, inverts the moral order. There would be a better excuse for worshipping matter, since it is matter that feeds and kills us, and these are the functions that popular religion first attributes to the deity. But to worship essence, which can do nothing, merely because it is infinite and ineffaceable, would be a refined madness, fortunately not likely to prove contagious when its true object is understood. Shreds and echoes of such aberrations nevertheless mingle in religious tradition, adding a touch of false mystery to honest piety, or of common superstition to spiritual life.

The realm of truth has a much closer relation to the object of human religion. Many truths are important, and all truth is a sublime standard of reference for science, for speculation, and for the conscience suffering from doubt or injustice. To appeal to God, or to feel God's eye upon us is a dramatic way of invoking the inexorable truth. But is the truth God, or is God merely a name for the truth? Not properly speaking: and we may verify this judgment by observing how the philosophers

Intellectual deification of the truth.

[1] See the motto opposite the title-page.

whose highest category might seem to be the truth, for instance Plato or Hegel, have to subtract all detail from nature in order to obtain Ideas or an Idea that might be identified with God: and how even after that thinning of the full truth, they would be unmistakable atheists, unless they added a living intuition, a personal psyche, to the Idea or Ideas, in order to raise them from the realm of truth into that of spirit.

When this is done, we reach the orthodox philosophical notion of God in Aristotle and Plotinus. Here Mythical God is by no means the truth, being ignorant deification of all facts: but he is an influence, radiating of the Good. from the realized enjoyment of all perfections in one act of thought; the effect being to diffuse those perfections, as far as matter permits, through the whole realm of matter and of created or fallen spirit. This theology is sublime, refining into pure spirit the turbid life of the universe: but that life remains as turbid as it was before, because this theology is mythical. The Good from which all goods are supposed to be derived, is a hypostasis of their common quality of goodness, not realizable psychologically, nor even ideally; because each possible good is specific, and the enjoyment of them all at once would be the enjoyment of none separately, as alone it can *exist*. So that as the God of Aristotle and Plotinus is avowedly ignorant of all facts, knowing only types of perfection, so he is ignorant of all actually realized goods, except the single one of his own rapture. This sun feels itself burning and sheds universal light; but it is blind to all refraction, to all colour, and to all shadow.

Truth, then, and excellence, even when reduced to a moral outline or programme of the cosmos, cannot A God must be sublimated into a deity. Deity must be be a spirit. spirit; and it must be a supreme instance of spirit, freed from all the trammels that depress spirit in ourselves. It must be posited, as spirit in any instance may posit spirit elsewhere, socially and naturalistically, as a separate invisible existence.

Does my philosophy compel or allow me to posit such a divine spirit or spirits? Certainly it does not compel me, nor does it even invite me to do so with any plausibility; because spirit, in my system, must be the spirit of some body, the consciousness of some natural life; and we find no bodies or psyches in nature that suggest to us, as they did to the ancients, a divine animation. I know that pantheistic poets retain that feeling, yet I have but scant respect for it. It seems to me to be vitiated by two childish fallacies: one, to attribute spirit to sunsets and storms known to be mechanical accidents; the other, to imagine that, if spirit animated such phenomena, it would have any kinship with human aspirations. Genuine mythology would see divine fecundity, where there is exuberance, and divine fury where there is destruction; and it would grow feebler and feebler, and more and more literary, as it began to humanize those fables, and to find "books in the running brooks, sermons in stones, and good in everything."

The genuine inspiration of modern religion is moral, and drawn from the difficulties, hopes, and joys of the spirit. In this capacity, as expressing the inner life, it may be interesting; but it has absolutely no standing-ground in external fact, and therefore supplies no evidence of the existence of non-human spirits.

That divine spirits may nevertheless exist, without their bodies being visible to us, or their influence such as to awaken in us any sense of their pre- Any existing
sence, I should be the last to deny. Our Gods would
science cannot fathom the realm of matter, be cosmic
incidents.
either inwards or outwards; and there can
be no just presumption that, beyond the dynamic cosmos to which we have access, other worlds rich in things unimaginable to us may not exist. But such

blank possibilities are uninstructive, and they benumb religion rather than stimulate it. The God of tradition might himself wonder how many other gods unknown to him might not exist, and he might be shaken by that thought in his presumptive omnipotence and omniscience. The bastions of any existing heaven may some day be stormed. Security lies in a different dimension, where no cosmic thieves can break in or steal. It lies not in being protected by spirits beyond us, but in the nature of the spirit within.

When this exclusively spiritual autonomy of spirit is thoroughly understood, the existential dependence of spirit becomes inoffensive. Inoffensive, I mean, to the philosopher examining the nature and dignity of spirit; not inoffensive to the spirit itself, enduring the accidents of fortune. But these accidents, cruel as they may be, are the indispensable occasions for asserting the autonomy of spirit now in one place now in another, and exercising all its spiritual rights. If spirit were not physically distributed and evoked among the animals, and perhaps among the stars, it would have no home in nature, no point of view fixed for each incarnation, no moral character, no tragic interests, no comic shifts of perspective. In a word, spirit could not exist unless its existence were natural. That it should be subject to all the accidents, lapses, conflicts, intermittences, and self-contradictions proper to life and death was set down once for all in its birth-certificate; yet the newborn creature, for all that, is born a spirit. Existence is not so jejune as an analytic positivism would make it; it is no collection of successive data; it vibrates with potentiality, momentum, interaction and tension. It is existence by being a perpetual passage from nonexistence back to non-existence, in respect to all its moments and most of its forms; and this fact, that makes existence painful to spirit, alone allows spirit to exist,

The existence of spirit is as natural as any other existence.

since it exists precisely by feeling potentiality, momentum, interaction and tension.   But in feeling them it ideally eludes them, in that it combines and unites their fleeting essences in single pictures and perspectives, whereas the facts themselves can never be fused or unified without being abolished.   Spirit, by being immersed in the flux, perceives the flux and by perceiving it lends it the only immortality of which it is capable.   Here, in the scope of vision, seeing the relations of things, it asserts an intellectual dominion over its parent world.   This is an absolutely unchallengeable dominion in its own sphere, into which matter can never rise; although by suppressing spirit in any given instance, matter may always dip again into the darkness of a total flux, and remain subject only to its own impetus.

Spirit, then, belongs here below, not yonder, ἐχεῖ, in the Platonic heaven.   In placing it here, in the animal psyche, my system takes its place in the train of Democritus and Epicurus who, although they did not deny the existence of gods, assigned to them no dominion over nature, and in that sense may be called atheists. [Analogy between this ontology and the doctrine of the Trinity.]

Yet, seen in another light, religiously rather than cosmologically, my treatment of these four realms of being may be regarded as a reduction of Christian theology and spiritual discipline to their secret interior source. In particular my analysis transposes the doctrine of the Trinity into terms of pure ontology and moral dialectic.

At the foundation there is one total groundless reality, breaking in upon nothingness with an overwhelming irrational force.   This reality lies in the primordial elements and motions of things, with their interlocked potentialities and momentum.   Here the presence and pressure of existence confronts us, the unfathomable mystery of the actual.   Reason, that loves [Matter, or primordial substance and power, corresponds to the Father.]

U

the perspicuous and the logically necessary, might like to dismiss this incubus, but cannot; and impatience towards unreason is itself irrational, since any different state of the facts would be equally groundless. Moreover, as Heraclitus perceived, everything existent does itself justice by presently disappearing, and soon this incubus ceases to oppress each particular soul. This, however, is no speculative solution; for not only will the incubus continue to oppress spirit in others, but even if everything save the present moment of spirit were abolished or had never existed, the truth would remain that here spirit had been confronted by fate: and this indelible fact suffices to prove the existence of a vehemently actual and absolute power.

This assault of reality, in the force of whatsoever exists or happens, I call matter or the realm of matter; but evidently this very power is signified by the First Person of the Trinity, the Father, almighty creator of heaven and earth and of all things visible and invisible.

Yet all things, according to the Nicene creed, were perforce created through the Son; and this dogma which might seem unintelligible, becomes clear if we consider that power could not possibly produce anything unless it borrowed some form from the realm of essence and imposed that form on itself and on its works. Power would be annulled before it began to exert itself unless it did or produced something specific, something eternally distinct and recognizable in its character. The Son is thus an indispensable partner and vehicle for the life of the Father.

Power cannot be exercised without appealing to form.

The same creed tells us that the Son was *begotten not made*, that is to say, came through an inner impulse, without plan or foresight, from the substance of the Father; as in nature it is absurd to imagine that the shape taken by things was an aim pursued in their taking it. Design and creation are secondary incidents, possible only when experience has supplied models for invention and when special organs, already formed, have acquired a definite capacity, for free play and variation. Blind spontaneity must generate, and not make, the instruments and the goals of deliberate action.

If we interpret in this way the Father to be power and the Son to be form, we see at once how the essence or quality of each is independent and incomparable, while their existence is one and inseparable. To exercise power is to select and adopt form: by which selection or adoption power ceases to be a merely explosive and empty strain, and form ceases to be an infinite undiscriminated field of possibilities.

In its own direction essence is entirely irrelevant to existence, equally necessary in every part, yet only logically necessary. But by the intervention of irrational power (as for instance in the propensity or compulsion to think) the infinity of essence is determined to a particular complex or series of forms: and this happens not only *The selective fiat of power limits actual form to the Logos or the truth.* at each moment in each thinking mind, but in the flux of existence at large. This complex or series of forms exemplified in the universe composes the truth about it; and this is the side of reality approachable by the intellect. It is the Logos, comparable with the heaven of Platonic Ideas, with the God of Aristotle, and with νοῦς, the second hypostasis in the trinity of Plotinus.

This Logos is just as much God as is the Father, since power or substance cannot exist without form. But form also cannot exist without substance and power to extricate it from infinity and render it actual; so that the Father and the Son are not two separable existents, but two *In the beginning the Word was with God.* incommensurable and equally original features of existence itself. And the priority of substance indicated by the name Father, who *generates* the Son, appears only on the naturalistic side; because in nature substance and power take up one form after another, and endure throughout the transformation, thus seeming fundamental, while the form, though there must always be *some* form, seems accidental.   But in a deity, or in the universe seen under the form of eternity, the Logos is as primitive as the Will; and to the intellect form might even seem the prior element, as if the Will were magnetized by the Idea, rather than the Idea evoked or generated by the Will.   Perhaps on this account Aristotle and Hegel place no power above the Idea or Logos of the world, making form magically dynamic; but I think this is doubly untenable.   It is untenable naturalistically, because, as Schopenhauer perceived, an inarticulate force, a blind compulsion or attraction, breeds, not indeed the forms themselves which are eternal and do not need to be begotten, but breeds the intuition or illustration of any form.   And the priority of the Logos is untenable dialectically, because the Logos is only a selection from the realm of essence, and nothing in pure essence could authorize the self-assertion or dominance of one feature to the exclusion of the rest.   Plato and Leibniz therefore had to introduce the Good or the notion of the Best Possible to make the inevitable selection.   But this, in both cases, was a subterfuge of apologetics, an appeal to moral considerations which are out of place.   Nothing can be more naturalistic than moral preference, in which the love of life, the fears and the lusts of the psyche speak the absolute language of passion.

Now love and pursuit of the Good, though they cannot be prior to power and to essence, also arise on
The procession of the spirit. occasion, when matter and form, by a contingent fusion, have themselves become actual; and this third dimension of reality is spirit. Christian theology has been much less curious and penetrating in regard to the Holy Ghost than in regard to the Father and to the Son; so that the Nicene creed,

as if to excuse the Church for its negligence, says that we virtually adore the Holy Ghost when we explicitly adore the Father or the Son. Yet, from the human point of view this is an anomaly, since it is the Holy Ghost that speaks through the prophets, vivifies us, and tells us all we know about the Son and the Father. But there is a secret reason for this silence on what is nearest to ourselves. The ancients could never outgrow their mythologizing turn of thought. When they conceived power or form they infused into them, poetically, the moral intensity of spirit. Power—the crash of a thunderbolt or the dark potentiality in a seed —had to be intentional and intelligent; and form had to become an intellectual intuition of form. The Father and the Son were accordingly conceived to be spirits on their own account: all the more when they were identified with Jehovah and with Christ, perfectly familiar as persons to the religious mind. Therefore, when it came to the Holy Ghost there was nothing positive to add, rather the positive character of those more individual divine persons to subtract, and only a vague influence to mention, which could perfectly well flow from them without involving a third personality.

Suppose, however, we abstain from personifications for a moment and consider our terms in their essential meaning and relations. We learn in the Nicene creed that the Holy Ghost *spoke* by the prophets, but this past tense is accidental, for we also hear that he proceeds from the Father and from the Son and is the universal lord and life-giver: a procession, dominion, and vivification that must be understood logically rather than temporally, like all crucial points in Platonic speculation. The spirit *gives* life in the sense that life would nowhere be morally worthy of the name if spirit were not actual there; but the *source* of spirit itself lies in the Father and the Son,

Its equal divinity.

or in my language in matter organized into the form
of a psyche.   It is not one instance of spirit that creates
another, but nature that rises into spirit at the crest
of every wave.   And this spirit speaks by all prophets,
that is, by all voices inspired by power and by truth:
an utterance which is itself the ultimate manifestation
of power, and the first pure and non-material actualiza-
tion of form.   So that it is in the Holy Ghost that the
Father and the Son are first truly vivified and united
and adore and glorify one another.   We may therefore
say that spirit, for all its dependence, is no less divine
than are form and power, and integral to reality.   For
without stretching over the physical continuum of
space and time after the manner of power, or being
indelible and eternal, like essence and truth, spirit has
its own supremacy.   It is original and morally prior
in its sphere, and necessary to the perfection of those
elements from which it flows.   It lives in moments
and in spots; yet from any station it may survey everything, rescuing its causes from ignorance of themselves.
By the least joy it can redeem them from futility, and
by the least pain it can wring the conscience of the
Fates and challenge their selfish somnolence.

   This moral cry and authority of spirit, unexampled
in the seething world, makes it the judge as well
as spectator of everything, and subjects it
inevitably to every sort of contrariety and
suffering.   I know that theology does not
say so directly: but indirectly we learn that Christ was
conceived by the Holy Ghost; and St. Paul often speaks
of "Christ" and of the "Spirit" indifferently as dwelling
within him; while speculative theologians are not wanting who say that the incarnation and passion of Christ
were essential features from the beginning in the design
of creation, and would have occurred even apart from
the sin of Adam.   And when we eliminate the mythical
and legendary parts of this theology, and consider only

*Its incarna-
tion and
passion.*

its spiritual burden, I think it becomes clear that the
divine element especially incarnate in human existence
is spirit; not that matter or essence can be wanting,
but that the novel fact and great characteristic here is
the passion of the spirit.   This passion would certainly
not have overcome the spirit in heaven, where the
harmony between power and form is perfect, and life
is for ever at its topmost ecstasy, as in the God of
Aristotle.   But that again is sheer myth; and as matter
can *exist* only in some form, and form only in some
matter, so spirit can *exist* only incarnate in the flux of
matter and form, where nothing is stable or is perfect,
if perfect at all, for more than a moment.   Passion is
therefore inseparable from spirit in its actual existence,
and exposes it to perpetual obscuration and suffering.

Obscuration and suffering bring temptation with
them, and spirit is tempted sometimes to love evil,
and be content with lies, and sometimes to   *Its degrada-*
defy its sources and conditions, to deny   *tion.*
matter, to despise form, and to pose as itself the only
power and the only arbiter of truth, self-tortured and
absolute.   But this is itself the greatest of lies and the
sin of the spirit against its own vocation.   Spirit proceeds, it is always proceeding, from the Father and from
the Son; and, if it would not grow mad and suicidal,
it must go about the Father's business, and repeat the
eternal Word that it hears spoken in heaven.

It was not the Holy Ghost that denied his dependence on the Father and on the Son: it was Lucifer.
And Lucifer thereby lost his brightness and quickly
became Satan, Mephistopheles, Caliban, and Puck.

That spiritual ruin should be possible is a proof
that spirit is secondary: spirit could not run into dissolution and death, as it does constantly, if   *Parendo*
there were not sources and conditions of its   *tutior*
life that might betray it, or from which its   *libertas.*
immediate organ might break away.   Nor will it do

to invoke the absolute contingency of fact, and to say
that the worst of dreams might as easily be groundless
as the best of philosophies, or that absolute free spirit
might indulge in both by turns.   For there is the inner
difference felt by spirit itself between the absurd and
the beautiful, between hell and heaven; and spirit,
though equally alive in both, is not equally at peace in
both, or in enjoyment of its chosen good.   This good
is therefore chosen for it, before being chosen by it;
a thousand errors must be corrected before that good
can be clearly distinguished and possessed.   There is
an order of reason, a Logos, prescribed for spirit, and
within which alone it can find its possible good.   If
spirit, taken abstractly, might embrace all essence
impartially, finding Being in evil as much or more
than in good, spirit in the concrete, as it actually exists,
is directed upon order, and upon a definite selected
order, beyond which it is swamped, lost, tortured and
maddened.   Chiefly, no doubt, this narrow path is
prescribed for spirit by the realm of matter, where its
organ and its fortunes must take shape; but even when
expatiating in the realm of essence, where freedom
might seem infinite, living spirit can make its way only
systematically, as in mathematics or in music.   Chaos
itself then seems only an infinite complex of orders.
In tracing any of these possible orders, a certain fidelity
of intention, a serious self-limitation and consistency
are requisite: whereby the vital presuppositions and
conditions of spiritual life are manifested.   In other
words, the Holy Ghost is not the first person of the
Trinity, but the third, proceeding both from the Father
and from the Son.   Consciousness is a gift of nature,
happiness is a fruit of piety and order: and spirit, being
the final fruition of existence, absolutely needs the
other realms to evoke and to feed it.

Nor is spirit brought to light once for all, in one
supreme instance; for its essence is to think, to love,

to be awake, watchful, and transitive. The Word must
be *uttered*; and such utterance cannot be either momentary or endlessly repeated; it must progress, Spirit exists
vary, and complete itself in endless ways. in multitudi-
As the potentiality of matter and life nous inspira-
is probably indefinite, and the variety of tions.
essence certainly inexhaustible, so spirit has an infinity of its own, the infinity of the renewable. One
cry of moral actuality breaking out from the heart,
leaves the heart free to repeat or not to repeat it; and
the repetition if it comes will vary it. One pleasure
cannot prescribe the quality of another pleasure, or
cause or prevent its existence; nor can one thought annul
the deliverance of another thought. The occasion and
the bounty of nature must provide. Authority thus
belongs to the Father, revelation comes by the Son, and
Spirit descends to those predestined by the Father to
receive it. Then, in the galaxy of spirit, the lesser with
the greater lights become partakers in his glory.

This analogy between Christian theology and my
ontology must not be pressed: the one is a dogma, the
other a language: a language based not on This system
inspiration but on analysis, and meant only not a cosmo-
to render articulate the dumb experience of logy but a
the soul. I am not concerned in these grammar of
the spirit.
Realms of Being with alleged separate substances or
independent regions. I am endeavouring only to distinguish the *types* of reality that I encounter; and the
lines of cleavage that I discern are moral and logical,
not physical, chasms. Yet I find this language applic-
able, and in that sense true. Theology could not
possibly be true unless revealed miraculously; and I
presume that most of my readers would agree that
miraculous revelations are creatures of the heart.
Religion itself sometimes calls its dogmas mysteries
and its creeds symbols, as if admitting the difference
in kind between imagination and truth. So discounted

and disinfected, the speculations of intense and consecrated minds have a great authority, especially when they have proved acceptable to mankind, and have become the companions and vehicles of a spiritual discipline.   They do not thereby become miraculously true; nevertheless they reveal inner and outer harmonies established with long labour and sacrifice in the human soul.   There they remain fountains of wisdom and self-knowledge, at which we may still drink in solitude. Perhaps the day may return when mankind will drink at them again in society.

INDEX

THE END